The Ages of
the Avengers

The Ages of the Avengers

*Essays on the Earth's Mightiest
Heroes in Changing Times*

Edited by
Joseph J. Darowski

McFarland & Company, Inc., Publishers
Jefferson, North Carolina

LIBRARY OF CONGRESS CATALOGUING-IN-PUBLICATION DATA

The ages of The Avengers : essays on the earth's mightiest heroes
   in changing times / edited by Joseph J. Darowski.
      p.   cm.
   Includes bibliographical references and index.

   ISBN 978-0-7864-7458-5 (softcover : acid free paper) ∞
   ISBN 978-1-4766-1849-4 (ebook)

   1. Avengers (Comic strip)   2. Avengers (Fictitious characters)
3. Literature and society—United States.   4. Comic books, strips,
etc.—United States.   I. Darowski, Joseph J., editor.
PN6728.A9A38 2014
741.5'973—dc23   2014032945

BRITISH LIBRARY CATALOGUING DATA ARE AVAILABLE

Printed in the United States of America

McFarland & Company, Inc., Publishers
   Box 611, Jefferson, North Carolina 28640
      www.mcfarlandpub.com

Table of Contents

Preface

JOSEPH J. DAROWSKI

After creating the Fantastic Four to launch Marvel Comics' new line of superhero comic books, Stan Lee and several artistic collaborators created individual heroes such as Iron Man, the Incredible Hulk, Thor, and Ant-Man. Soon, Marvel planned another team title to join their publishing line, *The X-Men*. There is a well-known story that one reason Stan Lee and Jack Kirby made the X-Men mutants, people who were just born with superpowers, is because Lee was tired of coming up with accidents that empowered his protagonists. It would be much easier if he could say the super hero was just born that way. The origin story could be told in a sentence. In a sense, laziness resulted in one of Marvel Comics' most successful franchises.

Similarly, *The Avengers* may have been born out of a lack of time with which to generate new ideas. As current Marvel executive editor Tom Brevoort explains, there were some quirks of the publishing industry, behind the scenes issues, and restrictions on Marvel's content that resulted in Lee and Kirby hastily putting together the first *The Avengers* comic book. In 1963, "you booked print time way ahead of time—and if your book wasn't ready, you paid for the printing time anyway. So it was vital to get something to press on time" (Brevoort). Because of artist Bill Everett's day job and other issues, production on the first issue of *Daredevil* fell behind after the printing time was already reserved. Marvel had to produce something that could take Daredevil's spot in the publishing schedule as quickly as possible. "In trying to solve this problem, Stan hit on the notion of doing a strip that brought all of the heroes together JLA-style—that would be a book that wouldn't require any ramp-up time, because the characters (and even the villain) all existed already" (Brevoort). Kirby was famous for his skill and speed in drawing comics, and without having to design new characters he was able to produce an issue with legendary quickness. "So [Lee] and Jack Kirby brainstormed the first issue, Kirby drew it up hastily, Dick Ayers inked it in what looks like no time flat, and it came out the same month as X-MEN #1" (Brevoort).

Thus, due to unforeseen circumstances and desperation, another long-running and profitable franchise was born.

This collection will explore the ways in which the comic book series has remained relevant while publishing stories across five decades. The audience expectations for entertainment have fluctuated dramatically throughout the years, and comic book creators have been forced to adapt to shifting hopes, fears, and concerns amongst the audience. Like any popular culture product, issues of *The Avengers* are reflective of the time period when they were produced. The entire team line-up was changed with the fourth issue of the series, and since that time *The Avengers* has had a reputation for significant changes in tone, team members, villains, and ideology. This narrative elasticity has allowed the title to remain relevant to readers even as the societal backdrop against which it is produced has changed dramatically.

Several of the first essays look at how the United States' involvement in international politics and wars affected the entertainment being produced for domestic consumption. In the first essay in this collection, "The Cuban Missile Crisis in Four Colors: 'The Avengers Meet ... "Sub-Mariner"!' as an Allegory to Armageddon," Liam Webb examines *The Avengers* #3 (Jan. 1964) and how several of the themes and issues explored in the story are reflective of contemporary American concerns. Fears from the Cold War in general and in response to the Cuban Missile Crisis in particular are highlighted in Webb's analysis.

Lori Maguire, in "'The Avengers always stand ready to do their part': *The Avengers* and the Vietnam War," discusses the transitions made in the series from the mid–1960s into the 1970s as the United States became embroiled in the Vietnam War. In "'The Kree-Skrull War' and the Growth of Uncertainty in the Cold War Era," Paul R. Kohl considers one specific storyline from the comic book series and how it reflects an evolving sense of American identity as the Cold War and the Vietnam War dragged on.

Jason Sacks' essay, "Earth's Mightiest (Dysfunctional) Family: The Evolution of *The Avengers* Under Jim Shooter," looks at the tenure of Jim Shooter as writer of *The Avengers* and the way his style altered the tone and content of the series. Nathan Gibbard considers some of the stories told during Shooter's time as writer and aligns them with significant movements in religion in America. "Madonna's Birth and God's Death: Marvel Comics, the Death of God Movement, and the Religious Climate of the 1970s" does an excellent job of examining how cultural shifts in one area of society, such as religion, can be reflected in another, such as entertainment. Giacomo Matteo Miniussi also addresses a Shooter storyline in "'The Korvac Saga': Exiles from Reason and Fragments of a Contemporary Mythology."

Peter W. Lee looks at gender issues and identity crises in "Stung by Stigmatization: Yellowjacket and Wasp Dis/Reassembled in the Age of Reagan." The trials and evolution of Yellowjacket and the Wasp served as a microcosm for changes happening to the Avengers and in America during the 1980s.

Jason LaTouche's "Everything Old Is New Again: Figuring Out Who the Enemy Is in the 1980s" focuses on the famous "Under Siege" storyline. A backlash against the counterculture movements of the 1960s and 1970s and a changing global geopolitical landscape had shifted American identity, and efforts to identify what that identity had become are reflected in this superhero adventure.

"The Earth's Mightiest Heroes and America's Post–Cold War Identity Crisis" by John Darowski examines several Avengers tales from the 1990s as the country shifted from a dual position during the Cold War to becoming the world's sole superpower. After decades of being defined as much by external threats as internal values, a massive upheaval was felt with the collapse of the Soviet Union and that change is seen in the stories of iconic American heroes at this time.

Todd Steven Burroughs' "The Spy King: How Christopher Priest's Version of the Black Panther Shook Up Earth's Mightiest Heroes" considers an important reimagining of an early Marvel character. When Christopher Priest wrote the adventures of Marvel's first African superhero he retconned some of the early tales so that the Black Panther was spying on the Avengers when he first joined the team in a 1968 comic book. This shift changed the role of the Black Panther on the Avengers then and now.

Morgan B. O'Rourke looks at a reimagined version of *The Avengers* that appeared in an alternate universe that Marvel referred to as the Ultimate line of comic books. "*The Ultimates* as Superheroes in the Age of Social Media and Celebrity" explores how the series both embraces and condemns aspects of America's celebrity obsessed culture.

"'No!' *Great Lakes Avengers* and the Uses of Enfreakment" by José Alaniz analyzes *GLA: Misassembled,* a mini-series that focused on a team that has traditionally been used as a joke. Alaniz uses the problematic tradition of the freak show and how it has evolved in American culture as a lens through which to explore the themes and plot of this mini-series.

Mark Edlitz and Dyfrig Jones discuss two different events that engulfed Marvel's publishing line. Edlitz's "The Uncivil Debate Within Marvel's *Civil War*" examines an extremely popular mini-series in light of post–9/11 politics. Similarly, Jones's "Islamic Invaders: *Secret Invasion* and the Post–9/11 World of Marvel" positions the storyline as indicative of attitudes and issues America was grappling with in the years following 9/11.

Finally, Joseph J. Darowski's "'The one with the kids on the island':

Avengers Arena and Teenage Dystopian Fiction" examines a recent 18-issue series that pitted teenage superheroes against one another in a battle to the death. While clearly similar to stories such as *The Hunger Games*, the series addresses contemporary concerns such as virtual identities and cyberbullying in intriguing ways.

The Avengers is one of Marvel's longest running franchises. With multiple spin-off titles and the core comic book series as well as successful adaptations in television, film, and video games, the Avengers series has come to represent an important part of the Marvel superhero universe. Published continuously for five decades, the series has changed and evolved or else it would have become a popular culture relic. Those changes provide insights into the culture that both produces and consumes this comic book series.

Work Cited

Brevoort, Tom. "Untitled Answer." Formspring.com. No date. http://new.spring.me/#!/TomBrevoort/q/180312428897141454. Accessed 15 May 2015.

The Cuban Missile Crisis in Four Colors

"The Avengers Meet ... 'Sub-Mariner'!" as an Allegory to Armageddon

LIAM WEBB

The Avengers #3 (Jan. 1964), "The Avengers Meet ... Sub-Mariner," has a cover date only fourteen months after the world almost fell into nuclear conflict due to the Cuban Missile Crisis in October 1962. Since comics were generally written approximately six months before publication, this book was likely written sometime in mid–1963, less than a year after the Crisis. The Crisis was likely still on the minds of Jack Kirby and Stan Lee, who, for the sake of this essay and history, I consider co-writers of the book.[1]

The Cuban Missile Crisis occurred when the U.S. learned that the Soviet Union was placing ballistic missiles in Cuba, a source of significant concern for the United States. The Soviets did this in part because the U.S. already had missiles in Turkey, within striking distance of the U.S.S.R., and they felt that this would make the situation more equal between the nations. Additionally, they felt it would deter the U.S. from invading their ally, Cuba, again ("Cuban Missile Crisis"). The Kennedy administration's response was to formulate many plans, including Cuban invasion plans, but Kennedy decided to set up a naval blockade of Cuba and gave the Soviets an ultimatum to remove the missiles currently there and not reintroduce them later (Cottrell; Rusk). In a television address Kennedy revealed to the American public what was happening. Soviet ships came up to, but then backed down from, the U.S. naval blockade, and an American spy plane was shot down over Cuba, all while both sides were rapidly negotiating with each other behind closed doors. Kruschev eventually offered to withdraw the missiles in Cuba in exchange for the U.S.'s promise not to invade Cuba and for the withdrawal of the American missiles from Turkey. Kennedy accepted both terms, the second one secretly, and the Crisis was averted. However, as Klein states, the American people and government did not know the true number of the Soviet soldiers in Cuba at the time, nor that the Soviets kept missiles in Cuba until December of that year. As a result of the Crisis, a direct hotline was set up between the U.S. and U.S.S.R. in case any similar tense situation should again arise.

As *The Avengers* #3 (Jan. 1964) starts, the Avengers are trying to locate Hulk who quit the team at the end of *The Avengers* #2 (Nov. 1963) because the Space Phantom, in a bid to invade America, impersonated him (and others) and caused the heroes to fight each other. Hulk was hurt emotionally that the other Avengers at first simply assumed Hulk was belligerent and did not question the Phantom's actions when the Phantom looked like the Hulk. Hulk accused them of feeling this way because they never quite accepted the Hulk as a "good guy" (Lee and Kirby, "Avengers Battle ..."). This "body snatcher" theme is not unlike the fear of Communist sleeper agents planted in the U.S. at this time in America's history (Klein). This, plus the Hulk's basic character idea—though only a man, he is powered by (and has the correlative destructive powers of) a radio-active bomb—positions the Hulk to fill the place of a small but destructive weapon, not unlike the missiles in Cuba, which could be used both for or against America. This atomic fear is also symbolized visually because the Hulk's skin is green, the "default" color for radioactive material in popular culture of the time. So while the Hulk can, and in some ways does, embody the fear of Communist agents in America, for the most part, he fills the role of weaponry/ brute force/the army of America's then-enemies. The Avengers, of course, symbolize American forces.

Iron Man's first dialogue in *The Avengers* #3 (Jan. 1964) includes the line "So long as he's running wild, there's no telling *what* he'll do!" (Lee and Kirby). Notably, Iron Man's anxiety seems related to the idea that the Avengers no longer "control" the Hulk, and not that the Hulk will hurt himself or others, or even that Hulk's feelings are hurt. This reinforces the text in the last panel of *The Avengers* #2 (Nov. 1963), when Wasp admits she is relieved Hulk is gone because he always "frightened her" and another member (either Thor or Iron Man depending on whom the reader believes the bubble stem goes to in this far shot) says "without the Avengers to keep him in check, what will he do next?" (Lee and Kirby, "Avengers Battle ..."). These concerns mimic the fears of the U.S. regarding the Cuban missiles because, up until this time in the Cold War, America were perceived as the "winning" side and it was this "edge" that Kennedy's administration was afraid of losing ("Cuban Missile Crisis"; "An Overview of the Crisis" 3, 6).

Iron Man video calls other Marvel heroes to search for the Hulk. These other heroes are either unavailable (Reed Richards, X-Men) or disinterested (Thing,

Spider-Man) in helping to root out the Hulk. Once this appeal to other heroes failed, Thor suggests contacting Rick Jones, which causes Giant Man to remember that Jones is "the only one who can control the Hulk!" (Lee and Kirby, "The Avengers Meet ..."). From a tactical standpoint, one wonders why the Avengers didn't call on Jones immediately, but practically, if they had, the readers would have been denied all those flashy cameos and the script may have fallen short a few pages. Jones finds Hulk in short order and persuades Hulk to ignore his destructive impulses and hide in a cave, turn back to Bruce Banner via nuclear "treatment," and stays with Banner at the latter's request. Jones here plays the role of nuclear diplomat by calming Hulk and guarding Banner, symbolically providing disarmament services, similar to the role Attorney General Robert Kennedy played when delivering the message to the Soviets that America would take their missiles out of Turkey.

However, Banner reverts to Hulk during the night since the treatment Jones gave him wears off because it wasn't "strong enough" of a dose (like any short-term disarmament action that addresses one situation but doesn't remove the source of the threat). After Hulk escapes, Rick warns the Avengers about the Hulk and gives them Hulk's location. Iron Man summons the other members and without waiting for the others' arrival, takes off alone for New Mexico. This "going it alone" action of Iron Man's is a classic "cowboy move" which parallels some of Kennedy's actions at this time, like the Bay of Pigs.

In this initial confrontation with the Hulk, Iron Man is first waved away by Jones (diplomatic to the end), then sucker punched by the Hulk. Iron Man reacts defensively to this sucker punch with a brief, short range pulse that Iron Man knows "won't *stop* him, but it's sure to slow him down!" (Lee and Kirby, "The Avengers Meet ...") and with some ineffectual diplomacy of his own. Iron Man asks Hulk to "stop fighting and let me talk to you" as he hides from Hulk's retaliation. These acts are similar to Kennedy's first attempts (with his advisors, known as the Executive Committee or ExCom) to talk the problem out. Both the superpowers and the superheroes favored this as the ultimate solution, since Hank Pym quickly (if more combatively) endorses the same position as Iron Man when he says, "Even Giant-Man can't match the Hulk's strength! This calls for cunning!" (Lee and Kirby, "The Avengers Meet ...") and prepares to weaken the ground under Hulk. Iron Man continues to try to talk to Hulk to no avail, and after the Hulk fights Iron Man, Giant Man and Thor, the Hulk momentarily defeats the Avengers and gets away.

Licking their wounds, the Avengers agree amongst themselves that Hulk got away mostly because they didn't really want to hurt him and so pulled their punches. This instinct was true of people on both sides of the Cuban Missile Crisis because, ultimately, there conceivably cannot be many (if any) people in high positions in any government that truly want a nuclear war.

Making his escape, the Hulk swims to the Gulf stream in the Atlantic "after days in the water" (Lee and Kirby, "The Avengers Meet ..."). For the story it is odd for the Hulk to be in the Atlantic, after just fighting the Avengers in New Mexico since, if an ocean is what he sought, the Pacific is closer (6,227 km Albuquerque to Pacific vs. 8,791 km Albuquerque to Atlantic). But, by specifically mentioning the Gulf Stream and Atlantic, Lee puts the Hulk in the neighborhood of Cuba, if not on the island itself. The Hulk then finds a "small, deserted island" in this area to land on, where he meets the second malefactor of the story, the Sub-Mariner.

The Sub-Mariner is first seen observing the Hulk's "every movement" with advanced spy equipment. Such equipment was, if not in the actual possession of the Soviet regime, certainly in their possession in the minds of Americans. The Hulk is then approached by Namor to make war on the Avengers, America's defenders. After a short fight between Namor and Hulk, they team up against all others and the reasons why they join forces is worthy of note. Namor tells Hulk, "We *both* share a burning hatred for the human race! If we act *together*, we can bring humanity to its knees!" It doesn't seem to be such a stretch to replace the words "human" and "humanity" for "American" and "America" in this particular line. This parallels the perceived strategy of the Russians and Cubans to "team up" or combine Cuba's proximity with Soviet nuclear muscle in order to subjugate democracy to socialism in the Cold War. The weapons are of course the true threat throughout. Hulk tells Namor "You're pretty tough for a little guy!" (Lee and Kirby, "The Avengers Meet ..."), and similarly, Cuba and for that matter even the Soviets, wouldn't have been seen as a credible threat to the U.S. if they didn't possess nuclear weaponry. Lee then immediately inserts thought bubbles to show that Hulk and Namor are only using each other and will betray each other when it is convenient. This is in line with the public's perception that the socialists' deal broke up quickly when they couldn't get what they wanted, and of course it also reflects the general attitude about trustworthiness of "evil" people and "undemocratic" governments.

Interestingly enough though, Lee then writes that the villains changed location to Gibraltar. There are many reasons why he might have wrote this. First, maybe Lee felt that he didn't want to make too obvious of a political statement—after all, these books were aimed at young readers and he may not have wanted things to either be "over their heads" or possibly "scare" them or agitate their parents. What was assuredly not accidental, however, was keeping the action on small islands, which not only enabled Namor to stay close to water, his power source, but also highlighted the fact that these interactions had a considerable maritime tint to them, which mirrored the well-known setting of a naval stand-off with the Soviet ships during the Crisis.

Now combined, the villains issue a direct challenge to the heroes to face off. In this confrontation, Namor's immediate concern is again for "superior weaponry": on one hand, he is concerned that the Hulk be uninjured while he needs Hulk's power, and at first attempts to debilitate Thor, the strongest Avenger and, when that fails, he instantly attacks Iron Man. In retaliation, Thor throws his hammer and Namor and Hulk retreat. This opening salvo in the longer battle to come also mirror the naval engagement in the Crisis: the "shot over the bow" appearance of the Soviet fleet mirrored by Namor's actual shot, but then the Soviets saw the superior American forces that made up the naval blockade, here embodied by Thor's hammer, and the Soviet force beat a hasty tactical retreat.

Next, while the Avengers revive Iron Man, Hulk tries to bring rock walls down on the oncoming heroes using his fists. The Wasp, who was nearby at the time, is incapacitated by Hulk's punch but quickly revives and employs the classic "Duck and Cover" defense, hiding on Giant Man's shoulder for the rest of the fight. Namor then takes the offensive and turns a "modified air raid siren" on the heroes but before he can use it, is grabbed by Giant Man who speaks a line that is representative of the popular opinion of the U.S. regarding Castro: "You're too *little* to be playing with such dangerous toys, fella!" (Lee and Kirby, "The Avengers Meet ..."). In the course of the battle, Hulk becomes "too stressed" which triggers the change back into Bruce Banner (a feature of the character in these early stories that is later dropped). Banner then runs away, speaking lines which seem applicable to the Cuban Missile Crisis: "In another few seconds, we might have *won*, or be destroyed ourselves! But now, we'll never know! Perhaps it's better this way! " (Lee and Kirby, "The Avengers Meet ...").

As Banner leaves, Namor states, "My power is leaving me..." (Lee and Kirby, "The Avengers Meet ..."). After a brief scuffle, Namor accesses water and runs away from the Avengers, though he does not admit defeat. This non-admission is reflective of Castro's position at the time (Hilsman). Wasp now appears on the third to last panel of the last page now that the main fight is over and asks Thor to press the advantage, but Thor and the rest reply strangely since it was the Avengers who were challenged to this fight: "*No* ! I have too much respect for his valor! Namor has *earned* his escape!" Giant Man adds, "Thor's *right* ! It's a pity the Sub-Mariner isn't on *our* side!" Iron Man offers a contradictory conclusion: "We've made a bad mistake! He doesn't fight by our rules! We may live to *regret* this!" Intentionally or not, these sentiments could very well be expressed as opinions of the American people following the Cuban Missile Crisis. Thor's lines can be interpreted as meaning that while the Soviets were never liked by the vast majority of the country, they were respected out of fear if nothing else. Giant Man's lines express the populace's wish for peace and cooperation between nations. Finally Iron Man's lines express the lingering fear, heightened by the Crisis, that all Americans felt toward the Soviet Union (Young).

The comic ends on a cautionary narrative note, which was perfectly apropos for the then-current feeling in the U.S. of mid–1963: "For they all sense that the adventure they just concluded is but the prelude to a far bigger, a far more dangerous adventure to come!" (Lee and Kirby, "The Avengers Meet ..."). Though the Crisis was averted, nervousness ran high in both populations, since the threat of nuclear war was still possible and now felt even more probable though it was averted. However, the fact that Captain American is revived in the next issue, and that his being found and revived was a direct result of Namor's "temper tantrum" after losing to the Avengers, indicates that while nervous, America felt vindicated by having come out "ahead" in the Crisis and this in turn led to an upswing in patriotism.

Note

1. The widely-known "Marvel method" of creating comics consisted of a story plotting session between Lee and the hired artist, and then the art was often, if not exclusively, created before the dialogue and other "script" items.

Works Cited

Coleman, David G. *The Fourteenth Day: JFK and the Aftermath of the Cuban Missile Crisis: The Secret White House Tapes*. W.W. Norton, 2012. Print.

Cottrell, Stephen J., Coordinator of Cuban Affairs, United States Government: National Security Council. Doc NLK-73–30. *Memorandum for the National Security Council's Executive Committee*. Unpublished, January 24, 1963, meeting minutes. *Archive.org*. The Internet Archive, 7 June 2012. http://ia600803.us.archive.org/10/items/CubanMissileCrisis Documents/Cuba-Missile-Crisis-2866.pdf. Web. Accessed 13 October 2013.

Cottrell, Stephen J. Doc NLK-78–5. *Memorandum for the National Security Council's Executive Committee: Subject—Cuban Brigade*. Unpublished, January 24, 1963, meeting minutes. *Archive.org*. The Internet Archive, 7 June 2012. http://ia600803.us.archive.org/10/items/ CubanMissileCrisisDocuments/Cuba-Missile-Crisis-2881.pdf. Web. Accessed 13 October 2013.

"Cuban Missile Crisis." Historywww. A&E Television Networks, LLC, n.d. http://www.history. com/topics/cuban-missile-crisis. Web. Accessed 13 October 2013.

"Cuban Missile Crisis Documents." *Archive.org*. The Internet Archive, n.d. http://ia600803. us.archive.org/10/items/CubanMissileCrisisDocuments/. Web. Accessed 13 October 2013.

Dobbs, Michael. *One Minute to Midnight: Kennedy, Khrushchev, and Castro on the Brink of Nuclear War*. Vintage, 2009. Print.

Evi.com. Evi Technologies Limited, n.d. Web. http://www.evi.com/q/how_far_from_albu querque_new_mexico_to_atlantic_ocean. Accessed 13 October 2013.

Hilsman, Roger, Director of Intelligence and Research, United States Government: Department of State. Doc 00999. *"Subject: The Situation in the Light of the Miyokan Talks and Castro Speech."* Unpublished, November 2, 1962. *Archive.org.* The Internet Archive, June 7, 2012. Web. http://ia600803.us.archive.org/10/items/CubanMissileCrisisDocuments/Cuba-Missile-Crisis-ii-999.pdf. Accessed 13 October 2013.

"History" (Spain). *LonelyPlanet.com.* Lonely Planet, n.d. Web. http://www.lonelyplanet.com/spain/history. Accessed 13 October 2013.

Klein, Christopher. "10 Things You May Not Know About the Cuban Missile Crisis." Historywww. A&E Television Networks, LLC, October 16, 2012. http://www.history.com/news/10-things-you-may-not-know-about-the-cuban-missile-crisis. Web. Accessed 13 October 2013.

Lee, Stan. *The Real Stan Lee.* Pow! Entertainment, n.d. therealstanleewww. Web. Accessed 13 October 2013.

Lee, Stan (w), Jack Kirby (p), and Paul Reinman (i). "The Avengers Meet ... Sub-Mariner." *The Avengers Masterworks*, vol. 1. Eds. Tom Brevoort and Mindy Newell. New York: Marvel Comics, 1993: 47–72. Print.

McElroy, Neil H., Secretary of Defense, United States Government. Doc MR 80–226 #6. Declassified 5.13.80. GPO, 1958. *Archive.org.* The Internet Archive, June 7, 2012. http://ia600803.us.archive.org/10/items/CubanMissileCrisisDocuments/Cuba-Missile-Crisis-005.pdf. Web. Accessed 13 October 2013.

"Old Newspapers: Cuban Missile Crisis." Kcmeeshawww, April 11, 2013. Kansas City with a Russian Accent. http://kcmeesha.com/2011/04/20/old-newspapers-cuban-missile-crisis/. Web. Accessed 19 January 2014.

Orsi, Peter. " Cuban missile crisis beliefs endure after 50 years." Public Opinion Online. Chambersburg Public Opinion, n.d. http://www.publicopiniononline.com/nationalnews/ci_21766506/cuban-missile-crisis-beliefs-endure-after-50-years Web. Accessed 13 October 2013.

"An Overview of the Crisis." *The Cuban Missile Crisis: Fourteen Days in October. The Crisis Center.* Oracle Education Foundation, n.d. http://library.thinkquest.org/11046/days/. Web. Accessed 13 October 2013.

Ping, Dan. "The Spanish Case: Was It Facism?" *UMich.edu.* The University of Michigan, n.d. http://sitemaker.umich.edu/spanishcase/francisco_franco. Web. Accessed 13 October 2013.

Rusk, Dean, Secretary of State, United States Government. Doc 00995. *"Confidential Letter from the Secretary of State to the U.N."* Unpublished, 2 November 1962. *Archive.org.* The Internet Archive, June 7, 2012. http://ia600803.us.archive.org/10/items/CubanMissileCrisisDocuments/Cuba-Missile-Crisis-ii-995.pdf. Web. Accessed 13 October 2013.

United States Government. *Memorandum for the Attorney General: Re: Legality Under International Law of Remedial Action Against Use of Cuba as a Missile Base by the Soviet Union.* GPO, n. d. *Archive.org.* The Internet Archive, 7 June 2012. http://ia600803.us.archive.org/10/items/CubanMissileCrisisDocuments/Cuba-Missile-Crisis-284.pdf. Web. Accessed 13 October 2013.

Young, John M. *When the Russians Blinked: The U.S. Maritime Response to the Cuban Missile Crisis.* Washington, D.C.: U.S. Marine Corps—History and Museums Division, 1990. *Archive.org.* The Internet Archive, n.d. http://archive.org/stream/WhenTheRussiansBlinked/When%20The%20Russians%20Blinked%20The%20US%20Maritime%20Response%20To%20The%20Cuban%20Missile%20Crisis#page/n207/mode/2up. Web. Accessed 13 October 2013.

"The Avengers always stand ready to do their part"

The Avengers *and the Vietnam War*

Lori Maguire

Although the Vietnam War was clearly a limited one for the United States, it remains among the most traumatic events in recent American history. Over 58,000 military personnel died there, and many others were seriously wounded both physically and mentally. It brought out massive divisions in American society and, although Richard Nixon claimed the conflict had ended in "peace with honor" (Nixon), it is difficult to see Vietnam as anything but a defeat for the U.S. The historian Marilyn Young has summarized its impact well:

> A fundamental axiom of U.S. foreign policy had been that this nation is always on the side of freedom and justice.... If axiomatic American goodness was brought into question by the war, so too was the axiomatic evil of the government's designated enemies. Everything that had been used to characterize the enemy—his indifference to human life, his duplicity, his ruthlessness—had at various times during the war been seen to characterize the United States as well. And while this might have been a surmountable problem in the name of a cause fervently embraced by a majority of Americans, it had become a very serious problem in the absence of such a cause [290].

The Vietnam War was bound to bring disillusionment with the war itself, with the nation's leaders and with the role of the United States in the world. The evolution outlined here—from a belief in American goodness on the world scene to one of questioning and then disenchantment had its reflection in popular culture and can be traced in *The Avengers* (Costello 1–2; Johnson, Jeffrey, 109–10).

This does not necessarily mean this transition was clearly expressed: while in progress there were relatively few references to the war in popular culture. Although around 450 films were made about World War II during that conflict, most of those about Vietnam only came out after the fall of Saigon (Cullen 81).

The same was true of *The Avengers* for, although there were direct references to Iron Man and, to a lesser extent, Captain America having roles in the conflict, they occurred in other comic book series. The first Avengers story set in a clearly-named Vietnam was only published in 1974, a year after American withdrawal. But we can notice its influence in a number of areas, such as attitudes to war, to patriotism and to communism and communists (notably Oriental ones). This essay will examine the evolution of these themes over eleven years. The first section considers the period from August 1964, date of the Tonkin Gulf incident, to late 1967, when polls showed that public support for the war remained relatively high. The second part will examine developments from the Tet offensive of 1968 until the withdrawal of combat troops in March 1973. A final section will then consider the presentation of Vietnam in the last two years of the war, when America was no longer an active participant.

From the Gulf of Tonkin Incident of 1964 to the Tet Offensive of 1968

President Dwight Eisenhower first sent military advisers to South Vietnam in the 1950s and John Kennedy had increased their number to over 16,000 by the time of his death (Anderson 101). Lyndon Johnson inherited the problem and his government immediately made clear in National Security Action Memorandum 273 that the U.S. would continue to assist South Vietnam (Bundy). He also vastly increased the number of American soldiers there and, of course, the casualty rate grew as well since the North Vietnamese were determined to win no matter what the cost and enjoyed significant support from the USSR (Zubok 198).

Much of the American escalation occurred after the Tonkin Gulf incident. On August 2, 1964, the destroyer USS *Maddox* was on patrol off the coast of North Vietnam for intelligence purposes. North Vietnamese authorities had been tracking the boat for days and were afraid it might fire on their territory. It seems that neither Ho Chi Minh nor General Giap wanted to attack the ship unless it struck first, but the increasingly powerful Le Duan issued the order on his own. (Moyar 310–11). Two days later the attack appeared to be repeated on both the *Maddox* and another ship. The key word here is "appeared"; American military personnel clearly believed that it had occurred but most of the information available now suggests that it did not (Guan 617; Moyar 312).

President Lyndon Johnson obviously thought that two attacks had taken place and insisted they had been unprovoked. He told the American people on the 4th:

> In the larger sense this new act of aggression, aimed directly at our own forces, again brings home to all of us in the United States the importance of the

struggle for peace and security in southeast Asia. Aggression by terror against the peaceful villagers of South Viet-Nam has now been joined by open aggression on the high seas against the United States of America.

He went on to say he was going to ask Congress for a resolution "to take all necessary measures." He got exactly this from Congress a few days later. In the absence of an official war declaration, over the next decade the Tonkin Gulf resolution would serve as the legal basis for American involvement in the war. Distinguished officer William Westmoreland received command of military operations and decided to follow a policy of attrition against North Vietnam and the National Liberation Front (NLF).[1] For this reason, he recommended the deployment of large numbers of additional troops. By the end of the year over 23,000 troops had been sent there and they would be continuously augmented, reaching over half a million by 1968 (Anderson 104). Air bombardment also increased substantially and North Vietnam was openly targeted. The U.S. had clearly changed from advising the South Vietnamese on how to fight the war to actively fighting it with (and often for) them.

Obviously, the Tonkin Gulf episode, even though Johnson tried to downplay it in the run up to the election, caused a patriotic reaction. Polls showed that Johnson's popularity rose from 42 percent to 72 percent and support for his policies in Vietnam went from 58 percent to 85 percent (Johnson, Robert David, 144; Wells 11). The election in November was a triumph for the Democrats but the situation began to change soon after. From the second half of 1965, polls clearly showed a decline in support for the war as casualties increased and victory remained elusive (Jacobs & Shapiro 600). By 1967 the war had descended into a bloody stalemate which was provoking more and more protests on American campuses. Meanwhile, the administration tried to keep an upbeat view on the situation, attempting to convince the public that victory was near.

The Avengers mirrored much of the administration's discourse during the period. Although it did not explicitly mention Vietnam, general support for America's policies in the Cold War—of which Vietnam was one of the centerpieces—was clear as was hostility to communists, especially Asiatic communists. One of the most obvious examples of this is "The Commissar Commands" (Lee) from *The Avengers* #18 (July 1965). This story takes place in the fictional communist country of Sin-Cong. Since Song Cong is the name of a real river and city in the northeastern part of Vietnam, an identification with North Vietnam seems obvious. Our first view of Sin-Cong presents us with a considerably less than subtle vision of communist tyranny as a character named Major Hoy lectures people on the need to obey the state. When someone voices disagreement, the giant Commissar is used to intimidate them.

The story then switches to New York where the Avengers receive a call for help from Sin-Cong's oppressed people. Captain America, hoping at this time to be recruited by SHIELD, is eager to go but the Scarlet Witch and Quicksilver have serious doubts. Strangely enough, it is Hawkeye who asserts the importance of the mission: "Let me spell it out to you! We're supposed to avenge injustice right? Well, when liberty's threatened, justice goes down the drain! That's it in a nutshell!" So the Avengers head to Sin-Cong and, after a number of adventures, eventually reveal the hollowness and tyranny of the communist dictatorship. The episode ends with a lecture from Captain America to the people of Sin-Cong:

> Be always on your guard! Their [the communists'] goal is nothing less than total world conquest and world enslavement! Only constant vigilance and devotion to freedom can stop them! And remember—the Avengers always stand ready to do their part!

No doubt is expressed here about the government's policy in the Cold War or about its explanations for such a policy. This entire episode effectively accepts and even justifies American involvement in Vietnam.

While this is the most obvious example, we should also note the appearance of a number of other Asian communists (although seemingly Chinese). The Mandarin, Iron Man's archenemy, appears in two issues of *The Avengers* during this period. We see him in "Vengeance Is Ours" (Lee) where he sends the Swordsman to infiltrate the Avengers. Later, in September 1967 the Mandarin reappears, trying to use hate-rays to make everyone in the world fight each other (Thomas, "The Monstrous Master Plan"). The idea of war itself is criticized which suggests a change in attitude from two years earlier. However, it also reflects the growing division of the nation that was revealing itself in increasing war protests.

Even more significant are episodes from 1966 which contain obvious Cold War plots with clearly Oriental villains. In "Frenzy from a Far-Off Land" (Lee) from July, the Black Widow is brainwashed by General Hu Chen to turn against America and attack the Avengers. Chen reappears in the next two issues which focus on a group resembling the Ku Klux Klan, the Sons of the Serpent. Here the drawings of Asian communists are particularly distorted making them look exceptionally angry and evil. General Chen, on a visit to the United Nations, is attacked by the Serpents, which leads him to a very vocal denunciation of "racist" America. He turns the event into a propaganda triumph for himself and his nation. Coming just after years of civil rights agitation, the comic book obviously wants to take a stand against racism. However its message is marred by the fact that the group's head turns out to be none other than Chen. Believing that division weakens a nation, he has used the group in an effort to split the U.S. (Lee, "To Smash a Serpent"). Bizarrely enough, in spite of all the dark history of slavery in America, this issue of *The Avengers* seems to say that racial problems are the result of foreign manipulation!

The Avengers return to the Chinese in 1967 when the Black Widow, now a SHIELD agent, pretends to defect to the other side. This highly complicated tale took place over a large number of episodes (often as only a brief update placed in the midst of another story). It ends with a confrontation between Captain America and communism's new superhero, the Red Guardian, whom we discover is none other than Natasha's husband whom she had believed dead (Thomas, "The Red Guardian"). Obviously the Red Guardian cannot win but it is interesting to note his generally positive image (as opposed to the negative one given to the Chinese). He dies protecting Natasha and actually saves Captain America (which gets the latter into an existential quandary). The fact that the episode is entitled "The Valiant Also Die" (Thomas) is highly significant for it obviously refers to the Red Guardian's sacrifice. It seems that simply being communist is no longer enough to deserve criticism. The drawings of the main Chinese villains, Colonel Ling and Dr. Yen, once again have racist overtones. It seems that race rather than communism are the key element in these characterizations.

As this period ends we can notice the increasingly negative portrayal of war. For example, in the 1967 adventure of Ixar. His people and those of another star system have fought an endless thermonuclear war and, by the time of the story, everyone but the two opposing leaders have died. However, this has not stopped the fighting, for the two leaders each build an army of androids, called ultroids. Ixar comes to earth to capture the Avengers and give their superpowers to his ultroids to gain an advantage that might, finally, allow him to win the war (Thomas, "To Conquer a Colossus"). The writers and artists present here the utter futility and devastation of eternal warfare and its resemblance to the arms race between the two superpowers is unlikely to have been an accident. The creators of *The Avengers*, like much of America's population, were becoming tired of the bloody stalemate in Vietnam. Further evidence of war weariness (and wariness) appears in the following issue in which the Greek god of war, Ares, figures prominently as antagonist (Thomas, "In Our Midst an Immortal"). Ares is undoubtedly a villain—and a cowardly one at that. By the end of the year, disillusionment had reached such a level that Captain America himself resigns, claiming he prefers to lead a normal life (Thomas, "Magneto Walks the Earth").

After Tet

By the end of 1967, total casualties had grown from 2,500 in 1965 to over 80,000 dead, wounded and missing in action (Willbanks, 6). Not surprisingly, the war declined in popularity at this time. The percentage who said "no" to Gallup's question: "Do you think the U.S. made a mistake sending troops to fight in Vietnam" went from 52 percent in February to 44 percent in October (Erskine 141). To counter this decline, the administration went on a publicity blitz. On 21 November 1967, at the National Press Club, General Westmoreland told reporters: "I am absolutely certain that whereas in 1965 the enemy was winning, today he is certainly losing" (Berman 115). This comment was only one of many cautiously optimistic statements being made by the administration, including by the president, and being widely carried in the news (Williams 292).

The Tet Offensive by North Vietnamese forces, which began on 31 January 1968, completely discredited all of these assertions. Surprise was intense because a truce had been declared for the Chinese New Year (Tet) holiday and this allowed the North Vietnamese and the NLF to make lightning progress—including a brief occupation of the American embassy in Saigon. The Americans quickly regrouped with the end result being a military victory for their forces but immense damage had been done to public confidence. While earlier polls had shown overwhelming public confidence in the conduct of the war, by the end of March the figure was dropping seriously (Braestrup, I 687). Johnson himself seemed broken by the event and soon after announced he would not seek re-election. One historian has well summed up the impact of Tet: "The Tet offensive of 1968 failed to defeat the American combat soldier on the battlefield, but it had defeated his general's strategy, his political leaders, and reversed the support of the people back home" (Arnold 91). Given the chaos in the Democratic Party, Richard Nixon won the presidential election of 1968. He promised to end the war quickly and introduced a policy of "Vietnamization"—the progressive hand over of military operations to the South Vietnamese Army in combination with American withdrawal. In reality, he extended the conflict into Laos and Cambodia. Not surprisingly, public support continued to decline (Lunch & Sperlich 25). Even more damaging, though, was the revelation in the Pentagon Papers, published in the *New York Times* in 1971 of the extent to which America's government had been deceiving the nation and the discovery of various atrocities committed by U.S. soldiers in Vietnam, notably the My Lai Massacre of 1968 and its subsequent cover up.

Paradoxically, though, this was also the period of détente, of improving relations between capitalist and communist countries. In 1969 meetings began between the U.S. and the USSR to discuss weapons reduction. Three years later this would lead to the first Strategic Arms Limitation Treaty (SALT). Furthermore, in February of 1972, Nixon went to China. However, although relations warmed between the blocs, the Vietnam War continued. Détente also brought into question earlier anti-communist rhetoric. If the U.S. was not in Vietnam for ideological reasons or because communism was so dangerous, then why was it there? Why had so many young Americans died (and were continuing to die)?

To protect the obviously corrupt government of South Vietnam? These questions would resonate throughout the next few years.

The comic book world reflected these changes. Consider the September 1968 adventure "The New Avengers vs. the Old Avengers" (Thomas). In this highly complicated story, the Avengers journey in a time machine to the past but when they return find that everything has changed dramatically—most especially themselves. The Avengers have become a group of fanatics, acting as dictators in order to impose peace on the world. Having destroyed alternative sources of power, there is no one left to challenge their authority. The two sets of Avengers end up fighting each other. Things are, of course, eventually set right (and the Avengers revealed to have been bewitched by Rama-Tut), but this story reveals a deep disenchantment with earlier Cold War rhetoric. In fact, after Tet there will be no more portrayal of evil communist spies, dictators or mad scientists in *The Avengers*. If they appear at all, their role will be much more ambiguous. Significantly when the Sons of the Serpent return in February and March 1970, the head serpent is no longer a foreigner but two Americans (one black and one white) trying to start a real race war in order to advance their own desire for power (Thomas, "Death Is the Hunter").

In a similar story from February 1971, the Avengers find themselves in an alternate universe where they meet a superhero group there, the Squadron Supreme (Thomas, "The World Is Not for Burning"). The Squadron is led by American Eagle who speaks in 1950s Cold War language, describing the Avengers as a "bunch of reds, or at least commie-symps" and who sits on a kind of throne. Once again, we see a rejection of earlier Cold War rhetoric and even a criticism of imperialist tendencies in U.S. foreign policy. Fortunately, the Avengers manage to reason with them and the two groups end up working together.

Another theme that occurs during this period is the inefficacy of the American army. For example, in "Hostage" (Thomas) of November 1970, the Zodiac crime cartel invades Manhattan and they easily defeat the army and subdue the population. Only after the Avengers intervene can the army enter Manhattan and arrest the criminals. In June 1971 (Thomas, "The Only Good Alien"), the first episode in the Kree/Skrull War, the army is shown once again as useless.

Indeed, the long series of episodes in this story is another, more developed condemnation of endless warfare. From that point of view this story can be seen as a criticism of the Cold War superpower rivalry and, more specifically, the Vietnam War. Indeed, both the Skrull and the Kree see earth as primitive and savage and only consider its strategic value (Thomas, "Behold the Mandroids"). In some ways this echoes U.S. rhetoric about the developing world, especially Vietnam (Bradley). The Avengers themselves come under the scrutiny of Senator H. Warren Craddock's Alien Activities Commission (an obvious reference to the Red scare activities of the House Un-American Activities Committee and Joseph McCarthy). Craddock goes so far as to surround Avengers mansion with tanks and helicopters and SHIELD's mandroids attack the Avengers themselves. At one point Rick Jones wishes for the simpler days of World War II and comments upon how difficult it has become to tell good guys from bad guys (Thomas, "All Things Must End"). The final message, however, is ambiguous for Craddock turns out to be a Skrull so that, once again, the comic book hedges away from clear condemnation by blaming exterior forces.

The negative vision of military conflict continues in spring 1972 when a group calling themselves Warhawks calls for preventive war. They turn out to have been enchanted by music played at Ares' command. Once again we see how easy it is to manipulate crowds and this time even the Avengers fall victim (Thomas, "The Coming of War Hawk"). The message is clear: the god of war plays an attractive melody but one that only leads to senseless destruction. In some ways, this story resembles the film *Apocalypse Now*, which presents a terrifying but strangely beautiful vision of war. An episode from July 1972 goes so far as to reflect on America's reputation, with Dr. Donald Blake (aka Thor) thinking that the poisoning of a Russian chess grandmaster was "one more example in the world's eyes of the violence they think is America, perhaps the last example they need" (Ellison, "Five Dooms to Save Tomorrow").

Indeed, disunion and internal fighting is another theme of this period with superhero battling superhero, perhaps reflecting the tension in the U.S. over demonstrations. We have already seen a number of such examples: the Avengers fight the Squadron Supreme; Ares gets the Avengers to fight each other through his enchanted war music; and the new Avengers even battle the old Avengers. The November 1970 issue has the tantalizing headline, "The Mighty Avengers Battle the Fabulous F.F. ... Or Do They?" In fact the Fantastic Four (or Three in this case) turn out to be Skrulls who have taken on their appearance (Thomas, "Hostage").

Interestingly enough, one of the rare direct references to Vietnam occurs at this time. In the September 1970 adventure "The Coming of Red Wolf" (Thomas) its Native American hero is said to have fought in an unidentified conflict that is obviously Vietnam. The main theme, however, is exploitation of Native Americans by unscrupulous capitalists.

From the American Withdrawal to the Fall of Saigon

Nixon's efforts at détente in 1972, notably his visit to China, and the disappointing results of North Vietnam's Easter Offensive that year worked together to resurrect the negotiating process. This would lead to the Paris Peace Talks and to the accord, signed on 27 January 1973, which officially ended U.S. participation in the war. Nixon hailed the agreement as bringing "peace with honor" (Nixon) and the last U.S. combat troops left Vietnam two months later. However, both North and South Vietnam almost immediately began to violate the agreement so war did not truly finish. The next two years saw the total collapse of the accord and in December 1974 North Vietnam began its final offensive against the South. Nixon had earlier promised to help the latter in such a case but he had resigned in August over Watergate and the Ford administration felt no need to honor these pledges. Communist forces progressively took control of South Vietnam until in April 1975 Saigon fell to them. Photos of helicopter evacuations from the massive U.S. embassy there humiliated the American superpower and seemed to show the world that the sacrifice of so many lives had been completely in vain. The feeling of bitterness and incomprehension was very real.

During this last period *The Avengers* continued to express disillusionment over American foreign policy. For example, when Captain America arrives in Japan he is greeted by protesters who call him an imperialist and tell him to go home. The Captain feels obliged to clarify his position: "I've come to Japan not as a representative of the American government or even an American." Times certainly had changed when Captain America himself felt obliged to downplay his nationality. Later, Sunfire, a Japanese superhero, protests his "invasion" and complains that he and the Sub-Mariner feel they are "above such petty details as international boundaries" (Englehart, "Holocaust"). This episode also shows the continuation of another theme from the earlier period—that of superhero fighting superhero. It is part of a series of issues in late 1973 in which the Avengers and the Defenders battle over the Evil Eye (Englehart, "It's Avenger vs. Defender to the Death") until they realize Loki and Dormammu have tricked them (Englehart, "Break-Through"). Once again, division comes from outside and is based on misunderstanding.

However, the most extraordinary development was the introduction of a half–Vietnamese character, Mantis, who appeared for the first time in June 1973 (Englehart, "The Lion God Lives"), as the girlfriend of the now reformed Swordsman. Mantis is from the beginning a cryptic figure, vaguely Oriental (although having blue eyes) and a martial arts expert imbued with elements of Oriental thought. It is only in March 1974 that the Swordsman reveals he met her in Vietnam (Englehart, "Houses Divided Cannot Stand").

Two issues later we discover that her father is a former German mercenary and present member of the Zodiac crime cartel. He had married the sister of the Vietnamese crime boss, Monsieur Khruul (Englehart, "Vengeance in Viet-Nam—Or—an Origin for Mantis"). This is very much in keeping with the well-known and widespread corruption of South Vietnam. After Khruul killed her mother and blinded her father, Mantis was raised by the pacifist priests of Pama (later revealed to be Kree) and taught their ways. Mysteries, however, remain and the Avengers go to Vietnam, making their first true visit in May 1974, over a year after the American withdrawal. (Englehart, "Beware the Star Stalker").

Soon after this, in November 1974, the bizarre story arc about the Celestial Madonna began. Supervillain Kang invades Avengers mansion, imprisoning its inhabitants (except the Swordsman) because he has discovered that one of the Avenger women is the Celestial Madonna and wants her for himself (Englehart, "Bid Tomorrow Good-bye"). In the midst of all this action, Iron Man finds time to regret his earlier involvement in the armaments industry, thinking: "You know, the longer I live, the sorrier I become for all the military contracts Stark Industries took in its time." Even that embodiment of the military-industrial complex has come to regret the war and, indeed, all his participation in the arms race (Johnson, Jeffrey, 64–5).

After a great deal of traveling, the Avengers return to Vietnam where they are attacked by three communist supervillains who are working with the NLF, the Crimson Dynamo (Alex Nevsky), Titanium Man (Boris Bullski) and Radioactive Man (Chen Lu). They form a group called the Titanic Three (Englehart, "The Reality Problem"). Communist villains had not appeared for a long time in *The Avengers* and it had been even longer since there had been a Russian one. One might expect that the renewed warfare in Vietnam and the obvious decline of the South caused earlier anti-communist feelings to resurface. However, the adventure bears little resemblance to previous ones. In fact, as they explain to the Avengers, they had grown tired of working for others so they came to Vietnam and allied themselves with the NLF/Viet Cong. Because of this, they became heroes of the communist Vietnamese and authority figures. The Avengers then go on their way although, admittedly Thor and Iron Man did quarrel over whether they should attack—illustrating, perhaps, the divisions in American society that the war had caused. The two groups do eventually fight each other but not for ideological reasons. Rather, they are both deceived and manipulated by a petty jewel thief called the Slasher who accuses the Avengers of a crime he committed. The Titanic Three then attack the latter but in defense of the law and, when both sides discover the deception, the battle ends. This story shows a remarkable evolution from earlier periods when communists were inevitable villains. Ideology is clearly out, yet the Titanic Three are not really heroes either. Their status is truly ambivalent and probably reflects how a lot of people felt at the time. Interestingly enough, Captain America does not even appear in this story because he is suffering a crisis of faith in his nation and its ideals. Instead he has adopted the name Nomad to signify that he is a man without a country (MacDonald).

The period from 1964 to 1975 saw growing division and disenchantment in the United States. Support ebbed for the Vietnam War as it became a bloody stalemate and as revelations about governmental deception came out. Of course, Vietnam was not the only thing responsible for this disillusionment since Watergate and other events played their role, but the war, and its rising toll of dead young Americans, undoubtedly had the greatest impact. Like much of America, the Avengers went from being strongly anti-communist supporters of interventionism to showing indifference and even bitterness and we can trace this metamorphosis in their adventures. During this period war, in general, was portrayed in an increasingly negative way and patriotism virtually disappeared from the comic book. However, the Avengers did retain and repeat one illusion—that the source of division and disagreement could be found in the exterior world and not within America herself.

Note

1. The National Liberation Front (NLF) is the official name for a group commonly called "Viet Cong" by most Americans. It was a nickname given to them by their opponents in South Vietnam, meaning Viet communist. I have preferred here to use the name they gave themselves.

Works Cited

Anderson, David. "The United States and Vietnam." In *The Vietnam War*, edited by Peter Lowe. Basingstoke: Macmillan, 1998.

Arnold, James. *The Tet Offensive 1968: Turning Point in Vietnam*. Oxford: Osprey, 1990.

Berman, Larry. *Lyndon Johnson's War: The Road to Stalemate in Vietnam*. New York: Norton, 1989.

Bradley, Mark. "Franklin Roosevelt, Trusteeship and U.S. Exceptionalism: Reconsidering the American Vision of Postcolonial Vietnam." In *A Companion to the Vietnam War*, 2d ed., edited by Marilyn Young and Robert Buzzanco. Oxford: Blackwell, 2006, 130–145.

Braestrup, Peter. *Big Story: How the American Press and Television Reported and Interpreted the Crisis of Tet 1968 in Vietnam and Washington*, 2 vols. New Haven: Yale University Press, 1977.

Bundy, McGeorge. "National Security Action Memorandum 273." 26 November 1963. http://www.lbjlib.utexas.edu/johnson/archives.hom/nsams/nsam273.asp. Accessed 4 November 2013.

Costello, Matthew. *Secret Identity Crisis: Comic Books and the Unmasking of Cold War America*. New York: Continuum, 2009.

Cullen, Jim. *Born in the USA*. New York: HarperCollins, 1997.

Erskine, Hazel. "The Polls: Is War a Mistake?" *The Public Opinion Quarterly* 34.1 (Spring 1970): 134–150.

Guan, Ang Chen. "The Vietnam War, 1964–64: The Vietnamese Communist Perspective." *Journal of Contemporary History* 35.4 (October 2000): 601–18.

Jacobs, Lawrence, and Robert Shapiro, "Lyndon Johnson, Vietnam and Public Opinion: Re-thinking Realist Theory of Leadership." *Presidential Studies Quarterly* 29.3 (Sept. 1999): 592–616.

Johnson, Jeffrey. *Super-History: Comic Book Superheroes and American Society, 1938 to the Present.* Jefferson, NC: McFarland, 2012.

Johnson, Lyndon. "Report on the Gulf of Tonkin Incident." 4 August 1964. http://millercenter. org/president/speeches/detail/3998. Accessed 13 November 2013.

Johnson, Robert David. *Congress and the Cold War.* Cambridge: Cambridge University Press, 2006.

Lunch, William, and Peter Sperlich. "American Public Opinion and the War in Vietnam." *Western Political Quarterly* 32.1 (March 1979): 21–44.

MacDonald, Andrew, and Virginia. "Sold American: The Metamorphosis of Captain America." In *The Journal of Popular Culture* 10.1 (Summer 1976): 249–58.

Moyar, Mark. *Triumph Forsaken: The Vietnam War, 1954–1965.* Cambridge: Cambridge University Press, 2006.

Nixon, Richard. "Address to the Nation Announcing the Conclusion of an Agreement on Ending the War and Restoring Peace in Vietnam." 23 January 1973. www.presidency.ucsb. edu/ws/?pid=3808. Accessed 16 November 2013.

Wells, Tom. *War Within: America's Battle Over Vietnam.* Berkeley: University of California Press, 1994.

Willbanks, James. *The Tet Offensive: A Concise History.* New York: Columbia University Press, 2007.

Williams, Kevin. "The Light at the End of the Tunnel: The Mass Media, Public Opinion and the Vietnam War." In *Getting the Message: News, Truth and Power*, edited by John Eldridge. London: Routledge, 2004.

Young, Marilyn. *The Vietnam Wars 1945–1990.* New York: Harper Perennial, 1991.

Zubok, Vladislav. *A Failed Empire: The Soviet Union in the Cold War from Stalin to Gorbachev*, rev. ed. Chapel Hill: University of North Carolina Press, 2009.

The Avengers Issues

Ellison, Harlan (plot), Roy Thomas (w), Rich Buckler (p), Dan Adkins (i), John Costanza (l). "Five Dooms to Save Tomorrow." *The Avengers* #101 (July 1972).

Englehart, Steve (w), Bob Brown (p), Mike Esposito (i), June Braverman (l). "Holocaust." *The Avengers* #117 (Nov. 1973).

Englehart, Steve (w), Bob Brown (p), Don Heck (i), Petra Goldberg (c), John Costanza (l). "Vengeance in Viet-Nam—Or—The Origins of Mantis." *The Avengers* #123 (May 1974).

Englehart, Steve (w), John Buscema (p), David Cockrum (i), George Roussos (c), John Costanza (l). "Beware the Star Stalker." *The Avengers* #124 (June 1974).

Englehart, Steve (w), John Buscema (p), Don Heck (i), Petra Goldberg (c), John Costanza (l). "Houses Divided Cannot Stand." *The Avengers* #121 (Mar. 1974).

Englehart, Steve (w), Sal Buscema (p), Frank Bolle (i), Tom Orzechowski (l). "Break-Through." *Defenders* #10 (Nov. 1973).

Englehart, Steve (w), Sal Buscema (p), Mike Esposito (i), Art Simek (l). "It's Avenger vs. Defender to the Death." *The Avengers* #116 (Oct. 1973).

Englehart, Steve (w), Sal Buscema (p), Joe Staton (i), Bill Mantlo (c), Tony Orzechowski (l). "Bid Tomorrow Goodbye." *The Avengers* #129 (Nov. 1974).

Engelhart, Steve (w), Sal Buscema (p), Joe Staton (i), Bill Mantlo (c), Joe Rosen (l). "The Reality Problem." *The Avengers* #130 (Dec. 1974).

Englehart, Steve (w), Don Heck (p), Frank Bolle (i), Petra Goldberg (c), John Constanza (l). "The Lion God Lives." *The Avengers* #112 (June 1973).

Lee, Stan (w), Don Heck (a), Dick Ayers (i), Artie Simek (l). "The Commissar Commands." *The Avengers* #18 (July 1965).

Lee, Stan (w), Don Heck (p), Frank Giacoia (i), Sam Rosen (l). "Frenzy from a Far-Off Land." *The Avengers* #30 (July 1966).

Lee, Stan (w), Don Heck (a), Artie Simek (i), Irv Forbrush (l). "The Sign of the Serpent." *The Avengers* #32 (Sept. 1966).

Lee, Stan (w), Don Heck (a), Artie Simek (i), Irv Forbrush (l). "To Smash a Serpent." *The Avengers* #33 (Oct. 1966).

Lee, Stan (w), Don Heck (a), Wally Wood (i), Artie Simek (l). "Vengeance Is Ours." *The Avengers* #20 (Sept. 1965).

Thomas, Roy (w), Neal Adams (p), Tom Palmer (i), Sam Rosen (l). "Behold the Mandroids." *The Avengers* #94 (Dec. 1971).

Thomas, Roy (w), Neal Adams (p), Tom Palmer (i), Sam Rosen (l). "This Beachhead Earth." *The Avengers* #93 (Nov. 1970).

Thomas, Roy (w), John Buscema (p), George Bell (i), Jerry Mann (l). "The Red Guardian." *The Avengers* #43 (Aug. 1967).

Thomas, Roy (w), John Buscema (p), Vince Colletta (i), Sam Rosen (l). "The Valiant Also Die." *The Avengers* #44 (Sept. 1967).

Thomas, Roy (w), John Buscema (p), Frank Giacola (i), Mike Stevens (l). "The World Is Not for Burning." *The Avengers* #85 (Feb. 1971).

Thomas, Roy (w), John Buscema (p), Tom Palmer (i), Sam Rosen (l). "The Coming of Red Wolf," *The Avengers* #80 (Sept. 1970).

Thomas, Roy (w), John Buscema (p), Tom Palmer (i), Sam Rosen (l). "Death Is the Hunter." *The Avengers* #74 (Mar. 1970).

Thomas, Roy (w), John Buscema (p), Tom Palmer (i), Sam Rosen (l). "Hostage." *The Avengers* #82 (Nov. 1970).

Thomas, Roy (w), John Buscema (p), George Tuska (i), L.R. Gregory (l). "Magneto Walks the Earth." *The Avengers* #47 (Dec. 1967).

Thomas, Roy (w), Sal Buscema (p), Sam Grainger (i), Sam Rosen (l). "The Only Good Alien...." *The Avengers* #89 (June 1971).

Thomas, Roy (w), Sal Buscema (p), George Roussos (i), Sam Rosen (l). "All Things Must End." *The Avengers* #92 (Sept. 1971).

Thomas, Roy (w), Don Heck (p), George Bell (i), Artie Simek (l). "In Our Midst an Immortal." *The Avengers* #38 (Mar. 1967).

Thomas, Roy (w), Don Heck (p), George Bell (i), Artie Simek (l). "The Monstrous Master Plan of the Mandarin." *The Avengers Annual* #1 (Sept. 1967).

Thomas, Roy (w), Don Heck (a), Sam Rosen (l). "The Ultroids Attack." *The Avengers* #36 (Jan. 1967).

Thomas, Roy (w), Don Heck (p), Werner Roth (p), Vince Colletta (i), Joe Rosen (l). "The New Avengers vs. the Old Avengers." *The Avengers Annual* #2 (Sept. 1968).

Thomas, Roy (w), Barry Windsor-Smith (p), Sal Buscema (i), Sam Rosen (l). "The Coming of War Hawk." *The Avengers* #98 (Apr. 1972).

Thomas, Roy (w), Don Heck (a), Artie Simek (l). "To Conquer a Colossus." *The Avengers* #37 (Feb. 1967).

"The Kree-Skrull War" and the Growth of Uncertainty in the Cold War Era

PAUL R. KOHL

The Cold War defined the United States' internal self-image and its international relations from 1945 to 1989. As Todd Gitlin has noted, "For four decades, anti–Communism remained a binder in the American cement" (66). The simplistic formula of Freedom versus Communism gave Americans a vision of what they were for and what they were against. So certain was the Cold War dichotomy that John J. Mearsheimer could write, after the fall of the Soviet Union, that "we may, however, wake up one day lamenting the loss of order that the Cold War gave to the anarchy of international relations" (44).

But the Cold War also contributed to a good degree of American uncertainty when that war went hot, embroiling the country in the conflict in Vietnam. It was at this point that consensus disappeared and great generational and political strife engulfed the nation. Todd Gitlin noted the change in his book *The Twilight of Common Dreams:*

> The seams of American identity began to give way. Growing numbers in the civil rights and antiwar movements began by rejecting American practices, went on to reject American ideals, and soon, since America *was* its ideals, rejected the conventional versions of American identity altogether [68].

Likewise Matthew J. Costello notes similar changes in American culture and in the pages of American comic books, especially those published by Marvel Comics. "As the Cold War consensus eroded," he writes, "the moral certainty of the comics also became a thing of the past" (90). The certainty of attitudes towards Communism and Communist foes in the first part of the 1960s is quite different from the handling of such matters later in the decade and in the early 1970s, when the war in Southeast Asia polarized the country.

This essay is a reading of one such "uncertain" text, the "Kree-Skrull War" from 1971 to 1972. It is a reading that recognizes the text in the same way as Marxist critic Fredric Jameson does, as a symbolic act that is grasped as the resolution to "determinate contradictions (80)." In the "Kree-Skrull War," writer Roy Thomas reflects the uncertain nature of American society at the time but attempts to resolve it by going back to a time when America was quite certain of itself, a time prior even to the Cold War: World War II.

The Marvel Universe was forged in the crucible of the Cold War. It's right there on page 9 of *Fantastic Four* #1 (Nov. 1961), the first entry by Marvel Comics into a renewed superhero narrative universe. As the members of the not-yet super-powered foursome debate whether to risk the effects of cosmic rays by being the first in space, Susan Storm takes Ben Grimm's fears to task. "Ben, we've got to take that chance ... unless we want the Commies to beat us to it!" she challenges him, adding, "I ... I never thought that you would be a coward!" (Lee and Kirby 9). It's also there in the origin of Iron Man, hit in the chest by shrapnel in the jungles of Vietnam. Likewise it can be seen in the radioactive undercurrents of the origins of the major heroes of the early sixties Marvel era: Spider-Man, Hulk, the X-Men and Daredevil. At the same time the appearance of Captain America in *The Avengers* #4 (Mar. 1964) brought a character who defined the certainties of the World War II era and brought them into the early Marvel Cold War period.

The consistent backdrop of the Cold War gave Marvel the contemporary feeling that its rival, DC Comics, lacked and attracted an older, more sophisticated audience. As the decade wore on, however, Marvel's representation of the Cold War became more sophisticated as well, an acknowledgement of the fissures that were opening up in American culture at the time. An example of the change at Marvel was the figure of the Black Widow, who started as a Soviet spy but later became a hero and member of the Avengers.

Those fissures were primarily the product of the Vietnam War and the disagreements over its handling and the issue of the Draft. In 1971 and 1972, as the war seemed all but lost Marvel published an epic story that contained elements that echoed the Cold War struggle and the troubles in Vietnam. Writer Roy Thomas and artists Sal Buscema, Neal Adams, and John Buscema produced "The Kree-Skrull War" in *The Avengers* #89–97 (June 1971–1972), presenting a retrospective of the previous thirty years of American history in the guise of an interplanetary battle with Earth stuck in the middle.

"The Kree-Skrull War" involves the two warring interstellar races of the title and the role of Earth as a battlefield in the far-ranging struggle. Both the Kree and the Skrulls had made their presences known on Earth in preceding Marvel history. The Skrulls first appear as early as *Fantastic Four* #2 (Jan. 1962), while the Kree show up for the first time in *Fantastic Four* #65 (Aug. 1967). The two races share a complicated history, with Earth as a constant proving ground.

The Kree originated on the planet Hala, and it was there that the Skrulls arrived, setting up a contest between the Kree and the intelligent species they shared their planet with, the plant-like Cotati. When the Skrulls declared the Cotati the winners, the outraged Kree killed the Skrull contact team, stole their technology, and declared war. Along the way the Kree took a particular interest in the Earth, creating the offshoot of humanity known as the Inhumans. The Skrulls likewise took an interest in Earth when they sensed a threat from its new superhumans. Their essential attribute is that they can shape shift to look like anyone, hence their skill as secret agents and spies.

What both the Kree and Skrulls have in common, in addition to their war, is the tendency of their races to be totalitarian in nature. The Skrulls, for example, naturally have a similar appearance, but possess the ability to disguise themselves as anything. Thus, the Skrulls are a perfect counterpart to the Communist threat Americans were alerted to by Senator Joseph McCarthy or allegorical films like 1956's *Invasion of the Body Snatchers*. The Kree, meanwhile, reflect a fascistic tendency with their leader, the Supreme Intelligence, "at once its supreme dictator and an object of religious worship" (*Marvel Encyclopedia* 292).

The true nature of the Kree and Skrulls are not essential, however, except for their totalitarian tendencies. As Matthew J. Costello points out in *Secret Identity Crisis: Comic Books & The Unmasking of Cold War America*, in the Marvel Universe of the early 1960s, both the United States' enemies of past and present were often conflated. As he notes, "the communists were frequently equated with (and often directly linked to) the Nazis of World War II, an objective evil against which to define an objective virtue" (61). As such, the Kree and Skrulls together continue that equation in the Marvel Universe.

However, the "Kree-Skrull War" storyline was also published in what Costello shows is a much more ambiguous time. He argues, "As the high Cold War tensions and certainties of the Cuban Missile Crisis were replaced by the ambiguities of the Vietnam War and Watergate, the world of the Marvel universe would become increasingly ambiguous, critical, and uncertain" (84). That ambiguity here is partially provided by the figure of Captain Mar-Vell, or Captain Marvel as he would later be known. Prior to this story Mar-Vell was sent to Earth to scout out a possible invasion, but defected, ultimately helping to defend the Earth. Mar-Vell's presence as an ally in the Kree-Skrull conflict creates a new dynamic between Earth and the Kree, especially given the role of the Supreme Intelligence in bonding Mar-Vell with Rick Jones. Now the Kree, unlikely allies against the Skrulls, take a role similar to the South Vietnamese, an ambiguous ally against the North Vietnamese.

As the story begins in *The Avengers* #89 (June 1971) Earth is in the middle of a major conflict. Here we are introduced to Mar-Vell and Rick Jones. Both have been joined together in consciousness but only one may appear on Earth at a time, the other forced to spend his time in the Negative Zone. That is until Mar-Vell figures out a way to break them both out. The Avengers discover that during his lengthy stay in the Negative Zone, Mar-Vell contracted a large dose of radiation, so they seek him out to cure him of potential side effects.

A small group of Avengers, Vision, Quicksilver, and Scarlet Witch, with the help of Rick Jones, find Mar-Vell. So too does the Sentry, sent by Ronan the Accuser, a Kree usurper to the Supreme Intelligence's power, who has come to kill Mar-Vell, who has been branded a traitor.

The scene then shifts in issue #90 and #91 (July and Aug. 1971), as the Sentry kidnaps Mar-Vell to the Arctic, where the Kree "Evo-Ray" is de-evolving the area and a group of scientists nearby back to the stone age. The threat is defeated but it sets up a greater conflict that will play out in the rest of the story.

In *The Avengers* #92 (Sept. 1971), the three Avengers, plus Rick and Mar-Vell return to New York. They are not given a hero's welcome, however, as the three scientists turned briefly into prehistoric men reveal what happened to them in the Arctic, against the suggestion of the Avengers. Mar-Vell is rumored to be part of the Kree plot and is branded by McCarthyesque senator H. Warren Craddock to be an alien spy. He is called to surrender to authorities, but is defended by the Avengers, who let him escape to refuge with the newly arrived Carol Danvers. It is the Avengers who are then branded traitors by the public and brought before Craddock's "Alien Activities Commission."

The charges of betrayal against the Avengers leads to Rick Jones (and Thomas) reminiscing about the simpler days of the 1940s, when things were black and white. Thinking back on the comic books he used to read, Jones notes, "They were just super-powered Joes with a clear idea of what truth was—an' justice—yeah, even law an' order...." Jones concludes that "these days you can't tell the good guys from the bad guys without a scorecard ... and there ain't no scorecard" (Thomas, "All Things...").

The Avengers are about to find out how true Jones' pronouncements are. As they return from the Alien Activities Commission hearing they find Avengers Mansion surrounded by protestors calling them traitors. They are then confronted by three founding members of the team, Captain America, Iron Man, and Thor. Captain America states: "We feel you acted irresponsibly in shielding Captain Marvel from investigation. Thus, by authority of our by-laws, we three hereby declare the Avengers disbanded—for all time" (Thomas, "All Things..."). Meanwhile Rick Jones has a vision of Mar-Vell in danger and runs to save him.

As issue #93 begins the Vision arrives back in Avengers mansion badly damaged. Ant-Man repairs the damage but is confronted by a surprise, "a mystery within an enigma, [...] one of which our readers may learn one day (15)." With the Vision repaired, the android tells of how he and the other Avengers were surprised by Skrulls disguising themselves as the Fantastic Four after they went in search of Captain Marvel at the upstate New York farmhouse he went to with Carol Danvers. He notes this was after Captain America, Thor, and Iron Man disassembled the team, which they deny, setting up yet another mystery.

Vision returns to the farmhouse with the other Avengers to defeat the Skrulls, but not before the Super-Skrull, who combines all the powers of the Fantastic Four, reveals that he has been disguised as Carol Danvers all along. The Super-Skrull's ship takes off with Mar-Vell, Quicksilver, and the Scarlet Witch aboard. They race towards the Skrull Empire. Here the mutant twins are threatened with death unless Mar-Vell creates an all-powerful weapon, the omni-wave.

Meanwhile the Kree have kidnapped Rick Jones, based upon "a momentary impulse" (Thomas, "Part VIII") and brought him to Ronan the Accuser. Ronan imprisons Rick with the captive Supreme Intelligence, who relates to Rick that he has been responsible for much of what has occurred:

> Indeed, my once-powerful mental waves cannot penetrate the energy-shields which protect the upper echelon of both Kree and Skrulls from those waves. Thus, I winged them instead across the void—to your globe, Rick Jones ... where, first, I indirectly caused the Avengers and Mar-Vell to be hounded ... by one H. Warren Craddock [Thomas, "Part VIII"].

The Supreme Intelligence admits as well that he is responsible for the courtroom vision that sent Rick after Mar-Vell, Mar-Vell's own abduction by the Skrulls, and Rick's abduction by the Kree, all for the purpose of sending Rick back to the Negative Zone.

This is where we find Rick as the final chapter of the saga begins, faced with impending doom at the hands of the Negative Zone's ruler, Annihilus. Rick is not in the Negative Zone for long, however, as he finds he has the ability to effect Annihilus and his existence in the Zone with his mind. He transports himself back to the Supreme Intelligence, who explains that within Rick Jones lies the human race's potential to make thoughts concrete. As Ronan and the Kree attack once more, the Supreme Intelligence coaxes Rick to think once more of the heroes of his youth, those from the comic magazines of the 1940s. And so appear a plethora of Golden Age heroes who fought during World War II who fight the Kree to a standstill. Rick then uses his enhanced mind power to immobilize the Skrull fleet in time for the Avengers to arrive and defeat them. Finally, it is revealed that H. Warren Craddock and the Captain America, Iron Man, and Thor were all Skrulls.

This labyrinthine plot synopsis can only begin to explain the complexity of Thomas' work. But it is clear that he is trying to overcome the ambiguity and the doubt of the 1970s by returning to the clear days of the 1940s. Roy Thomas is noted for his love of the World War II era heroes and was one of the first fans to take them seriously enough to begin his own fanzine, *Alter-Ego*, in 1961.

Rick Jones is the hub upon which the whole plot revolves because his history contains the contradictions which Thomas is here trying to overcome. Originally introduced into the Marvel Universe in *The Incredible Hulk* #1, Rick was the teenager saved by Dr. Bruce Banner just as a Gamma Ray bomb was about to go off. Banner was, of course, caught in the blast and ended up as the Hulk. Rick stayed with him and as the Hulk joined the Avengers, Rick tagged along.

This set him up for his second major incarnation, as Captain America's partner, the modern-day equivalent to Bucky Barnes. In his first appearance of the 1960s, in *The Avengers* #4, Cap notes Rick's resemblance to Bucky. This direct reference to World War II fits the pattern that Costello notes. There is a certainty to Rick taking Bucky's role that disappears when Rick begins sharing the mind of Captain Marvel.

Rick Jones' journey is the journey of Marvel Comics in the 1960s, from innocence to assuredness to doubt. Rick brings the journey full circle by conjuring up the superheroes of the past, from those days in the 1940s and 1950s when the enemy was clear. What writer Roy Thomas does in the "Kree-Skrull War" is create a story that combines the ambiguity of the late '60s Marvel period with the tropes of the earlier era.

Oh, yes. And the secret that Hank Pym discovered in the Vision? It was later revealed that the body of the Vision was originally the android body of the original, World War II era, Human Torch. And so it comes full circle.

Works Cited

Costello, Matthew J. *Secret Identity Crisis: Comic Books & the Unmasking of Cold War America*. New York: Continuum, 2009.

Gitlin, Todd. *The Twilight of Common Dreams*. New York: Henry Holt, 1995.

Jameson, Fredric. *The Political Unconscious*. Ithaca: Cornell University Press, 1982.

Lee, Stan (w), and Jack Kirby (a). *Fantastic Four* #1. New York: Marvel Comics, 1961.

The Marvel Encyclopedia. New York: Marvel/DK, 2006.

Mearsheimer, John J. "Why We Will Soon Miss the Cold War." In Richard K. Betts, ed., *Conflict After the Cold War: Arguments on Causes of War and Peace*, pp. 44–61. New York: Macmillan, 1994.

Thomas, Roy (w), Sal Buscema, Neal Adams, and John Buscema (a). "The Kree-Skrull War." In *The Avengers* #89–97. New York: Marvel Comics, 1971–72.

Earth's Mightiest (Dysfunctional) Family

The Evolution of The Avengers Under Jim Shooter

Jason Sacks

The Avengers was one of the most stable titles of the Marvel Comics Group during the 1960s and '70s. During the 13-year period between *The Avengers* #1 and #150, only Stan Lee, Roy Thomas and Steve Englehart chronicled the adventures of Earth's Mightiest Heroes[1]—a record matched only by *Fantastic Four* and *Amazing Spider-Man*.

During that decade-and-a-half run, those three writers placed the series squarely at the center of the ever-burgeoning Marvel Universe; *The Avengers* was where Marvel's readers could always find epic adventures combining several of their favorite heroes into one team. But when Englehart was forced off of *The Avengers* in an internecine struggle with editor-in-chief Gerry Conway, *The Avengers* had two new writers within a year. Conway, covering the dual task of editor-in-chief and writer, only lasted a half-dozen issues as scripter of the series before giving way to Jim Shooter, a man recently arrived from DC who had an influential future in front of him at Marvel.[2]

Shooter's ascension to the reins of one of Marvel's flagship series added a new level of energy to the Avengers' epics. One of his first innovations emphasizing events that had deep emotional impact for members of the Avengers and bringing back characters that had histories with the team. He thereby deepened the stakes of his stories. All of the returns and revivals led to a sense that Shooter was creating a large (and dysfunctional) family around Earth's Mightiest Heroes.

When Shooter then brought in the nigh-omnipotent Korvac as an enemy of the team, it seemed *The Avengers* had gone full circle, back to its roots as both the center of universe-spanning action and the home of a very large collection of super-heroes in the Marvel Universe. But while the Korvac Saga appears to be a typical Avengers action epic on the surface, it also became emblematic of a number of major changes in the Marvel Universe that would play out in unexpected ways in the 1980s under his influential and controversial tenure as editor-in-chief at Marvel.

The Life and Times of Jim Shooter

Jim Shooter has one of the most unusual careers of any comic book professional. He was possibly the youngest writer ever to script comic books when he assumed the writing chores on "Legion of Super-Heroes" in DC's *Adventure Comics* at the age of fourteen. A high school student from Pittsburgh, Pennsylvania, with a family that was frequently desperate for income, the young Shooter urgently needed to earn money to help keep a roof over his family's head. As he reflects:

> At age thirteen, I was ready to write a comic book. I had desperately sought copies of Marvel Comics—borrowed, traded for, or managed to scrape up twelve cents to buy. I studied them. Analyzed them. Read till I knew them by heart. So, I wrote and drew, as best I could, a story of the *Legion of Super-Heroes* starring Superboy, for National's *Adventure Comics* and sent it off. I picked the *Legion* because I judged it to be the worst comic book National published, and therefore, it seemed, the one where they needed me most. I waited, alternating between confidence and despair. Months passed. Finally an encouraging letter came! Essentially it said "send us another one." In almost no time, I sent them two more. I waited. Months passed. On February 10, 1966, the suspense ended with a phone call from Mort Weisinger, Vice President of National Comics and editor of the Superman family of titles, which included *Adventure Comics*. He was a little worried over my age, fourteen by then, but, nonetheless bought the first three stories I'd sent him and commissioned others. The money from those stories couldn't have come at a better time for my family [Shooter, "I Aimed"].

Shooter took over the "Legion" strip with *Adventure Comics* #346 (July 1966) with a tale called "One of Us Is a Traitor." The story showed his youthful enthusiasm as he immediately introduced four new characters: the beautiful Princess Projectra; Karate Kid, a hero created because the Legion members generally didn't engage in physical combat; the doomed Ferro Lad; and Nemesis Kid, who would betray the team.

Shooter brought a teenager's love for epic and emotional drama to the series. He played up romances and rivalries between team members. He also added a strong element of many teen's favorite concept, tragedy, as Ferro Lad sacrificed himself to fight the preternaturally powerful Sun Eater. Ferro Lad's death in *Adven-*

ture Comics #353 was a bracingly emotional moment that stuck in readers' minds and stood in contrast with the blandly presented death of Lightning Lad in *Adventure Comics* #304 and destruction of Triplicate Girl's third body in *Adventure Comics* #341, both of which had only a tiny impact on their teammates.[3]

Though Shooter was working hard on the series, earning fan acclaim both in the fan press of the day and in the comic's letter pages, he had a hellish time working on the Legion strips due to his excruciating working relationship with tyrannical editor Mort Weisinger. Weisinger was by all accounts a vicious bully, a man who frequently berated even his most experienced creators in the most vicious of terms, always looking to strip their self-esteem for his own sadistic reasons. As Shooter muses in retrospect:

> People don't believe how nasty Mort was. They think I'm exaggerating. Nah. It had nothing to do with "strictness" or "professionalism." He was nasty. Ask Roy Thomas, who worked for him for a couple of weeks and quit. Ask Carey [*sic*] Bates.
>
> I suspect he was especially tough on me. [Weisinger's assistant E.] Nelson [Bridwell] said so. Our theory was that he was "grooming" me (with a bull-whip) for a staff position [Shooter, "I Aimed"].

Shooter soon moved into writing other titles for Weisinger along with the "Legion" strip: *Superman, Action Comics, Superman's Pal Jimmy Olsen, Captain Action* and more. His ability to channel the then-popular Marvel style into a DC comic served him well, despite the terrible gauntlet he had to navigate in order to remain employed. Weisinger would call Shooter every Wednesday evening after the end of the *Batman* TV show to discuss his comics, ready with enough abuse and fury about his work to traumatize the young man. In fact, the teenage writer was so distressed by the phone calls, it reportedly took years before he could answer a ringing phone without his hands shaking. And though he was making enough money to keep his family out of poverty, the decent income wasn't worth all the terrible abuse.

At eighteen, after four years of that manipulation, Shooter graduated from both high school and DC Comics. After leaving DC's offices, Shooter first stopped at Marvel, where he had always hoped to work. Though he was offered a seemingly lucrative $125 per week contract to write for the House of Ideas, it was impossible to survive financially in New York on a $125 per week salary and thus he had to move back to Pittsburgh to take a job in the advertising industry rather than comics. As Jim Shooter put it, he was washed up at age 18 (Shooter, "Washed Up").

Though the comics industry moved on without him, Shooter's passion for comics never left him and he returned to New York four years later. After a quick stop at Marvel—which he felt moved on without him so quickly that he had trouble understanding the comics of that era—Shooter quickly received an offer to return to *Superboy and the Legion of Super-Heroes,* recently returned to their own title after several years as a back-up feature, and now with a different editor. The malicious Mort Weisinger had retired shortly after Shooter left; benign new *Legion* editor Murray Boltinoff had no concerns about the former wunderkind, who was ready to report to duty. However, Shooter lamented that "the editors I worked with were easier to endure than Mort was, but even more formula-oriented" (Shooter, "Here I Go").

In December 1975, then Marvel editor-in-chief Marv Wolfman offered Shooter a job as assistant editor, essentially his second-in-command. Shooter subsequently retained the job as assistant editor under Wolfman's successor Archie Goodwin, and on January 2, 1978, was appointed as editor-in-chief himself. During his time on staff, Shooter wrote a number of comics for Marvel, including several issues of *Amazing Spider-Man, Daredevil,* the *Spider-Man* newspaper strip, and *The Avengers.*

Jim Shooter felt that clear storytelling was the key to quality comics. While writing the Legion in the 1960s, he would provide hand-drawn layouts for the artists to follow. During that era, Weisinger tutored the young man on key storytelling principles. Throughout Shooter's early tenure as an assistant editor at Marvel, Stan Lee would meet frequently with him to share his own theories on how to tell a great comics adventure. Shooter was struck by how similar the two men's approaches were.

Shooter's time at the helm on *The Avengers* displays a command of those techniques and principles. In his stories, it is always clear who the characters are on each page. Characters are almost always introduced in an unambiguous manner, and an attempt is always made to differentiate the heroes both by their look and their personality. As Shooter explained, "I want good stories. That's all I ever ask for. Because it's comics. I want visual stories. Because it's a story I want conflict and some kind of resolution and so forth" (Groth).

Most importantly, in the most radical break from the creators who preceded him as editors at Marvel, Shooter believed that an editorial presence was an essential part of the creative process. Regarding his days at Marvel as an assistant editor, Shooter concluded that writers who were able to produce their own material without supervision would tend to repeat bad patterns, deliver stories that required too much inside knowledge, and didn't introduce a reader to the plot they were to read.

The Avengers Family Unit

One of the key motifs of Shooter's development of *The Avengers* is the enormous number of heroes that appear. He seemed enchanted with the idea of creating a giant team of super heroes, perhaps channeling his experiences with the 25-member Legion. The first hero to return was Thor, whom Steve Englehart had written out in *The Avengers* #151 (Sept. 1976) because he was too powerful to have teammates (reader mail disagreed strongly with that idea). Shooter brings back Thor in his third issue as writer, *The Avengers* #159 (May 1977), without explanation. In a subtle tip to the larger saga he's creating, In the same issue, the Black Panther returns to the ranks without explanation.

Indeed, there seems to be a concerted element in Shooter's tales to return as many classic Avengers as possible to the series. In *The Avengers* #160 (June 1977), founding member Henry Pym's mind snaps; he flashes back to the early days of the Avengers, dons the Ant-Man uniform that he wore in that premiere issue. Readers are shown Iron Man searching for Thor in Asgard, in Attilan for the Inhumans, and even on a Western ranch looking for Hawkeye and the Two-Gun Kid. Clearly Shooter, now at the center of the Marvel Comics Group due to his professional commitments, saw *The Avengers* as his opportunity to explore the heroes of the universe that he was controlling. Later, *The Avengers* #163 (Sept. 1977) returns Hercules—then a member of Marvel's '70s super-team the Champions—to the pages where he hadn't appeared for several years. Anybody and everybody in the Marvel Universe could pop up in the Avengers during Shooter's tenure.

Shooter clearly saw the Avengers as a family, a large and inclusive team of heroes around which many of the Marvel characters orbited. It seemed any hero from the Marvel Universe might appear in these stories—Captain Marvel, only a loose ally of the team, joins the group for a handful of adventures, as does Ms. Marvel (both of whom had their own comics at the time and thus could profit from cross-promotion) and the Guardians of the Galaxy (whose series had been canceled earlier that year). Even characters like Daredevil and Spider-Man, who never crossed the Avengers' orbit during those years, made cameos in the book.

If the Avengers were a giant extended family, they were a family that has its own unique level of dysfunction. Many of the key elements in Shooter's early issues center on the strange relationship that Wonder Man has with the Vision. The "synthezoid" Vision (essentially a living robot built upon the android body of the original Human Torch) has the brainwave patterns of the recently resurrected Wonder Man; that shared pattern causes anger, resentment, and fury between the two characters—they engage in a vicious brawl in *The Avengers* #158 (Apr. 1977)—and in *The Avengers* #160 (June 1977), Shooter has the Grim Reaper, Wonder Man's bereaved brother, hold the Vision and Wonder Man hostage as part of a bizarre trial that would determine who is his real sibling.

In another key storyline, Golden Age hero the Whizzer, then believed to be the father of Avengers Quicksilver and the Scarlet Witch, joins the team (despite his advanced age) before he's forced to the sideline. It's unusual to see a real father figure in comics, especially one who's fighting a struggle with advancing age alongside battling evil villains.

The whole tangled incestuous web of the Avengers becomes even more twisted with the two-part Ultron saga beginning in *The Avengers* #162 (Aug. 1977), when Ultron (who created the Vision and was created by Hank Pym, a.k.a Ant-Man and Yellowjacket) attempts to create a robotic bride for himself by transferring the mind of Pym's wife Janet (a.k.a. Avenger the Wasp) into a female robotic body. Shooter gives the robotic wife the name Jocasta, a resonant name that causes Black Panther to consider: "Hank himself created Ultron— and if I remember my Avengers history right, Ultron immediately turned on his father and tried to kill him—like a living, mechanized manifestation of the Oedipus complex. In classical literature, Oedipus murdered his father—and married his mother. And now Ultron has kidnapped Jan, Hank's wife—his— mother?" (Shooter and Perez, "The Bride of Ultron"). Despite these convoluted family links, if there's any ethos around family shown in Shooter's *Avengers* run, it's that of inclusion, of the idea that conflicts can be overcome or ignored and that differences should be sublimated to the ideas of responsibility and teamwork. Wonder Man and the Vision become friends after their fight; the Whizzer is respected by his allies; even Jocasta finds a home of sorts with the team.

The Slow Burn

Shooter's writing is powerful in the way he slowly builds up the series of issues that have been dubbed the Korvac Saga; many of the elements that he sets in motion pay off over a long period of time. In a style that perfectly fit the episodic nature of comics in the 1970s, Shooter would frequently introduce major story elements one month, step away from those concepts for several months to follow other threads, then return to his overriding topics when everything was in place for the next step and an eventual payoff. In that way, he would reward longtime readers and intrigue new readers while, ideally, never making either feel confused.

Thus, it's slightly hard to peg an issue of *The Avengers* as the beginning of the Korvac Saga. However, for the purposes of simplicity in this essay, the first chapter that introduces the threat is *The Avengers* #167 (Jan. 1978). The time-spanning galactic heroes the Guardians of the Galaxy come back to 1970s Earth to confront a menace that they had recently fought in the 31st century in 1977's *Thor Annual* #6: a strange cybernetic man called Korvac. As the Guardians tell the story, Korvac has come back in time to kill the young Vance Astro, in the future a Guardian, as a way of reversing the events in the *Thor Annual*. Though that sounds like a classic science fiction plot—not to mention a clichéd trope—Shooter immediately gives Korvac's adventure a twist in his own characteristic way.

In an apparent non sequitur, the story shifts from the Guardians' spaceship to a fashion show on Park Avenue, hosted by Janet Pym, who is both a superhero and a fashion designer. Watching the models on the runway are two men. One, Kyle Richmond, a.k.a. Nighthawk of the Defenders, will be another of Shooter's Easter eggs, the other is a strange blonde man in a tuxedo, who will be crucial to future events. As the Wasp and Nighthawk battle the Porcupine, who wandered into the fashion show to steal jewels, the strange man wanders backstage at the fashion show. He locks eyes on a beauty with golden tresses, extends his hand to her, and "he does not speak. She feels his desire, senses his offer. It is received with awestruck wonder—but no trace of disbelief. It is unquestionably real. She accepts. Gratefully. Totally. Together ... unseen ... they depart" (Shooter, Stern, and Perez, "Tomorrow").

Readers had to be wondering just what that moment was all about, and what it meant in the larger scheme. There was no easy way to correlate the Korvac storyline with what the readers had just seen. But in the next chapter, readers would be able to easily make a connection between Korvac and the mysterious man.

The scene at the fashion show also plays with another of Shooter's favorite themes: the juxtaposition of the fanciful and the ordinary. One of the most striking aspects of the Korvac Saga is the way Shooter plays with the idea that some of the most fantastic events imaginable are happening in the midst of ordinary everyday life—demigods visit fashion shows and live in upper class New York suburbs; Hercules rides in taxis and has his luggage lost by airlines; the Avengers commandeer an ordinary city bus to get to Korvac's house when their quinjets are grounded; the Guardians spend much of their time sitting in trees protecting young Vance Astro. The contrast of the grand and the prosaic helps give this narrative a sense that it could be happening right outside readers' windows.

The following issue emphasizes that juxtaposition and explores it in terrifying detail. In *The Avengers* #167 (Jan. 1978), the near-omnipotent Starhawk journeys to a "large, comfortable home" in suburban Forest Hills Gardens to confront the strange being that lives there. As the beautiful fashion model from the previous issue answers the door, Starhawk and Korvac confront each other with a strange exchange. Starhawk mutters, "Therein lies the hope of the universe!" to which Korvac replies, "I ... am the hope of the universe" (Shooter, Stern, and Perez, "Tomorrow"). Grandiose thoughts from this man who quickly introduces himself as Michael (and his model girlfriend as Carina). Starhawk is invited into the home for what appears to be the most civilized clash in the history of the Marvel Universe. The two great cosmic avatars wage war on every place of existence, clashing on a physical scale and a cosmic scale at the same time. In the struggle, we witness Starhawk punch Michael, "the stunning impact of the blow ripping through the sum of his being. Somewhere in the depths of the cosmos within his mind, a planet shatters—and in unison, the billion souls who inhabit the sub-realty of the enemy's id scream in utter terror as their entire dimension trembles" (Shooter, Stern, and Perez, "Tomorrow").

In a series of progressively inventive layouts by artist George Pérez, readers witness the battle cross dimensions and realities, and progress in surreal and cosmic ways. Michael finally triumphs, turning Starhawk to dust, "though a few of the most subtle earth-dwellers sensed the psychic and physical disruptions our battle caused, none divined the source. The greatest powers of the universe remain unaware of our meeting" (Shooter, Stern, and Perez, "Tomorrow"). With perhaps the most frightening and symbolic of Michael's powers, he then returns Starhawk to life, identical to his previous make-up, with the only exception that "henceforth you will not remember this incident, nor the fact of my existence ... and never shall your senses perceive me" (Shooter, Stern, and Perez, "Tomorrow").

This initial encounter has shown Michael/Korvac in all of his complexity. He's powerful beyond the comprehension of mortal man. He's a vicious fighter who will do anything to triumph. But perhaps most notably, Michael is not quite evil in the ordinary sense of the term. He may be incomprehensible to mortal ken and may be operating on a completely different plane from humanity and the aliens that live inside his head, but he is not, strictly speaking, an evil being. He could have chosen to leave Starhawk dead and wipe all memory of his nemesis from the world; instead, Michael chooses to show mercy to Starhawk's family by reviving him and taking action to simply be left alone. That mercy and the depth of character it demonstrates gives this writing its considerable power and complexity.

Again showing his love of the long game, Shooter then moves away from the Korvac storyline for several issues as he brings back Ultron for a return appearance and takes the opportunity to tie up loose ends. But even while addressing other plot lines, Shooter keeps his eyes on the Korvac plot: heroes start to disappear without explanation; first Two-Gun Kid disappears in front of his best friend Hawkeye, then Quicksilver disappears from in front of his wife, the Inhuman Crystal, then Captain America disappears at the end of the second battle with Ultron. Scarlet Witch reacts to the stress of the moment with the despairing comment, "It never ends ... and each trial is harder than the last" (Shooter and Buscema, "Holocaust"). Finally, the last page of *The Avengers* #172 (June 1978) shows the impact of these disappearances: as Iron Man states, "Our main ... our only concern is to keep trying to find out how our people are being abducted ... and by whom!" readers are shown a high-tech chamber in which heroes are trapped in giant test tubes. Quicksilver, Captain America, Moondragon, Vision, Two-Gun Kid and Jocasta are shown, along with other tubes that can't be easily seen (Shooter and Buscema, "Holocaust"). The reader has to wonder what other heroes have been captured, and how all of this relates to Korvac's apparently pernicious plans.

The Avengers #173 (July 1978), a transitional chapter, answers those questions at last. It shows the turmoil that these events have caused our heroes. The Scarlet Witch is near a nervous breakdown thinking about the kidnapping of her husband and her brother; meanwhile, several other members of the team mysteriously are beamed from Avengers Mansion without explanation. Finally, as the issue ends, the truth behind the abductions is revealed: the being who kidnapped the heroes is the strange alien titan the Collector.

While the Avengers confront the Collector, Korvac continued his planning. Michael surveys all the realms of existence to prepare for his "proprietorship," as he calls it. He observes the Watcher, the Greek and Norse gods, even the devilish Mephisto, but "none yet guess that I even exist!" (Shooter, Mantlo, and Wenzel, "Captives"). He even observes the nearly omniscient Eternity, swearing to soon take what is rightfully his—a barely-hidden threat of galactic hegemony.

In *The Avengers* #174 (Aug. 1978), the Collector reveals that he has kidnapped the team as a kind of celestial Noah, preserving these life forms from a terrible fate at the hands of the enemy. The Collector says, "The enemy, in his rash attempt to achieve universal sovereignty, might cause a war among the great powers of the cosmos—a war which could obliterate all reality." But just as he's about to reveal the name of his enemy, Korvac blasts the Collector from tens of thousands of miles away.

For the subsequent two issues the team tries to locate Korvac, and Shooter strives to humanize him. We witness Korvac swimming to keep in shape but also forgiving Carina for being the daughter of the Collector and for initially conspiring against her lover. The couple fall in love right in front of readers eyes, then make love in a way that bonds them cosmically, rising above the bonds of mere mortality. Their love had truly become transcendent. With that, Korvac/Michael seems to find peace. By the end of *The Avengers* #175 (Sept. 1978), he states, "I have no enmity towards the Avengers, and it would be a pity indeed to have to destroy them!" However, if the team did find him, he adds, "I'm afraid they will most fervently wish that they had not!" (Shooter, Michelinie, and Wenzel, "The End...").

Finally in the climactic pages of *The Avengers* #176 (Oct. 1978), the Avengers find their way to Michael's home, a normal abode with furniture that is "all in good taste," as the Wasp declares. But just as the team is ready to walk away and leave Korvac/Michael alone, his own machinations cause his scheme to fail. Neither Iron Man, nor Moondragon, nor Captain Marvel, nor Jocasta can sense anything wrong about the man. But Starhawk is startled by the fact that these heroes seem to be talking to a man who is not there. Korvac had previously prevented Starhawk from perceiving him; now that lack of vision leads to his ultimate discovery. With a look of profound unhappiness on his face, Korvac proclaims, "I'm afraid you've found the one you call ... the enemy. And you can't imagine how very, very sad that makes me." He continues, "There is so much cruelty in the cosmos, much injustice. And I was in the unique position to alter that, to bring all of existence under my sane and benevolent rule." Turning cosmic, Korvac screams, "Your meddling heroics have destroyed the hopes of a universe, the dreams of a god! And for that—you shall pay!" (Shooter, Michelinie, and Wenzel, "The Destiny").

In *The Avengers* #177 (Nov. 1978) Korvac massacres the Avengers and Guardians one after the next so callously and quickly that it's difficult to keep track of all the devastation. Michael is too strong and too ruthless for the valiant Captain America and the super-powerful Wonder Man. But in a moment of weakness, Moondragon is able to manipulate Michael's brain and Thor staggers him. The cosmic being is then slain on the bizarre battlefield of suburban New York.

But in the heat of battle, events turn on the most powerful force of all: that of the human heart to love. As Shooter tells us in his narration:

> In his moment of trial and pain, Michael casts his gaze towards Carina, his beloved. Once she was the daughter of the Collector, who was, in truth, one of the elders of the universe. He perceived Michael's existence, though no other could. Fearing Michael, her father sent her to Michael's side, that she might betray him—but, when the moment came, she was torn, for she had grown to love Michael. And so, she hesitated—and in that moment caused the end of her father's life! Now Michael reaches out to her ... for love ... for respite ... for strength to go on. And though she loves him beyond all earthly ken, the panorama of bloodshed before her and the dark prospect of cosmic war ahead have wrought turmoil in her soul. She is torn ... and she hesitates—and in that moment ends the life of her beloved [Shooter and Wenzel, "The Hope..."].

Carina strikes out at the heroes with her own superpowers, but Thor's hammer strikes her dead, her hand only inches away from that of her beloved Michael. Moondragon reports that Michael left a breath of life in the seemingly dead Avengers and thus the shattering clash is over. But the lingering question remains, at least in the head of Moondragon: was the war worth it?

The slow burn of Shooter's well-learned storytelling techniques help to lead to a satisfying conclusion. Shooter showed the attentive reader that the stakes of this clash were both incredibly high and thoroughly human. Readers feel the pain of the deaths of the Avengers' family, as well as the profound horror of perishing within inches of your beloved. By showing the twists and turns of the love between Michael and Carina, Shooter underlines the fact that death will forever separate Korvac from the woman he loved. Carina and Korvac were a tight family unit but were permanently separated in death.

The Evil (or Not) of Korvac

Hanging over this entire grand tale is a crucial question: was Korvac actually an evil being? This is the type of question many Americans were struggling with following the long Vietnam War, when the question of right and wrong became much murkier than it had been in previous fights. Superhero comic books, the home of clearly delineated battles between good and evil since their rise to popularity during World War II, were asking deeper questions about morality and the nature of good and evil. Shades of gray in both heroes and villains were becoming more common.

Keep in mind that even when Korvac kills our heroes, he goes out of his way to bring them back to life almost immediately—and that Starhawk, whom he dispatched in a heated flurry, is turned back from sand to a human. Perhaps more important is the fact that though Korvac has it completely in his power to kill the Avengers in *The Avengers* #177 (Nov. 1978), he chooses to restore the lives of all those who fought him. Moondragon the psychic reads Michael's mind and reports that "in the heat of battle I dared to walk the planes of Michael's mind. I have seen inside his heart—and touched the souls of Michael and his beloved. He was not evil, Thor! He sought not to rule us ... nor even to interfere with our madness. He wished only to free us from the capricious whims of Eternity" (Shooter and Wenzel, "The Hope...").

It's a remarkable statement, one that clouds this story filled with death, confusion, and fear, with an unusual level of moral ambiguity for an Avengers epic. An empathetic reader is forced to stare at the compelling, silent panel of Michael's and Carina's hands separated in death and wonder if the equivocal ending paints Earth's Mightiest Heroes as the heavies. Looking back through the adventure, it's hard not to think Korvac is at worst a benign creature, a formerly malevolent man who—despite the concerns of the Collector and his angry previous life—appears to have found some real personal peace. Is it possible that this cosmically powered soul basically just wanted to be left alone? It's an elegant thought, and one that bears thoughtful consideration. Where Korvac's previous writers, Steve Gerber and Len Wein, made him a one-dimensional baddie,[4] Shooter renders the being in a more complex way, showing the godlike depths of his emotions and demonstrating that the human heart is the most powerful force of all.

Jim Shooter: All-Powerful and Misunderstood?

Just as interesting for armchair analysts is the question of whether Korvac's complexity in some ways reflects Shooter's ambiguous place in the comics industry. Though Bill Mantlo and David Michelinie co-scripted several issues, the plot and framework of this epic tale were Shooter's, and it was written as he began his first struggles to reform Marvel Comics into his own vision for the company. Many of Marvel's creators accused him of megalomania as he created order out of the company's chaos, even as the company's sales surged and positive reforms were instituted. Like Korvac, Shooter made small and subtle changes to the reality of comic book creators, reforms that would have reverberations for decades to come. And yet, he was also seen as the villain; in his eyes, misunderstood as the man who was destroying the old Marvel.

Just as interesting, Shooter returned to the idea of an omnipotent and often misunderstood super-being in his vastly popular *Marvel Super-Heroes Secret Wars* and *Secret Wars II* comics in 1984 and 1985. Shooter created a character named the Beyonder, who whisks the Earth's super-heroes to a strange alien planet as a way of learning about humanity; *Secret Wars II* has the Beyonder come to Earth in order to learn about "strange human customs." There are echoes of the Korvac Saga in the all-powerful but ambiguously motivated outsider who wants to bring his own vision to the world, though the Beyonder takes a much more active role in destruction than Korvac does.

The Korvac Saga, part of Jim Shooter's first run on *The Avengers* in 1977 and 1978, is a fascinating and complex adventure that stands as the ideal companion for earlier grand Avengers epics. But just as the Kree-Skrull War showed the approach of writer Roy Thomas and the account of the Celestial Madonna displayed that of writer Steve Englehart, the Korvac Saga is informed by the worldview of Jim Shooter, circa the late 1970s. Readers can see the forces that made Shooter into the man and the professional that he became, showcasing his anxieties about family and his approach to his work. More than anything, however, the Korvac Saga shows Shooter's deep and abiding humanity.

It's easy to read this and feel that either the Avengers or Korvac are villains, but under Shooter's scripting, it's clear that neither side in the struggle was ultimately good or evil. Indeed, a key reason the Korvac Saga stands as one of the finest of its time is precisely because of that complex ambiguity. This was an era when moral ambiguity was rising as moral certitude was waning. This societal concern was reflected in this storyline. Intriguingly for the man who took control of Marvel Comics during this period, Shooter delivered a comic book with a plot that was decidedly outside the norm.

Notes

1. With a brief two-part storyline written by Tony Isabella.
2. At the same time that Shooter arrived from DC, Conway went over to DC, where he created his own sub-line of comics dubbed "Conway's Corner"; in effect, he was the editor-in-chief of a mini-comics group at DC.
3. The destruction of Triplicate Girl's third body became a running joke among Legion fandom for the heroine's bland smiling acceptance of a terrible trauma.
4. Despite the fact that both of them wrote many notable comics in their careers.

Works Cited

Groth, Gary. "Pushing Marvel into the '80s: An Interview with Jim Shooter." *The Comics Journal* #60 (Nov. 1980). Stamford, CT: Fantagraphics Books.

Shooter, Jim. "Here I Go Again." Accessed 15 January 2014, at http://www.jimshooter.com/2011/03/here-i-go-again.html.

_____. "I Aimed to Be Better Than the Worst." Accessed 15 January 2014, at http://www.jimshooter.com/2011/03/i-aimed-to-be-better-than-worst.html.

_____. "A Leap of Fate." Accessed 15 January 2014, at http://www.jimshooter.com/2011/03/leap-of-fate.html.

_____. "Washed Up at Eighteen." Accessed 15 January 2014, at http://www.jimshooter.com/2011/03/washed-up-at-eighteen.html.

Shooter, Jim (w), and Sal Buscema (a). "When Avengers Clash!!" *Avengers* #158 (Apr. 1977). New York: Marvel Comics.

_____, and _____. "Holocaust in New York Harbor." *The Avengers* #172 (June 1978). New York: Marvel Comics.

Shooter, Jim (w), and John Byrne (a). "To Fall by Treachery!" *The Avengers* #164 (Oct. 1977). New York: Marvel Comics.

Shooter, Jim, and Bill Mantlo (w) and Dave Wenzel (a). "Captives of the Collector!" *The Avengers* #174 (Aug. 1978). New York: Marvel Comics.

Shooter, Jim, David Michelinie (w) and Sal Buscema (a). "Threshold of Oblivion!" *The Avengers* #173 (July 1978). New York: Marvel Comics.

Shooter, Jim, and David Michelinie (w) and Dave Wenzel (a). "The Destiny Hunt!" *The Avengers* #176 (Oct. 1978). New York: Marvel Comics.

_____, and _____. "The End ... and the Beginning!" *The Avengers* #175 (Sept. 1978). New York: Marvel Comics.

Shooter, Jim (w), and Sheldon Moldoff (a). "One of Us Is a Traitor!" *Adventure Comics* #346 (July 1966). New York: DC Comics.

Shooter, Jim (w), and George Pérez (a). "Beware the Ant-Man!" *The Avengers* #161 (July 1977). New York: Marvel Comics.

_____, and _____. "The Bride of Ultron!" *The Avengers* #162 (Aug. 1977). New York: Marvel Comics.

_____, and _____. "First Blood!" *The Avengers* #168 (Feb. 1978). New York: Marvel Comics.

_____, and _____. "...Though Hell Should Bar the Way!" *The Avengers* #170 (Apr. 1978). New York: Marvel Comics.

_____, and _____. "The Trial." *The Avengers* #160 (June 1977). New York: Marvel Comics.

Shooter, Jim (w), Roger Stern (w), and George Perez (a). "Tomorrow Dies Today!" *The Avengers* #167 (Jan. 1978). New York: Marvel Comics, 1978.

Shooter, Jim (w), and Curt Swan (a). "The Doomed Legionnaire!" *Adventure Comics* #353 (Feb. 1967). New York: DC Comics.

Shooter, Jim (w), and George Tuska (a). "The Demi-God Must Die!" *The Avengers* #163 (Sept. 1977). New York: Marvel Comics.

Shooter, Jim (w), and David Wenzel (a). "The Hope ... and the Slaughter!" *The Avengers* #177 (Nov. 1978). New York: Marvel Comics.

Siegel, Jerry (w), and John Forte (a). "The Stolen Superpowers!" *Adventure Comics* #304 (Jan. 1963). New York: DC Comics.

Siegel, Jerry (w), and Curt Swan (a). "Colossal Boy's One Man War!" *Adventure Comics* #341 (Feb. 1966). New York: DC Comics.

Madonna's Birth and God's Death

Marvel Comics, the Death of God Movement, and the Religious Climate of the 1970s

Nathan Gibbard

The changing role of religion in Marvel comics from the 1960s to the 1970s can be seen in the juxtaposition of two of its major editors-in-chief. For Stan Lee, his guiding principle in regards to religion in comics was "I wanted these stories to be palatable for readers of every type" (*Stan Lee's Mutants, Monsters, and Marvels*), further noting elsewhere, "I scrupulously tried to avoid any reference to any specific organized religion. I thought of myself as an equal opportunity writer" (Lee, xii). For Jim Shooter, the use of religious ideas and images were acceptable, as long as they did not attempt to definitely raise one religion as corresponding to the reality of the Marvel Universe: "If a character expresses a belief, that's fine. It's that character's opinion. Bringing in God or his Son and definitively proving that Christianity is the official doctrine of Marvel is another thing entirely" ("Rooting out corruption"). There was a subtle shift during the 1970s from the use of general themes of myth and culture, to a willingness to embrace more explicit religious images and ideas.

Given the cultural tumult at the time, this is hardly surprising. From the 1960s to the 1970s religion became a topic of conversation in a way it had not been before. If religion is connected with culture, then drawing upon any culture necessarily connects one with religious ideas of one form or the other. Indeed, Anthony Mills' recent work on how Marvel comics re-structured the traditional American monomyth, corresponding to theological developments during the 1960s and 70s, as well as Jeffrey Kripal's *Mutants and Mystics: Science Fiction, Superhero Comics, and the Paranormal,* are both modern, theological considerations of the intersections between American religious developments and superheroes.

The Avengers during the 1970s is a particularly good example of this. Looking at the Avengers, the Korvac Saga especially draws on images that any theological student of the 1960s and 70s would have recognized as belonging to a particular stream of radical theology. The claim for the literal death of an omnipotent, omniscient, benevolent deity was hardly striking, but belonged to the popularization of the death of God theologies in the mid–1960s.

Two controversies, with very different results, arose during the 1970s regarding religion within the Marvel universe. The first was Steve Englehart's work with Dr. Strange. In one storyline in particular, Dr. Strange chases an entity backward through time as it gathers magical energy in order to recreate reality. Arriving just prior to the Big Bang, the entity—Sise-neg—creates the universe, but stops short of creating it in its own image, realizing that the universe is already in harmony and as it should be (Englehart, "Sise-Neg"). Sise-neg— Genesis spelt backwards—was an obvious play upon the Jewish-Christian conception of God. This was made explicit when Sise-Neg states at the end of the two issue arc, just before the Big Bang: "When you think of this think not of the man called Sise-neg—but the God called Genesis" (*ibid.*). Upon reading it after publication, Stan Lee sent a letter to Englehart and Brunner (the artist) saying they needed to print a retraction, clarifying it was not God but *a* god. As Brunner notes, "Steve and I said, 'Oh, come on! This is the whole point of the story! If we did that retraction of God, this is meaningless!'" (Cooke). Instead, they wrote a fake letter from a fictitious pastor in Texas, and Roy Thomas—the then editor-in-chief—printed that instead.

Conversely, when Tony Isabella, the writer of *Ghost Rider* from 1974 to 1976, wanted to have Ghost Rider be saved both literally and spiritually by Jesus, his powers turning from demonic to divine, the final issue was instead re-written by Shooter at the last minute. Instead of Jesus being revealed as the story was clearly leading up to, Shooter rewrote the ending so that it was Satan creating an illusion of someone looking like Jesus.[1] While writers could play with religious imagery, they could not make the Marvel universe an explicitly Christian one, wanting to leave it up to personal interpretation, but that did not mean they could not play with particular Christian and Jewish conceptions of God.

In regards to *The Avengers*, religion, comics, and culture it is interesting to note the relative explosion of covers that make mention, or reference religious imagery or terms in some way during the 1970s. One reason for this increase was undoubtedly a result of that fact that Thor, the Norse god of Thunder was a recurring character in *The Avengers*, yet this does not fully account for the increase in specific usage referencing religious imagery—including words—on the covers and in the story titles. If this was the reason, one might expect to find such references at a steady rate throughout the 1960, 70s, and 80s, but this is not the case. During the 1960s, looking at *The Avengers* titles for references to "god," allusions to religious imagery (e.g., titles taken from Bible passages), and religious iconography, 7 comic books fit those characteristics. In the 1970s, that amount almost doubled to 13. The 1980s also had 13, but six of them were directly connected to the "Assault on Olympus" story arc. We can compare this with the Fantastic Four, a title that also dealt with cosmic issues on a regular basis, but had a strikingly less frequent prevalence of such titles. For both the 1960s and 1970s, there were 6 such covers in each decade. Such covers and titles still only account for 11 percent of the total covers and titles for *The Avengers* during the 1970s, but those statistics alone don't reveal the provocative nature of many of those titles. "Godhood's End" and "The Day of the Godslayer." These titles are out of place when compared to the wider Marvel family.

Two Avengers story arcs in particular fit this pattern of religious influence. The first is the Celestial Madonna story arc, written by Steve Englehart after his previously mentioned Sise-Neg storyline. Englehart had no particular fear of dealing with religious themes, and drew heavily on Christian sources in the story's development. While the term "Messiah"—the Celestial Messiah being born from the Celestial Madonna—is more generally Christian, the term "Madonna" is particular to Roman Catholic tradition. The term itself was not used by Protestant denomination which dominated the American religious cultural landscape at the time, making it a particular metaphor for a certain kind of grouping of characteristics. The term "Madonna" (literally, "My Lady") is a term used to designate the Virgin Mary, the mother of Jesus, usually when she is portrayed in artistic representations of some sort. According to Catholic and Orthodox tradition, Mary remained "pure," chaste and virginal throughout her entire life, not even wanting to be married to Joseph in the first place but desiring to give her life wholly to God as a sort of proto-nun.

It is only in the context of this *earthly* Madonna that Englehart's *celestial* Madonna makes full sense, and also is suggestive of a normative view regarding the idea of which would be the *better* Madonna. Within Catholic tradition Mary is seen as born without original sin and living a sinless life, a near model of perfection. Mantis, as the Celestial Madonna, is chosen because she *is* "the perfect human" (Englehart, "Let All Men..."). While Mary is pure and virginal, wanting to abstain from the world, it is precisely Mantis's willingness to embrace the world, including her sexuality, that completes her training as the Celestial Madonna. "She was selected to abandon her temple and walk amongst other humans to seek perfect humanity.... Mantis was learning the secrets of mankind ... on the streets of mankind" (*ibid.*). Historically, it is important to remember that without the context of the 1960s and the sexual revolution, this idea of sexuality adding an element to a person's wholeness and perfection would have made little sense. A certain religious conflict is being articulated, here, with a particular side being chosen. Against previous models of purity, Mantis' "perfection" includes her earthly, instinctual desire and sexuality, preparing her for her role as the bearer of the Celestial Messiah. This is a long way from the traditional image of a pure, chaste Catholic Madonna.

In keeping with his own counsel regarding religion and Marvel Comics, in Shooter's own work as writer of *The Avengers*, he also engaged directly with religious imagery and ideas while skirting particulars. In *The Avengers* #171 (May 1978), in pursuit of Jocasta, the trail leads to a convent, complete with traditional, iconic images of nuns. This visual metaphor would have most likely been factually erroneous in the wake of Vatican II, where the vast majority of female religious orders shed the traditional garb for more secular looking clothing, but is necessary for effect. George Pérez drew here upon the visual connection to nuns, strictness and goodness, in order to set-up a dichotomy with the fact that the Avengers arch-foe, Ultron, is using the convent as his hiding place. If Pérez would have used as his visual representation what most female religious orders in 1978 really looked like, he would have risked the audience not being able to understand the visual metaphorical juxtaposition.

In the same issue, after the nuns whom Ultron had kidnapped had been saved and freed by the Avengers, the Scarlet Witch notices the Norse god Thor is uncomfortable. Thor responds to Wanda's concern, "Aye, Wanda, verily! This house of Christian worship hath no regard for the Asgardian god of thunder!" When asked if the nuns should honor him, Thor replies, "Nay, milady! E'en my father, mighty Odin, who is called all-powerful, doth lay no claim to supreme divinity ... and yet t'would seem that many mark my very existence as an affront to this edifice!" This exchange is sometimes perceived as a tacit acknowledgement that Thor recognizes a higher authority than Odin and himself, but such a reading is not necessarily the only one. While Thor later has no difficulty in acknowledging a higher authority by swearing on the Bible (Byrne) that has no bearing on the reading of Thor at the time it was first published. Unfortunately, no letters from fans regarding this moment appear in *The Avengers* to indicate how the line itself was taken. However, given the rising secularism and the appeal to the counter-cultural movement that influenced Marvel Comics, it can just as easily be seen as an indictment against any single entity claiming omnipotence.

It is the Korvac Saga, though, which seems to bare the most connections with certain religious impulses at the time. *The Avengers* #171 (May 1978) is part of the overall saga, and so Thor's statement must be seen in the context of the overall arc. In the Korvac Saga, the titular Korvac travels back in time, fleeing from Thor and the Guardians of the Galaxy. There, in the past, he finds himself on Galactus' cosmic ship. Wandering over the vastness of the ship, and unknown to the Devourer of Worlds, Korvac manages to steal a small portion of the power cosmic, expanding his knowledge immensely. Indeed, his journey to omnipotence is interesting in that it seems to go by way of omniscience. In Galactus' ship, Korvac plugs himself in "only to find that knowledge is, indeed, power ... and that he had underestimated the impact of absorbing knowledge as boundless as infinity!" (Shooter, "The End..."). In Korvac's pursuit of knowledge, he gains power and a different view as to the nature of reality as a consequence. This alone is different than many other near-omnipotent characters who pursue power for power's sake. Indeed, instead of a megalomaniacal villain clamoring for domination, Korvac turns himself into "Michael," living quietly and unobtrusively in Forest Hills Gardens, New York, as he tries to figure out a way to unravel the weight of fate imposed by Eternity on sentient life. Rather than directly trying to take over the world, Michael's goal is "correcting the chaos, healing the injustice that civilization had heaped up on a battered universe." In the end Moondragon, who alone among the Avengers chanced to walk Michael's mind, says of Michael, "He was not evil, Thor! He sought not to rule us..., nor even to interfere with our madness! He wished only to free us from the capricious whims of Eternity!" (Shooter, "The Hope..."). It is interesting to note that only one letter, published in *The Avengers* #180, talks about Michael as a villain (St. Germaine). Even at the time there seems an awareness of the subtlety of the character.

It is interesting to note that it is not Michael who causes the Avengers grief, requiring an intervention, but rather the Collector. Starting in *The Avengers* #168 (Jan. 1968), the Collector starts "collecting" the Avengers as he feels something major is about to happen, wishing to preserve them. It is only as a result of this action by the Collector that the Avengers pursue this perceived new threat. Eventually the Avengers, accompanied by the Guardians of the Galaxy, find out the location of Michael and attack him. Despite Michael's reticence, the Avengers hurl themselves at the near-omnipotent Michael and he is forced to defend himself. In the end, it is not the Avengers or the Guardians of the Galaxy's physical or moral might that defeats him, but love. Seeing the destruction he is causing to the superheroes, Michael's wife, Carina, loses faith in his purpose. Seeing it in her eyes, Michael wills himself to die. With his dying breath, he brings the fallen Avengers and Guardians of the Galaxy back to life (Shooter, "The Hope...").

If the letters page in *The Avengers* #181 (Feb. 1979) was indicative of the letters received, many of those reading the Korvac Saga were aware that they were reading a story that played off of traditional expectations. As David J. Welsh from Austin, Texas, said, "I must congratulate you on your conclusion to the Michael/Korvac storyline.... To begin with, there's the clever way you manipu-

lated and even reversed the fundamental superhero-supervillian dichotomy."
He then goes on to note, "Michael was not another malicious, power-hungry
tyrant bent on controlling the cosmos. He was, in fact, just what he claimed to
be—an all-powerful, all-knowing benevolent being with a desire to liberate the
universe from the chaos and injustice of blind, unthinking chance." Jacob Lasky,
in the same vein (in defense of the Avengers) notes, "None of them [the
Avengers] could truly grasp the concept, none of them really understood what
was going on. The true battle, therefore, was being fought on a much higher
place, Michael contesting against the fabric of the universe, fate, if you will."
Especially with Welsh's letter, there is an indication of an awareness that Michael
was far more than normal, portrayed in God-like (not god-like) terms. All-
powerful, all-knowing, benevolent: this particular combination of terms is not
random but specific to the Christian tradition and recognizably so.

What is interesting here in this story is the particular constellation of characteristics within a comic book character, and the end result. Many characters
are benevolent, but few are either all-powerful or all-knowing. The Watcher and
Odin may come close to being All-knowing, but are either not categorically
benevolent or all-powerful. Galactus and most other universe-spanning threats
might be close to being all-powerful, but are seldom all-knowing, and never
benevolent. "Michael" is unique here, and a clear aberration in the standard
trope of cosmic entities in superhero comics as almost uniformly being defined
by their power. A key part of the aberration is that "Michael" seeks to free creation itself from the whims of Eternity, entering into and changing creation for
the better. And all as a result of his cosmic love for Carina. And then "God"
dies.

The idea of the "death of God" was not a foreign concept to those of the
late 1970s, or even early 1970s, death of God theologians having entered public
consciousness in the mid–1960s. In their April 8, 1966, issue, *Time* magazine
published what the *Los Angeles Times* named one of the top 10 magazine covers
"that shook the world," and which the *New York Times* called "a signpost of the
1960s, testimony to the wrenching social changes transforming the United
States." The cover featured no images, only a black background with red bold
letters, asking the question "Is God Dead?" Within, following up on an article
with a similar topic published in their October 22, 1965, issue, the magazine
raised the prominence of several key radical theologians that were part of the
"death of God" movement in theology. One of the chief of these figures was
Thomas Altizer, professor of theology at Emory University at the time.

Altizer, unlike some other death of God theologians such as George Vahanian, did not believe that the "death of God" was a figurative turn of phrase, but
rather argued that God literally died, totally emptying himself and becoming

immanent within creation. Christ died, was not resurrected, but instead stopped being apart from humanity, and was rather dispersed into it. Indeed, for Altizer, "the original heresy was the identification of the Church as the body of Christ" (Alitzer, *Gospel* 132). He even goes so far as to claim in *Oriental Mysticism and Biblical Eschatology* that "the world of Christian theology ... is irredeemably satanic insofar as it is bound to the dead body of that God negated and left behind by the forward and apocalyptic movement of the incarnation" (626).

The key part for Altizer's thought is Jesus' kenosis, or self-emptying into the world. This was part of God's purpose from the beginning, to slowly empty God's self into humanity, precisely doing away with the need to look outwards to some sort of transcendent law-giver for authority, but rather to own the moral call to action: we are freed from a transcendentally imposed fate which does not require human action, to live in a fully profane world where meaning is not given from the outside but within. Jesus enters into the world to do away with the capricious whims of fate, not unlike "Michael" a decade later. In such a way, God is present in everything and is fully immanent within creation, in good, bad, sacred and profane. This view as very different than someone like Vahanian, one of the first death of God theologians, who argued that the death of God that Nietzsche's prophet had predicted had come about, not as a literal death of God, but in the death of a certain conception of a God that acts within history.

Death of God theologians, such as Altizer and Vahanian, but also William Hamilton and Paul van Buren—all identified in the 1965 and 1966 *Time* articles—were part of the cultural, but also religious, tumult at the time and heavily influenced by Nietzsche's death of God and Dietrich Bonhoeffer's religionless Christianity. As a backlash against the rigid social construction arising from the 1950s and the Cold War, the 1960s saw a questioning of many of the assumptions that had informed American cultural life. Considering the role religion had played in that cultural life, it was in many ways natural that traditional religion was also caught in this backlash. It was in this context that Nietzsche was Americanized, and thus made more suitable for an American audience. Indeed, as Jennifer Ratner-Rosenhagen points out in *American Nietzsche: A History of an Icon and His Ideas,* there is something odd about the embrace of Nietzsche by American intellectuals as his anti–Christian, anti-democratic views seem to be in stark contrast with American societal roots. This embrace of Nietzsche is not so foreign, though, if we trace the way in which he was received, translated, and domesticated within the American context.

Ratner-Rosenhagen points out that it was often theologians and religious thinkers that started laying this groundwork for transmission into the American context. Glossing over the more strongly-worded anti–Christian sentiments in

Nietzsche, they focused on the idea that religion was judged by what it did to help people, rather than on belief. This focus on doing coincided well with the supporters of the social gospel movement prevalent in the late 1800s and early 1900s. Conversely, the reception of Nietzsche was a different sort of reception than most other philosophical texts, appealing to the emotions of the readers rather than strictly the intellect: "Likening it to a 'romp in the hay,'" these readers "described their experiences of reading Nietzsche as intoxicating, bracing, challenging, ennobling. But most of all, the experience taught them about the value of ideas as an experience, and words as a vital form of action" (166).

But it wasn't just counter-cultural students and non-conformists that were leading this charge, but academics. Harvey Cox's *A Secular City*, was almost ubiquitous on college campuses during the 1960s. As Patrick Allitt notes in *Religion in America Since 1945: A History*; "In the mid-sixties every intellectual who didn't have a handy copy of Marshall McLuhan's *Understanding Media* in his or her back pocket had *A Secular City* there instead; it sold almost a million copies" (74). Cox argues that with modernization comes the inevitable secularization of society, and the retreat of religion. This was not a new argument, being seen in Max Weber's analysis of religion and production in *The Protestant Ethic and the Spirit of Capitalism* in 1905, but Cox made the theory popular and accessible to a much larger number of people, especially non-specialists. "Like Thomas Merton's *Seven Storey Mountain* in the 1940s," Allitt notes, "it is marvellously representative of its age, and as long as you are in the midst of reading it, it seems unquestionably right" (*ibid.*). With the apparent retreat of religion an inevitability, this opened up the door for other practices to gain in popularity. But this apparent retreat also tapped in to a general torpor among some within society of the ability of religion to answer the bigger questions at all. Religion might not have caused the mass destruction of life during the Second World War, but it was certainly seen by some as a contributing factor. It was with the horror of the Second World War, and the hardening of ideologies during the Cold War, which hammered the final nail into the coffin of Enlightenment ideas of human progress. It is in this context that theologies that posited the death of God grew.

In this context, New Age spiritualities proliferated, drawing upon a plethora of material already available, but largely underground during the 1950s. As Philip Jenkins notes, "Very little of the New Age was terribly novel to the 1960s or 1970s, and a great deal of it was based on movements and writings firmly rooted in the age of Guy Ballard and Aleister Crowley" (166). What was different from their predecessors was the wide-spread use of drugs, and the element of UFOology that permeated the movement, but also a more conscious recognition that previous forms of religion and societal boundaries did not seem capable of addressing the reality of existence. In the same way that superhero comics through Marvel's evolution of the genre benefited from the malaise regarding traditional approaches to the genre, so too did former occult and theosophic practices benefit from the malaise captured in the song by Peggy Lee, "Is That All There Is?" Indeed, out of this context arose what Charles Taylor identifies in *A Secular Age* as an embrace of the idea of authenticity, and especially views that supported the Immanent Counter-Enlightenment view of the world (473–535). Both religion and reason were insufficient for living in the world, and so a new way that rejected both in key ways was needed.

This counter-cultural turn on campuses, and among teenagers is significant also because it is precisely during the 1960s and 1970s whereby superhero comics, notably Marvel comics, begin to attract an audience of teenagers and young adults. Marvel, especially, was at the forefront of this charge. According to *Esquire* magazine in 1965, Spider-Man and the Hulk were ranked along with Bob Dylan and Che Guevara as favorite revolutionary icons (Wright 223). Nietzsche's works, modified by theologians and philosophers for an American audience, gave impetus to a reaction against a dominant culture that was increasingly seen as corrupt and backwards. Traditional views of religion itself were also implicated within this matrix, and served as an easy source of rebellion.

It is within this confluence of sources that the 1970s Avengers should be read, providing us a way to re-examine other comic book sources during the 1960s and 70s for their religious influences. Jim Shooter himself has acknowledged that it was the characterization of Marvel superheroes, a characterization that also resonated with students on university campuses, which attracted him to write comics as a young person. The same climate that permeated the 1970s, including the rise of the Christian right which threatened the apparent developments of the 1960s away from certain religious ideas, influenced and affected cultural industries including Marvel. In this context, it was easy to tap in to certain imagery prevalent at the time, sometimes making religious statements without their meaning. In the letters page of *Ghost Rider* #21 (Dec. 1976), following after the controversy regarding the identity of the 'friend' that had helped Ghost Rider, the editor's note:

> We've had many readers write and tell us that *Ghost Rider* has religious overtones, but the consensus among us "hicks" is that this mag—like all other Marvel comics—has many overtones. Sure, we can take credit for the stories and the artwork—but *not* the overtones. They're partly our subconscious and partly your imagination. You and all the other readers bring part of yourselves to our stories, and a lot of what you draw out of them is what you put in.

While this is a nice statement, and one must assume that it truly is trying to capture a view that they considered true, it is difficult to reconcile with what had occurred in the context of other Marvel storylines. Five short year before, in

The Amazing Spider-Man, it was precisely the overtones that the comic sought to convey to the reader: in that case an anti-drug message. Considering that in the case of *Ghost Rider* the overtones were consciously there on the part of the plotter and writer, it is a little questionable to claim that they are not.

There is always the danger in an argument of this sort of going too far. What is not being argued in this essay is that Shooter was trying to consciously utilize the works of Altizer and other death of God theologians in order to write the Korvac Saga. He might have, but that is beyond the claim being made. I am also not arguing for a particular theological viewpoint informing the work of Marvel writers during the 1970s. That would be attempting to make a theological claim and would entail a different sort of engagement with the material. It is the sort of engagement that is quite frequently seen in attempts to examine religion in the contexts of superhero comics. Kripal's work in *Mutants and Mystics* posits an occult influence throughout the superhero industry, based on a human potential belief system. This sort of argument is just as theological as Anthony Mills more traditionally theological work. Rather, what I am arguing and have attempted to show is that the Avengers during the 1970s was influenced by certain religious trends known at the time, and thus when religion does feature, cannot be divorced from the overall religious climate at the time. More often than not the claim is made that the words of people like Stan Lee and Jim Shooter should be taken that there was no religious orientation expressed in the works of Marvel at the time, or else that a particular theological orientation is the hermeneutic key to understanding superheroes as a whole. In the middle is the more modest claim, advanced here in the particular examples provided, that we can only understand the *use* of religious imagery and images within the stories in the context of their overall cultural placement.

Notes

1. The truth of the matter, as to whether or not Isabella's storyline was cleared by Marv Wolfman or any previous editors-in-chief is largely a matter of opposing viewpoints. Shooter maintains on his website that no one approved of what Isabella had done. While Isabella, for his part, claims that it was a personal vendetta by Shooter, who used editorial confusion to impose a different ending to the storyline.

Works Cited

Allitt, Patrick. *Religion in America Since 1945: A History*. New York: Columbia University Press, 2005.
Altizer, Thomas J. J. *The Gospel of Christian Atheism*. Philadelphia: Westminster Press, 1966.
_____. *Oriental Mysticism and Biblical Eschatology*. Philadelphia: Westminster Press, 1961.

Byrne, John (w&a). "Reap the Whirlwind." *Namor, the Sub-Mariner* #13 (Apr. 1991). New York: Marvel Comics, 1991.

Conway, Gerry (w), and Gil Kane (a). "Deathplay!" *Ghost Rider* #21 (Dec. 1976). New York: Marvel Comics.

Cooke, John B. "Of Doctors and Ducks: Interview with Artist Frank Brunner on His Marvel Days." *Comic Book Artist* #6. Web. November 9, 2013. http://twomorrows.com/comic bookartist/articles/06brunner.html.

Elton, John T. "Toward a Hidden God." *Time Magazine.* 8 April 1966. 98–109.

Englehart, Steve (w), and Frank Brunner (a). "Sise-Neg Genesis." *Marvel Premiere* #14 (Mar. 1974). New York: Marvel Comics, 1974.

Englehart, Steve (w), and Don Heck (a). "...Let All Men Bring Together." *Giant-Sized Avengers* #4 (June 1975). New York: Marvel Comics, 1975.

"The 'God Is Dead' Movement." *Time Magazine.* 22 October 1965. 79–82.

Grimes, William. "John T. Elson, Editor Who Asked 'Is God Dead?' at Time, Dies at 78." *New York Times.* 17 September 2009. Web. November 9, 2013. http://www.nytimes.com/2009/09/18/business/media/18elson.html?ref=obituaries&_r=0.

Isabella, Tony. "Creator Interview: Tony Isabella." Vengeance Unbound. C. Munn (webmaster). Aug. 2003. Web. November 9, 2013. http://ghostrider.omegacen.com/interview01.html.

Jenkins, Paul. *Mystics and Messiahs: Cults and New Religions in American History.* Oxford: Oxford University Press, 2000.

Kripal, Jeffrey J. *Mutants and Mystics: Science Fiction, Superhero Comics, and the Paranormal.* Chicago: University of Chicago Press, 2011.

Lasky, Jacob. "Letters." In *The Avengers* #181 (Mar. 1979). David Michelinie (w) and John Byrne (a). New York: Marvel Comics, 1979.

Lee, Stan. "Foreword." In *The Gospel According to Superheroes: Religion and Pop Culture.* B. J. Oropeza, ed. New York: Peter Lang, 2005.

"Magazine Covers that Shook the World." *Los Angeles Times.* 2 September 2010. Web. November 9, 2013. http://www.latimes.com/entertainment/news/la-et-10magazinecovers14-july14-pg,0,5472017.photogallery#axzz2kAU48ciA.

Mills, Anthony. *American Theology, Superhero Comics, and Cinema: The Marvel of Stan Lee and the Revolution of a Genre.* New York: Routledge, 2014.

Ratner-Rosenhagen, J. *American Nietzsche: A History of an Icon and His Ideas.* Chicago: University of Chicago Press, 2012.

St. Germaine, Julie. "Letters." In *The Avengers* #180 (Feb. 1979), Tom DeFalco (w) and Jim Mooney (a). New York: Marvel Comics, 1979.

Shooter, Jim. "Rooting Out Corruption at Marvel—Part Two of a Bunch." 14 June 2011. Web. 9 November 2013. http://www.jimshooter.com/2011/06/rooting-out-corruption-at-marvel-part_14.html.

Shooter, Jim (w), Roger Stern (w), and George Perez (a). "Tomorrow Dies Today!" *The Avengers* #167 (Jan. 1978). New York: Marvel Comics, 1978.

Shooter, Jim (w), and David Wenzel (a). "...Where Angels Fear to Tread." *The Avengers* #171 (May 1978). New York: Marvel Comics, 1978.

Shooter, Jim, David Michelinie (w), and David Wenzel (a). "The Destiny Hunt!" *The Avengers* #176 (Oct. 1978). New York: Marvel Comics, 1978.

_____. "The End ... and the Beginning!" *The Avengers* #175 (Sept. 1978). New York: Marvel Comics, 1978.

Shooter, Jim (w), and David Wenzel (a). "The Hope ... and the Slaughter." *The Avengers* #177 (Nov. 1978). New York: Marvel Comics, 1978.

Stan Lee's Mutants, Monsters, and Marvels. Dir. Scott Zakarin. DHG Productions, 2002.

Taylor, C. *A Secular Age.* Cambridge: Belknap Press of Harvard University Press, 2007.

Welsh, David J. "Letters." In *The Avengers* #181 (Mar. 1979). David Michelinie (w) and John Byrne (a). New York: Marvel Comics, 1979.

Wright, B. W. *Comic Book Nation: The Transformation of Youth Culture in America.* Baltimore: Johns Hopkins University Press, 2001.

"The Korvac Saga"
Exiles from Reason and Fragments of a Contemporary Mythology

Giacomo Matteo Miniussi
Translated by Laurie Schwartz

> "I ... I do not understand all this, woman!—Can it be that Michael was just ... and we were the villains?—Verily, then, his innocent blood is on our hands!"—Shooter, "The Hope"

With these dramatic words, the Mighty Thor compels the reader to recall the entire saga of Korvac to verify this incredible admission of guilt: for the first time in the history of the "Earth's mightiest heroes," they doubt their own conduct. The greatness of this tale also certainly lies in its capacity to make you re-read it, but even more than that, in the fact that also after a second or even third reading, the doubt remains. In the story Moondragon plays the role of a classic literary *topos*: the alien, who, observing the actions from outside, manages to maintain a view of the facts that is objective and disenchanted. Moondragon causes Thor to question what success actually means in this story. The shock provoked by the crisis of mimesis with the heroes quickly leads us to an analysis of conscience.

The Avengers, of course, are those who fight and defend liberty and democracy, and who are represented, more or less, as the guardians of our civilization: the Western, consumer, bourgeois civilization. In comic book reality, they are represented as an institution that is subordinated to the government of the United States. They are therefore the emblem of the establishment brand United States and their belonging to that civilization is displayed in such a consistent way throughout the course of the story[1] so as to leave little doubt that it is toward such a society that criticism is directed and thus directly singled out.

This essay intends to illuminate how the Korvac Saga amounts to a disenchanted reflection not just on American civilization, but indeed, on global civilization at the end of the 1970s. A civilization, that is to say, which took stock of ten years of history during which, for the first time, a profound crisis of ethical values had gripped individuals and, above all, ten years during which reflection on the defense of liberty and democratic principles in their relationship to power brought divergent social classes to be at loggerheads with one other. The hopes that young students of '68 nurtured for a renewal and improvement of society, the utopia of a global civilization that was not repressive, the rage against the "machine"[2] that sought to flatten the political, cultural and ideal planes into one single dimension; all of this was foundering. Much of it had already foundered in the disenchantment prophesied by Max Weber, dragged adrift by the epilog of the war in Vietnam and by the recurrence of significant economic recessions. A period which—as Hobsbawm said—"is that of a world which lost its bearings and slid into instability and crisis" (403). This essay suggests an interpretation of the Jim Shooter story from a hermeneutic perspective, attempting to follow authors who have most influenced social criticism in American culture after the Second World War: Herbert Marcuse and Hannah Arendt.

The God Who Dies

The saga of Korvac has a spiral movement, the plot winds round and round its own center, only skimming it, to finally collapse into itself, suddenly, at the end of the story: the sad and incomprehensible death of a god! The nucleus of this plot, or rather, its end, is the moral *epochè*, the suspension of judgment on what happened. The reflection suggested by this saga is thus colored by disenchantment, delusion and fear. Nevertheless, even in this swan song of dreams of social progress, the comic books bring a critique ("Innocent blood in on our hands") and raise a question ("and we were the villains").

The dying god in the first instance functions as a key for reflecting on the meaning of existence, but most of all, about death exacted as a sacrifice in the name of a cause (the nation rather than the democracy, or an ill-defined concept of liberty). The significance of this cause, however, is made more complex and opaque here in the penultimate panel of the story: what is staged is only the devastating force of war, a force beyond the human that does not leave any winner on the field (Shooter, "The Hope..."). This fatal final image is like a cry that arises against the perceived inanity of war and of death which gripped the America of the post–Vietnam era.

In face of such devastation what sense does the hero's existence have? In the real world in which this cartoon saga was born, heroes had undergone a horrendous metamorphosis: the Vietnam veterans transformed the figure of the hero into the evidence of a grave error, if not directly for the atrocities committed in the name of freedom, a reminder of events many Americans don't want to remember. For the first time, the silent expanse of the tens of thousands of crosses in the burial grounds marking those fallen in Vietnam speak of war in its brutality, and not in its ideal of the struggle for good: these silent multitudes have entered into the consciences of people and have stained them irreparably.[3] What price has liberty? Is it right to wage war in its name? And what if we get it wrong, albeit in good faith and with the hope of making the world free and just? In the Korvac saga, these questions manifest themselves in their ambiguity while assuming, at the same time, the dual personification of Korvac and the Avengers. Both the one and the others, indeed, fight for these principles: Korvac wants to emancipate the cosmos from the tyrannies (of Eternity, Odino and Mephisto), just as Captain America, standing before the gravestone of Korvac, renews his promise to battle all despots.[4]

The god who dies is also a clear reference to Nietzsche, that is to say, a metaphor of an increasingly perceptible collapse of a horizon of sense, a symbol of the stifling sensation of alienation that the individual experiences in a technological society. Such a society is a dystopia that is realized step by step in proportion to the propagation of a kind of schizophrenia between *homo faber*—modern man capable of controlling nature and bending it until it is transformed into commodity—and *homo sapiens*—the individual who requires a sense and a canon to guide the *praxis*. This civilization, however, winds up being more and more automated, to the point of transforming the person himself into a mere cog in the chain of production, and in the end, a commodity of the market. In the Korvac saga, this fate does not even spare the Avengers: they become products destined to be objects of consumption, worthy of being appreciated and collected by the cosmic being known as the Collector (Mantlo).

The death of a god, therefore, not only drives us toward a critique of society, but also strips bare the fragility of the symbol of the hero: "Western civilization has always glorified the hero, the sacrifice of life for the city, the state, the nation; it has rarely asked the question of whether the established city, state, nation were worth the sacrifice" (Marcuse xix). In such a reality, the existence of superheroes is pure fiction, mythos. The figure of the hero, like that of god, must die to leave us with a narrative that helps us to understand our world, as well as to have vision of it that is as liberal and critical as possible.

Fragments of a Contemporary Mythology

It is within the terms of a contemporary mythology, then, that the Korvac saga asks to be read. Like a classical epic poem, in this saga the good and the bad do not simply confront one another. The two factions are, rather, the symbol of something else. It is necessary then to analyze the dynamics of the story in such a way as to reveal how a larger element looms over two fronts: it is not important which of the two will win—in fact, both have lost—but how these two factions are represented to reveal what exactly is at stake. Our analysis will start with the figure of Michael Korvac.

At the beginning of the story, Korvac is represented as the exasperation of technological society: he is a horrible hybrid of machine and man created by the Badoon, and his dreams of revenge and emancipation converge in a perverse craving for power. At first, the attempts at this revenge, as recounted in the prologue of the saga, amount to a mere struggle to obtain political power, that is to say, they aim to subvert or topple the *status quo*, "to overcome my masters" and establish a private empire (Wein). This struggle, for all practical purposes, seems to be a simple class struggle.

Nevertheless, after an initial failure, Korvac manages to achieve power, which he obtains through the knowledge that he absorbs in the spaceship of Galactus (Shooter, "The End..."). Now, even if the delineation of the personality apparently continues to be that of the deviant greedy for power, in truth, here we are witness to a bone fide conversion: he reaches for truth through knowledge and enters into symbiosis with the universe. This event transforms him profoundly. From this moment on, his goals change. He now wants to emancipate not only himself, but the entire universe: "correcting the chaos, healing the injustice that civilization had heaped up, on a battered universe" (Shooter, "The End..."). His are no longer the egotistical goals of one who craves power, or the simple vendetta of injustices suffered, but the altruistic aims of someone who wants to make progress and fight for liberty and global justice and no longer just as a class struggle. What is suggested here is a purpose for the struggle that goes beyond the level of political-social status, as in the previous case, but aims at a superior level, at a betterment of the conditions of life for every single individual which this society—of technology and of consumerism—has perverted into injustice and chaos. A purpose that can't be anything other than the aspiration of a self-styled "new-made god" (Shooter, "The End..."). The choice of terms here proves to be starkly similar to a mythological language: chaos, in Greek cosmology is the condition in which material is found before it is shaped by the gods.

It is particularly interesting to note that the authors, however, keep a proper distance from this new status of Korvac: while he proclaims himself to be a new-made god, they clarify instead that Korvac is only "Like unto God" (Shooter, "The End...").[5] This distinction is important because it defines the behavior of Korvac as insolent and overbearing, a veritable *hubris*, and it is as such that he must be considered and, above all, punished. Feeling himself akin to the gods, Korvac opposes their excessive power like a new *Prometheus*, who, in the presumption of possessing the knowledge of the righteous, wants to illuminate people so that they emancipate themselves from the tyrannical gods.

But does the parallel to Prometheus really work? The text offers a cue to believe otherwise. For classical mythology, Prometheus certainly represents a civilizing hero, he who gave the flame of rationality to man, thus permitting the formation of a civilization. But for Korvac it is civilization itself that nurtures chaos. He himself affirmed this as soon as he obtained cosmic consciousness in the spaceship of Galactus. The rationality proposed by Prometheus, in other words, is that concept of reason "which contains the domineering features of the performance principle" (Marcuse 130), directed at "the progressive replacement of an uncontrolled natural environment by a controlled technological environment" (155) and at the repressive organization of the instincts. "Even at the beginning of Western civilization [...] reason was defined as an instrument of constraint, of instinctual suppression; the domain of the instincts, sensuousness, was considered as eternally hostile and detrimental to reason" (159).

This repression, as Freud noted, is structural in Western civilization, where instincts and Eros are repressed and transformed into productivity. The individual is de-sexualized, and his instincts, Eros and Thanatos, are transformed into performance through the notion of guilt. Nevertheless, such repression is necessitated "less by the 'struggle for existence,' than by the interest in prolonging this struggle—by the interest in domination" (Marcuse 130). Modern democracies hide their dark side behind this concept of reason and civilization: as Hannah Arendt indicated, totalitarianism, rather than being an anomaly or historical accident, is something inborn in the development of modern society, it is one of the possible responses to those questions posed by modernity to which democracies have not managed to find solutions. Prometheus is indeed disobedient to the gods, but it is he who creates civilization and, for this, suffers eternal pain. He is the symbol of productivity, of ambition, and of incessant striving to control life. But this productivity of his is malediction and benediction at the same time, and binds progress to effort in a way that is unavoidable. In this, Prometheus is the archetypical hero of the performance principle.

Prometheus is, therefore, not the mythological figure that Korvac refers to. We must turn to precisely his opposite if we want to identify the symbols for another principle of reality, namely, Orpheus and Narcissus.

> Orpheus and Narcissus (like Dionysus to whom they are akin: the antagonist of the god who sanctions the logic of domination, the realm of reason) stand for a very different reality. They have not become the culture-heroes of the Western world: theirs is the image of joy and fulfillment; the voice which does

not command but sings; the gesture which offers and receives; the deed which is peace and ends the labor of conquest; the liberation from time which unites man with god, man with nature [Marcuse 161–162].

If we read the story carefully, we will realize that the figure of Korvac seems to be constructed along the lines of the myths of Orpheus and Narcissus. First of all, it is important to notice that truth and consciousness have embraced Korvac as in a kind of fusion of man with nature, with the cosmos. Here, his own humanity has been restored to him, and not just the spiritual. It is no coincidence, in fact, that "his last self-directed thought" was to give himself, once again, human features (Shooter, "The End..."). Korvac abandons the civilization of technology (represented by that of his body as half machine) and aspires to a liberation of Eros (represented by a new body, young, strong, and beautiful). This passage is decisive. And what does Korvac do immediately afterward? He gives himself a name—Michael ("Like unto God") and finds a partner, she, too, beautiful and young. Now Korvac is truly ready to embark upon the real struggle.

But what does this struggle consist of and what form does it take? One of the more incredible aspects of this saga is probably the diversity of rhythms that punctuate the lives, on the one hand, of Carina and Michael and, on the other, of the Avengers. From the beginning, both members of the couple prove to be static and reflective figures, opposites of the hyper-dynamism of the Avengers, who are constantly involved in struggles, journeys, and quarrels. Carina and Michael, however, are always portrayed in their dwelling, a beautiful home in a residential neighborhood, not dedicated to any particular activity if not utopian reflection: the creation of a free society.

What we are told of Michael and Carina is their love story, the liberation and satisfaction of their libido. Their life, as it is described to us, could almost seem hedonistic, but in truth it is something more. Hedonistic is indeed often synonymous with lustful. Whereas here, the enjoyment of life, and above all, the enjoyment of life "together" has a higher significance. The importance of being together here and now is elevated to a creative principle. Perhaps for this reason, Michael Korvac, unexpectedly, declares that he feels pity for Jocasta, a machine "created in the name of love" (Shooter, "The Hope...").

The resumption of his own humanity through the liberation of instincts and of Eros thus represents hope for the creation of a new world. So, like the images of Orpheus and Narcissus, Michael and Carina, too, reconcile Eros and Thanatos and dream of a world that is not dominated and controlled via science and technology, but liberated. This is the critique, but also the political message[6] that Korvac brings to mankind. Here, he takes a stand against his adversaries, the Avengers, who, as the defenders and perpetrators of not just one bourgeois *status quo*, but also of an oppressive and class-structured society, "slew first the dream, then ... the hope" (Shooter, "The Hope...").

Serving as a counter-weight to the polyhedral complexity of Michael Korvac, the Avengers appear more deliberately superficial. The element that stands out most during the course of the story is a continuous centrifugal force that jeopardizes the cohesion of the group. The frontline of the heroes is constantly besieged by these disintegrating tensions, which not only place the importance of the group in doubt on an institutional level, but also the valor of the role of their leader. Thus, for example, with the entrance of Gyrich, the Avengers' priority status is revoked, and at the same time, we witness continual disputes between Captain America and Iron Man regarding the integrity of the latter in command. The united group of heroes demonstrates a tendency toward disintegration, toward individualism. Such contradiction functions as the key to reflect on what exactly social cohesion is, and what political power provides the glue for this cohesion. Power, as Hannah Arendt maintains, is, first of all, the capacity to put together a community, and that is why this not only requires action, but also having a history in common in which a context of diverse actions, their meaning, takes form as a whole.

It is interesting that the possibility for creating this adhesion for the Avengers comes from identifying Korvac as the enemy. The identification of the enemy in this case turns out to be systematic for political power (Schmitt). Defining the distinction between enemy and friend can be understood as the point of departure for gathering real political consensus from members of a community with regard to the community itself. Such distinction functions as a real social contract inasmuch as it creates the idea that citizens of a state can understand only if that state is ready to defend itself against its enemies. In other words, the identification of a common enemy to hate and fight becomes exaggerated and distorted until it unleashes the aggression that is hidden in the subconscious. This introjection proves in fact to be the true social glue and the true political power, not only of absolutist states, but of every modern nation state as well. As pointed out by Michel Foucault, inasmuch as there have been historical experiences of totalitarianism to exacerbate the mechanisms of biopower, investing the body itself with control, such a mechanism is deployed, in varying degrees, in the operation of all modern nation states. With the advent of late modern society, in fact, social control is no longer managed via a network of systems that create and control customs, habits, and production practices by means of disciplinary institutions, but is extended far beyond the locations organized by the institutions, becoming more and more socially immanent and diffuse in the body of citizens. A totalitarian "other," then, less visible but no less insidious (Foucault).

In the narrative, such "other totalitarianism," such biopower (that extends into space and time) capable of hiding itself, just to make us believe that the choices of the collective are spontaneous, merges into one single personality, that of the Collector. He indeed proves to be the emblem of consumer society, not just for his passion of collecting luxury goods and placing them in a display case, but because he demonstrates that he possesses real power over the bodies of the Avengers (a nearly total power from the moment that he was able to kidnap them, make them disappear and reappear at his whim from every place and time). And after having finally collected them together in a single place, he reveals to them the existence of a looming threat, not coincidentally defined simply as "the enemy" (Mantlo). The Collector is the character of the saga who, probably more than all of the others, symbolizes the repressive society that Michael wants to liberate. He in fact is the one who manipulated the Avengers like puppets and sabotaged the peace of Korvac himself through Carina, his daughter. And it is perhaps because of this that the Collector is still, on balance, the only real victim of Korvac.

The Ruins of Temples

Throughout this saga, a contemporary mythology is sketched out in which its heroes and martyrs undergo a metamorphosis. They become *persistence*: like the ruins of temples, they testify to something that is no more, and thus, perhaps, are summoned to announce the arrival of something that not yet is.[7]

What remains at the end of the saga, in fact, are images of the dead, disillusion, and even of oblivion. Only in this final moment, the Avengers go back to being true heroes. The Avengers are obliged by Moondragon to recognize the failure and in so doing they oblige us to recognize it as well. In rallying together in the face of a possible better reality, a lost paradise, already vanished because of the short-sightedness of mankind (masterfully represented by the final scene in which all of the heroes reunite in the presence of the tombs of Michael and Carina), there is an assumption of responsibility for the mistakes, a cathartic integration of these within a real horizon of meaning, capable of making us grow, as individuals and as a political community.[8] In order for this to happen, however, thought must remain imagination. Thought, namely, that is not an instrument of repression, that resists death with the great refusal of Orpheus the liberator. Such thought is philosophy, where mythology indeed meets imagination. Through it, events and things can be understood in the light of their possibilities and anticipations. With it, even death can be turned into a sign of liberty!

Notes

1. From the fashion show of protagonists Janet Van Dyne and Henry Pym, to the oft recurring *topos* in this story of the superhero who travels on public transportation, to absurd situations such as the God of Thunder seated in a cafeteria.

2. "The political machine, the corporate machine, the cultural and educational machine which has welded blessing and curse into one rational whole" (Marcuse xvii).

3. The title of the second story of the Avengers reasserts the shadow of Vietnam in the conscience of the reader: "First Blood" (*The Avengers* #168, Feb. 1977), which marks a tribute to the well known 1972 book by David Morrel, later adapted in the 1982 film *Rambo: First Blood.*

4. This happens in the four pages added at the end of the story by Mark Grunwald (w) and Tom Morgan (a) in the reprint of the Korvac Saga of 1991.

5. For additional discussion relevant to this phrasing, please see Nathan Gibbard's "Madonna's Birth and God's Death: Marvel Comics, the Death of God Movement, and the Religious Climate of the 1970s" in this collection.

6. "Today the fight for life, the fight for Eros, is the political fight" (Marcuse xxv).

7. Cfr. Maria Zambrano, *El hombre y lo divino*, 1955.

8. An assumption of responsibility that is characterized precisely by its view toward the future (Jonas).

Works Cited

Arendt, Hannah. *The Origins of Totalitarianism*. New York: Schocken Books, 1951.

Foucault, Michael. *L'Archéologie du savoir*. Paris: Gallimard, 1969.

Freud, Sigmund. *Das Unbehagen in der Kultur*. Frankfurt am Main: Fischer Bücherei, 1955.

Hegel, G. F. W. *The Philosophy of History*. Ontario: Batoche Book, 2001.

Hobsbawn, Eric J. *The Age of Extremes. The Short Twentieth Century, 1914–1991*. London: Vintage, 1995.

Jonas, Hans. *Das Prinzip Verantwortung*. Frankfurt am Main: Insel, 1979.

Mantlo, Bill (w), and David Wenzel (a). "Captured by the Collector!" *The Avengers* #174 (Aug. 1978). New York: Marvel Comics, 1978.

Marcuse, Herbert. *Eros and Civilization*. Boston: Beacon Press, 1955.

Schmitt, C. *Der Begriff des Politischen*. Berlin: Grünewald, 1938.

Shooter, Jim, David Michelinie (w), and David Wenzel (a). "The End ... and the Beginning!" *The Avengers* #175 (Sept. 1978). New York: Marvel Comics, 1978.

Shooter, Jim (w), and Dave Wenzel (a). "The Hope ... and the Slaughter!" *The Avengers* #177 (Nov. 1978). New York: Marvel Comics, 1978.

Wein, Len, and Roger Stern (w), and Sal Buscema and Klaus Janson (a). "Thunder in the 31st Century." *Thor Annual* #6 (Dec. 1977). New York: Marvel Comics, 1977.

Stung by Stigmatization
Yellowjacket and Wasp
Dis/Reassembled in the Age of Reagan

Peter W. Lee

In the early 1980s, Earth's Mightiest Heroes briefly became zeroes. During the previous decade, the Avengers explored the farthest reaches of space and the core of the human spirit, which kept fans coming back for more. But as the team prospered in this formative period, individuals struggled. In their own titles, Iron Man fought inner demons he kept bottled up as a Vietnam War profiteer and Captain America, disillusioned with dirty politics, became a nameless nomad in search of an identity (Wright). In 1980, *The Avengers* celebrated its two hundredth issue, advertised as "a double-sized anniversary" blockbuster. Eleven months later, the team fell apart. In issue #211 (Sept. 1981) "the old order changeth," the cover blurb declared, ousting the longtime roster. In its stead feline rookie Tigra enthusiastically jumped in, but didn't quite land on her feet in her one-week stint in comic book time (Shooter, "...By Force"). Issue #216 (Feb. 1982) pictured her cowering before a villain to spare her nine lives. Having turned "scaredy cat," she mused, "I'm just not in the same league as you guys! [...] I think I'll quit while I'm ahead!" (Shooter, "To Avenge...").

While Tigra recognized her shortcomings, her teammates also let their cats out of the bag. By issue #212 (Oct. 1981), the Avengers had regressed to the founding members, with Captain America assuming the Hulk's place. In issue #217 (Mar. 1982), Hank Pym—the Yellowjacket—believed this was a rebirth of sorts. "I had such hopes. The 'new' Avengers were practically the original group. This time I thought I could be the kind of man Jan wanted me to be" (Shooter, "Double-Cross"). Pym was wrong, the founding members were not immune to change. While Tigra soul-searched, the Big Three (Iron Man, Thor, and Captain America) revealed their alter egos to each other. The other two founders, Pym and his wife, Janet Van Dyne—the Wasp—experienced greater re-directions mirroring shifts in American gender roles. Pym, the big-brained Yellowjacket, reflected the fall and revitalization of the Cold Warrior, echoing President Ronald Reagan's rhetoric to rally the nation around the flag. Van Dyne, too, experienced new times: a shrinking violet since her 1963 debut, the Wasp embraced the empowerment of the women's movement, even if the Reagan administration and other facets of American culture did not (Faludi). The Pyms' subsequent divorce symbolized the deep fissures running through the United States in the late twentieth century. While assembling to battle the foes no one hero could withstand, the Avengers fragmented when facing each other. Their world, as the old comic book tagline reads, would never again be the same.

Great Expectations Dashed:
Giant-Sized Identity Crisis

In the 1970s, Americans stumbled from the quagmire of Vietnam, only to sink into a bleak malaise. The Cold War fortitude of the 1950s and the hopes of the counterculture of the following generation remained unfulfilled, leaving many Americans in limbo. As historian Christopher Latch describes the national retreat, "after the political turmoil of the sixties, Americans [...] retreated to purely personal preoccupations": a self-directed look inward he terms "psychic self-improvement" (4). Journalist Susan Faludi characterizes the American man as "stiffed," due to the hyper-masculinity of the postwar era giving way to disillusionment (Faludi). The Civil Rights, youth, and feminist movements seemingly rallied against the white male as the symbol of rottenness in America's apple pie (Kimmel). As historian Matthew Pustz noted, this melancholy pervaded even the bright garish colors of the comic book world.

For Earth's Mightiest Heroes, shifting masculine standards mandated a dramatic struggle. Fittingly, the Avengers of 1981 comprised of the original team, a throwback to the black-and-white simplicity of the optimistic Silver Age. But as the team simmered with internal angst leftover from the 1970s, Janet Van Dyne seemingly remained immune to the nation's mood. Although she never attained stardom, the Wasp had faithfully served throughout the decades, had social status as an heiress with limitless wealth, and remained on the cutting edge of haute couture as a social butterfly. Hubby Hank Pym fared less well: writers had long written him out of the roster as a dead-end scientist with little fan appeal. Despite numerous costume changes and super-powered gimmicks, Pym was a goliath-sized bore. Writer Jim Shooter summarized Pym as "never the Avenger who saved the day at the end [and was] usually the first knocked out or captured" (Shooter, "Hank Pym").

Pym's spotty record wasn't about to change. In issue #212 (Oct. 1981), Van Dyne notices he's already on a downward slide. After he refuses to cuddle in bed, she sniffs, "Oh, *Hank*! Why are you such a cold fish lately?" Pym hints at the source of his frustrations when he disintegrates one of her costumes. When Captain America jokes, "The Wasp has arrived with her new partner—uh, Yellowjacket!," Pym glowers at the chairman's giving him second billing. Thor and Iron Man then reject his proposal to elect new leadership and Pym sees this as proof of his second-tier status: "I've just been away too long—locked in my lab wasting time on research that led nowhere and you've all *forgotten* me—Hank Pym, the has-been." His self-pity escalates when his wife offers to replace a broken gadget. Pym explodes, "You *love* doing that, don't you? You love taking every opportunity to flaunt your blasted money. Well, I don't *need* your butlers, your cars, or your money—and I don't need *you*!" A sobbing Jan flees and the other heroes stand dumbfounded. Cap mutters, "As Chairman, I feel as though I should *do* something ... but *what*? It—it's a family matter!" Pym's attitude becomes Avengers business when his shooting mouth gives way to outright belligerence. When Yellowjacket attacks a disarmed villainess, she turns on him. Wasp intervenes but the damage is done. Pym cries, "Why *her*? *WHY*?" (Shooter, "Men")

In the next issue, #213 (Nov. 1981), the Avengers respond to Pym's actions with a court martial. Captain America accuses Pym of negligence which "could have cost us all our lives ... and left the city defenseless!" Yellowjacket inwardly concurs he "was a jerk" because he "was so eager to do well on my first case since rejoining the team—desperate to be the star!" Out loud, he maintains a facade of stoic manliness. Tigra has no such qualms in her observations: "I've never seen a woman so hung up on a guy! And such a *strange* guy! He seems like a cold fish—all wrapped up in whatever murky stuff is churning around inside himself! He gives me the *creeps*!" (Shooter, "Court-Martial").

The others echo Tigra's doubts. Iron Man reviews Pym's biography stretching back to the character's 1962 origin. Stark had upgraded Iron Man to stay current over the years, but Pym's situation was a continual quest for endorsement—self-approval, if not fan appeal from comic readers—through new identities. Stark recognizes Pym's Ant-Man/Giant-Man/Goliath identities masked a deep disturbance. In a two-page spread, Iron Man reflects, "He seemed *uncomfortable* as an Avenger! I always sort of suspected that he felt *outclassed* by the rest of us—that he was troubled because he never had the raw power" of the others. He hypothesizes this was "the reason he kept abandoning the team and going back to the lab! It seemed as though he was trying desperately to achieve a scientific breakthrough to *prove* himself!" Stark wonders, "Can he ever be more than a haunted, hollow man drowning in a sea of guilt over the wrongs done by his monstrous creation [robot villain Ultron]? Can he ever rid of the desperate need he has to *redeem* himself in his own eyes?" (Shooter, "Court-Martial"). In *The Avengers* #216 (Feb. 1982), fan Kevin J. Dooley commented on Iron Man's revisionism: "The intertwining of Hank Pym's past was a good touch. Iron Man's comments made obvious something that seemed to have been building for some time." In issue #222 (Aug. 1982), reader Reggie Smith emphatically answered the Golden Avenger's rhetorical question: "*Yellowjacket's mental condition has been developing for years*" with no way out.

Pym himself agrees with this assessment. Prepping for the trial in #213 (Nov. 1981), he sobs, "I'm a failure as a husband ... just like I'm a failure as a hero." He turns to villainy and builds yet another robot, "Salvation-I," to unleash on his teammates, planning to charge in at the pivotal moment. When Van Dyne intervenes, Yellowjacket smacks her in the face, sending her reeling. "Shut up! I've got to do this! I've got to save the day right before their eyes! Don't you see? It's my only chance to redeem myself! It's the only way!" He storms out, concluding, "You've got to understand-! I can't let them drum me out of the Avengers! I *can't*! It's all I have *left*!" (Shooter, "Court-Martial"). His final remark omits his wife on the floor.

At the trial, Captain America stands firm. "We're the Avengers, not the Brooklyn Dodgers! One 'error' by one of us can cost thousands of lives!" Yellowjacket strikes out, accusing Cap of fraternizing with the enemy while he played hero. With this tactic not gaining any traction, Pym implores his wife for support. She tells him to "let it end" and Hank does so, summoning his robot. Salvation-I runs amok until Wasp saves the day. "Why?" Hank asks again. "Why did it have to be Jan? If—if I couldn't do it ... why her? Why? Why?" (Shooter, "Court-Martial"). Like before, Pym's open inquires linger in the air, unanswerable from a standpoint of a crisis in masculinity. He leaves the Avengers a failure.

By issue #217 (Mar. 1982), Pym hits rock bottom. As a former American hero who had battled assorted communist baddies during his early 1960s run, he becomes a dupe at the hands of his old foe Egghead, a failed atomic scientist turned un–American with dreams of world domination. Egghead tells Pym he wants to make amends with his disabled niece, Trish Starr, another relic from Pym's more glorious past. Pym initially resists; he knows capitulation to Egghead would morally crack him: "I haven't sunk so low that I'd have anything to do with murderous scum like you!" (Shooter, "Double Cross"). He changes his minds when Egghead sheds tears and offers a $500,000 fee—enough for Pym to establish himself without a woman's fortune propping him up. Egghead's penitence turns easy over when Pym learns his nemesis has scrambled Starr's mind to force him rob a government warehouse. The Avengers arrive, his former wife orders the team to "bring him down," and does so herself. With no ready alibi, Pym surrenders, a traitor to his country.

In *The Avengers* #227 (Jan. 1983), a jailed Pym comes to the same conclusion as Iron Man. Psychiatrist Paul Edmonds visits the former hero to judge his mental stamina to stand trial. Pym admits he, too, was an egghead: "It was easier to deal with chemicals than with people." His first wife, Maria Trovaya, died in a Hungarian revolution against the Soviets (presumably the 1956 revolt, but Marvel omitted the date) and Van Dyne became a coping mechanism. As a superhero, Pym realized he "would constantly be overshadowed by the more powerful teammates—at least one of whom the Wasp found most attractive," meaning Thor. Trying to match the Thunder God as Giant-Man made him "clumsy ... inept ... and all the changes in size were playing hob with my cell structure." Pym asserts he wanted out, but "the problem was that Jan wanted to be an Avenger—and wanted *me* to be an Avenger, too! I had to keep trying for her, even though my heart wasn't in it!" A break down in issue #161 (July 1977) led him to "take on the Avengers single-handed and nearly beat them! My finest hour as a 'hero' ...and I wasn't even in my right mind!" After electro-shock therapy, Pym happily had "a reason ... an excuse ... to return to the lab full time" even though Van Dyne remained on the team. "I wouldn't see her for days. I felt alone ... lost." Pym returned to superheroics as Yellowjacket, "but I was only fooling myself. By then, I was in no state of mind to be an Avenger!" He adds "all I want back is my dignity" (Stern, "Testing").

Pym's quest for manhood proved elusive. In issue #213 (Nov. 1981), fan T.M. Maple asked in disbelief, "This is ol' regular dependable Hank? [...] Well, why not? [...] Heaven knows that many people in real life drive themselves around the bend chiefly by their own imaginings and not be pressures of the 'real world.'" Ken Morrissey observed, fearing the character's impending death, "His career as a super hero is finished, he's lost his wife, he's lost his self-respect, and he's broke," Avengers' butler Edwin Jarvis held out more hope. In issue #214 (Dec. 1981) the English manservant brings the American Dream before Captain America. Jarvis asserts, "Any man was free to go as far and high as his wits, courage and determination might carry him [... but] these days many people want to eliminate the risk! They think that some *Big Brother* should ensure that everyone succeeds!" Pym had fallen between those cracks. Cap agrees life isn't fair and adds "no one ever said it should be! Whatever the goal, there will always be some good men who fall short for some reason—but the *best* of them will pick themselves up and go at it again." Jarvis hopes Pym will "pick himself up again." (Shooter, "Three Angels"). In #227 (Jan. 1983), Edmonds doubts Cap's assessment, reporting Pym "suffered at least four nervous breakdowns in the last decade! He has a massive inferiority complex" but can stand trial. Unbeknownst to all, a hardboiled Egghead smiles at Pym's flagging spirits. "Henry always did have faith in the legal system," he laughs. "I suppose I shall have to shatter that faith for him!" (Stern, "Testing"). For Pym, the American way—the means to pull oneself by their bootstraps from the dregs of defeat—itself was at stake.

Buyer and Boss-Lady: Wasp Rising

While Hank Pym stewed in prisoner's garb, Janet Van Dyne did more than pull bootstraps—she redesigned them. Despite logging more panel time than Pym throughout the decades, fans regarded the giddy glam-gal as a throwback to the outmoded 1960s. As reader Philip Fishman bitterly wrote in *The Avengers* #216 (Feb. 1982), "If it wasn't for Mr. Pym's lab work, Janet Van Dyne Pym would still be 'Dingaling Jan, the airhead heiress' and nothing more. *Hank* was the one who gave her her wings, sting, and shrinking powers [...] This realization would probably be even more galling to Hank if he thought of it, but I feel that it should have been brought up." Van Dyne's reputation as a clothes horse and free spender was legendary; in issue #213 (Nov. 1981) fan Gary Morgan catalogued thirty-three costume changes for the bug-sized heroine, with the editor commenting, "by no means a complete list." Iron Man agreed, quipping in issue #217 (Mar. 1982), when a villain trashes her car, "She usually buys a new limo every month ... or whenever the old one gets dirty!" In issue #216 (Feb. 1982), reader Ken Morrissey darkly dubbed Van Dyne a "nowhere character" and suggested "as long as you're getting rid of her ex-husband, why not get rid of her too? It's worth a thought."

Writer Jim Shooter already had plans for Van Dyne. With Pym off the rails, his wife climbed uphill for self-empowerment. *The Avengers* #214 (Dec. 1981) describes Van Dyne as

> heiress to a large fortune [and has] anything that she desires, if money can buy it. Most women would envy her—and yet in recent times she has been unhappy. The contentment she feels now has grown only during the last two days—since the disappearance of her husband [Shooter, "Three Angels"].

Writer Roger Stern, succeeding Shooter, seized the opportunity to expand her character. When Yellowjacket drops by to apologize for her shiner, Van Dyne responds with a divorce: "For years I lived for you, clinging to you and worshipping you and supporting your fragile ego! I submerged myself completely to prop you up! No more! Ever again!" (Shooter, "Three Angels").

With no husbands or kids, and with a steady income and glamorous job, Van

Dyne adopts the new eighties lifestyle in vogue: the yuppie, then on the ascent for career women in law and medicine (Ehrman 108–09). In #217 (Mar. 1982) she boasts, "No more *Mrs. Hank Pym*—I'm *Janet Van Dyne* again, free and simple!" (Shooter, "Double-Cross"). No longer a sidekick to a deadbeat hero, she flexes her wings and flies to the top of her profession. When the Avengers assemble, Van Dyne proposes the election of a new chairman: herself. Yellowjacket had attempted to do so in issue #212 (Oct. 1981) but Van Dyne pressures Iron Man and Thor to back her. Cap grins, "I can't say it's the easiest job I ever had, Jan, and I can't believe you *want* it, but let's make it unanimous" (Shooter, "Men of...").

The team follows Wasp's lead. In her first assignment in issue #217 (Mar. 1982) she takes down Pym for poaching government property on Egghead's behalf. Van Dyne's sunny side demeanor notwithstanding, her life was not free and simple. Jarvis observes, "I also see that you are far more troubled by what happened than you will admit—even to yourself!" (Shooter, "Men of..."). The Wasp earned admiration from her teammates, but struggled to balance her old and new selves. In issue #220 (June 1982), the team battles Moondragon, who had instigated the Avengers' earlier breakup in issue #211 (Sept. 1981). The giddy Wasp admires her fashion taste: "This little costume Moondragon gave me is *tres chic*!" A brainwashed Thor also captivates Wasp with his unleashed masculinity: "Those eyes! Those shoulders! That voice! *Yum*!" She finally snaps out of her reverie ("Oh, pooh!") and takes on Moondragon: "Since Cap and Iron Man are too polite to clobber an unarmed woman, us girls will settle this one-to-one!" (Shooter, "By Force..."). The leader of the Avengers is the woman left standing in the next panel. In issue #224 (Oct. 1982), Raymond Mann approved Van Dyne's new assertiveness: "The Wasp has been put down, let down, bounced around, and abused by nearly everybody in times past. But in this issue, she shone! Without her, the mighty Avengers would never have gotten past Thor, much less have defeated Moondragon [...] And I especially loved the fact that she delivered the knock-out punch."

Mann appreciated Wasp's strength but Janet Van Dyne was not about to turn Avengers mansion into a "feminazi" camp. Wasp balances her traditional flightiness with a new direction for the team. When they consider adding "new blood" to their ranks, Wasp knows "*exactly* what this team needs. More girls!" The Big Three settle on old-timer Hawkeye—the hot-headed archer hardly qualified as "new blood." In contrast, Van Dyne hosts a tea party and selects Jennifer Walters, the She-Hulk. The Wasp's choice generated some minor controversy: the She-Hulk was persona non grata in the Marvel Universe. Stan Lee created her as a copyright protection for television executives as Marvel branched into other media (Daniels 182, 211). Appropriately, Wasp sees She-Hulk as a tabula rasa and remakes Walters in her own image: "We want a complete image that'll drive men wild at the sight of you!" As fan Tony Sprague wrote in the letter page in #226 (Dec. 1982), "I'd like to see She-Hulk get a costume of some kind. After all, the Wasp *is* a fashion designer!" In the same issue, reader W. Gregg Stamey, Jr., acknowledged, "The scene with the super-women's brunch was different and interesting, showing that Janet Van Dyne—while maturing—still has a bit of the airhead heiress in her system." When She-Hulk rushes into battle in her new duds in the next issue, Wasp stops her: "That outfit is an *original*! Tear it—and I'll never speak to you again!" (Stern, "Testing..."). In *The Avengers* #222 (Aug. 1982), reader Chad Scott wanted to see "the poor guy [Pym] redeem himself ... but keep him away from Jan for a while. Speaking of Jan, her election to chairman of the Avengers should be the start of something more interesting. Let's hear it for Jan and her new-found freedom!"

Wasp's newfound assertiveness went beyond selecting She-Hulk for the team. In *The Avengers* #227 (Jan 1983) she strong-arms Monica Rambeau to active membership as the new Captain Marvel, explaining: "I know the First Lady. We have the same masseur!" Old-hand Hawkeye openly grouses, "Hey, am I the only one who's noticed how bossy our boss-lady's gotten lately?" She-Hulk teases him about strong women and Cap defends Jan. "The calling of special meetings is the group-leader's privilege, Hawk—you know that! I think Jan is just growing into her post as Avengers Chairwoman ... and doing a good job of it, I might add!" Seeing Hawkeye's narrow vision, Captain America—the World War II hero who usually found himself uncomfortable in modern times—quips, "Welcome to the future, Hawkeye" (Stern, "Testing...").

Despite her empowerment, the Wasp's initial leadership masked an inner tension. In 1976, novelist Tom Wolfe described Americans living in the "Me Decade" and highlighted their self-absorbed hedonism. By 1983, this same naval gazing threatened the team. Marvel's heroes were hardly invincible but these weaknesses heightened during this period. Self-doubt plagued Van Dyne's tenure: in issue #231 (May 1983) inactive teammate Jocasta, Van Dyne's robot sister of sorts, is killed, bringing another blow to the Wasp personally. In the same issue, Iron Man abruptly resigns over the telephone. After a hot, one-issue romance with Van Dyne, which she terminates, he trades his armor for the bottle. In issue #232 (June 1983) a distraught Wasp considers stepping down. She cites the current roster: Hawkeye injured, reserves Vision and Scarlet Witch on an extended honeymoon, reserve Hercules in editorial limbo, reserve Beast serving the rival hero team The Defenders, and reserve Wonder Man finding a new career as a clown in a kids' television show. The team's lack of assembling has become an unbearable burden on her shoulders.

Van Dyne would bear the responsibilities alone. In issue #224 (Oct. 1982),

Tony Stark attempts to catch Van Dyne on the rebound from her divorce. Reflecting that the Avengers have offered "real comfort to her ... besides giving her a sense of pride and purpose after her ugly break-up with Hank," his libido turns on: "Gee, for an ol' playboy like Tony Stark, I should have noticed sooner ... she's looking absolutely terrific!" While Pym pours out his troubles in jail ("I let my personal problems overwhelm me ... I got in trouble and took it out on—on Jan! I deserved to be kicked out of the Avengers!"), Stark strips his armor and zeroes in on Van Dyne (Shooter, "Two From..."). In issue #229 (Mar. 1983) reader Kathryn Newman gushed, "So, here's hoping that Jan gets over her guilt towards Hank and realizes that Anthony Stark is the right man for her."

The creators disagreed. Lounging in his arms, Jan muses, "When I think of how Hank used to keep himself cooped up in that lab of his all those years, when we could have been enjoying life and each other, just like this!" She confides Pym was a stuffed shirt "wrapped up in himself, his bio-chemistry, his robots. That's how I became a social butterfly. Just to get out, do something different." Listening to her thoughts, Stark feels a little guilty with her on the rebound and not opening up his secret double life as her teammate. When Iron Man reveals his identity in a three panel layout, Van Dyne realizes the folly of mixing business with pleasure: "Oh Tony, this isn't what I needed ... not a member of the team. Not Hank's *friend*." Captain America encourages Stark to get over it. "We all make mistakes. The important thing is to learn from them ... to bounce back. You can do it, mister! You're an Avenger!" But Stark is not as strong as the invincible Iron Man's suit: he trades the Avengers for alcohol. In issue #232 (June 1983) Van Dyne tells him, "We just don't want to see you throw your life away ... like Hank did." Stark snaps, "I am *not* Hank Pym, lady! I'm nothin' like you ex-hubby! I don't need your help—an' you don't need mine!" (Stern, "And Now..."). Their attempts at personnel management a failure, the Avengers give up and leave Stark to stew in his stupor. Despite his intoxication, the former Iron Man knew neither he nor Van Dyne needed each other. She had gotten over Pym quickly and ascended to team leader singlehandedly, balancing the dual roles of socialite and superhero.

Nevertheless, the Avengers' solo pursuits came at the expense of the group. Their personal lives—literally separate comic book titles with different creative teams and storylines—threatened to tear the team apart. In issue #228 (Feb. 1983), the Wasp breaks down in front of Thor. "Oh, Thor! Why has this happened to us ... to all of us? We're *Avengers*!" Thor respectfully remains silent, but rookie She-Hulk, unencumbered by two hundred issues of continuity, pinpoints the problem. "It's that blasted Avengers' tradition of 'respecting the privacy of members' personal affairs.' The Founding Members carry it too far! Can't they see how it hurts them?" (Stern, "Trial..."). Indeed, the Avengers clearly are out of their depths when they attempt group counseling: Wasp and Captain America initiate a full retreat when a tipsy Stark tells them to scram. When facing their inner vulnerabilities, Earth Mightiest Heroes went down in defeat.

Morning in America, Mourning in *The Avengers*

Henry Pym's trial as a national traitor marks an Avengers apex in the early 1980s. Van Dyne's ascent and Pym's downfall end in the court of law while a communist villain schemes in the background. Despite Van Dyne's leadership, the team totters on shaky grounds. Soon after Pym's arrest, Tigra departed as well, admitting she didn't have what it takes. In #218 (Apr. 1982), fan T.M. Maple noted, "Tigra's bewilderment at the fast pace and big stakes of the Avengers' world, her uneasiness with her performance, and her sometimes rash attempts to prove herself all ring true." Maple concluded, "Incidentally, this makes a nice counterpoint to Yellowjacket, the bitter veteran, also anxious to make good in company more powerful than he thinks he can keep up with."

Like Tigra, rookies She-Hulk and Captain Marvel sense the group's uncertainty. In #228 (Feb. 1983), She-Hulk wishes Van Dyne would let her emotions turn savage. "Why does she hold in all that grief and heartache? Why doesn't she scream and shout and get it out of her system?" (Stern, "Trial..."). In #227 (Jan. 1983), Van Dyne's long-time friend Susan Richards also sees through Van Dyne's transparent bravery. When her husband Reed—a brainy scientist whose behavior is similar to Pym's remoteness at times—applauds the Wasp's courage, Mrs. Richards explains the facade is *"just* a front [...] She's keeping everything bottled up inside her! And she's been through so much lately.... Hank's expulsion from the Avengers, the divorce ... and now that she's become chairperson of the Avengers—! I'm afraid for her, Reed!" Wasp echoes Mrs. Richard's clairvoyance, recognizing her identity is at stake. "I can tough it out! I'll show 'em ... I don't need him ... don't need anybody! After all, I'm an Avenger." She fixes her hair. "I'm the *leader* of the Avengers!" (Stern, "Testing...").

Pym's trial eludes Van Dyne's control. As he prepares to take the stand, the self-explanatory Masters of Evil, led by Egghead, rescue him. Wasp charges into battle, barking orders. Cap reflects, "Jan's really coming into her own as group leader! Even Hawkeye's snapping to at her orders!" Similarly, Pym has new possibilities, as his foe eggs him on: "Join the Masters of Evil, Henry. *We* will give you a new life!" With Pym working for his old enemy, Iron Man resigned, and the She-Hulk temporarily depowered, Thor comments, "The Avengers have known happier times." In issue #229 (Mar. 1983), while the team struggles to flag their sagging spirits, Pym rewires Egghead's machine to defeat the Masters of Evil with a dramatic monologue:

> I did a pretty good job of screwing my life recently. You just about finished the job for me! You used me, Egghead ... and you tried to make me a criminal. But you couldn't. I've come to terms with myself in the past months. I know who I am and who I'm not! I'm not Ant-Man anymore. I'm not Giant-Man ... or Goliath ... or Yellowjacket! I'm Henry Pym! And it was Henry Pym who defeated the Masters of Evil! You, Egghead ... you turned to crime because you thought your scientific knowledge made you better than everyone else ... put you above the law! But you were wrong. You weren't above the law, and you weren't better! I'm the better scientist ... I just proved that! [Stern, "Final Curtain"].

Having reaffirmed his identity through American individualism, Pym's reclaimed manhood extended through the cultural milieu of the 1980s. As film historian Tony Shaw points out, several motion pictures produced during Reagan's early presidency, including *Rambo* series and *Red Dawn*, confronted the Vietnam Syndrome feeding the American malaise since the 1970s. In the movie's revisionism, however, the heroes "get to win this time" (Shaw 275). Pym's triumph over his demons in the rotund embodiment of Egghead, equates a personal victory in the Cold War. Fittingly, Egghead cracks in the final battle when Hawkeye storms in and inadvertently fries him to save Pym's life.

In issue #230 (Apr. 1983), the Avengers recognize Pym's victory through another court martial. Pym accepts his past: "I made my mistakes ... and I have to live with them." So does Hawkeye, who answers charges for Egghead's death. The surprised bowman asserts he has no regrets. "I don't deny that my actions caused the death of Egghead [...] But in no way did I use undue force! I found Hank Pym in mortal danger, and I used the necessary means to save him ... period. After all, we are suppose to be Avengers, right?" The panel closes in on a close-up of Hawkeye's gritted teeth. The gung-ho archer denies revenge as a motive (Egghead killed Hawkeye's brother in a 1964 story), and instead turns philosophical: what do the Avengers avenge? Pym provides an indirect answer, "The only thing Hawkeye is guilty of is being a good Avenger." He adds, "When I last spoke before this body at my court-martial, I was not in a rational state of mind. I was unfit to be an Avenger. You wisely expelled me. I never expected to speak before you again." But now Pym stands avenged, having redeemed himself from old ghosts; a shorthand for the American way as a conservative United States aligned itself with their president's vision of America—the greatest role Reagan ever played, as biographer Lou Cannon maintains. In revisiting the past, Pym reassembles his identity through reliving the Cold War struggles. Hawkeye, too, had a legitimate grievance against Egghead, but kept his cool and never lost control. The archer, Pym acknowledges, is "a good Avenger" (Stern, "The Last Farewell").

Pym ties up some loose strings, planning to live the Horatio Alger narrative and the American Dream. He will begin anew in a "small research foundation in the Midwest." Captain America offers reserve status as an alternative, but Pym refuses: "Trying to play super-hero was the biggest mistake I ever made with my life! I was only fooling myself in ever thinking otherwise but if you ever really think you might need a Yellowjacket again some day ... here!" He hands Cap his costume and gadgets: the next Yellowjacket would not be Pym. To his ex-wife, he comments on his failure to live up to a fabled masculine image. "You thought you'd found the strong, silent hero. But I was never that strong, Jan. You know that now. We both have other lives to lead" (Stern, "The Last Farewell").

When Pym made a dramatic exit after his court martial in #213 (Nov. 1981), a defeated shell of a man, Van Dyne mused, "You know, I feel like crying ... but I just don't have any tears left" (Shooter, "Court-Martial"). Now, as Pym plans to rebuild his life, she turns on the waterworks. Although no longer married, the story concludes with each finding security in traditional gender roles: Pym strides out the door as the confident male, ready to take on life, Van Dyne the weeping woman left behind, despite her responsibilities as leader of Earth's Mightiest Heroes. The caption portends this traditionalism in optimistic terms: both could carry on with "joy and hope tomorrow" (Stern, "The Last Farewell"). While in mourning, it might be Morning in *The Avengers* once more.

As America's premier superhero team, the Avengers also had no place for small dreams. In issue #211 (Sept. 1981), the team reverted to the original line-up. But the Silver Age of flawed, yet triumphant, heroes was long gone. In issue #215 (Jan. 1982), fan Ellis R. McDaniels, realized, "for too long, the Avengers have tried to be something they are not: social workers. Avengers Mansion is not a home for wayward heroes, nor is it a sanctuary for those with identity crises or personal problems." Those personal failings cumulated in Pym's court martial, mirroring the crisis of masculinity in the late 1970s. In issue #214 (Dec. 1981), while the Pyms' marriage disintegrated, Captain America blames himself, telling the press, "I regret that I did not have the wisdom, understanding, foresight, or compassion to prevent the events of the last few days, or change their course once they were in motion." Thor's alter ego, Dr. Don Blake, offers his professional opinion: "obviously he's had a mental breakdown! [...] Since he recently rejoined the Avengers, I suspect he was demanding too much of himself—but then I think he always has!" Tigra's feline instincts labels Pym a "first class rat" but Jarvis says she is mistaken. "Men are fallible—even heroes—and Dr. Pym, like any man, must bear the consequences of his actions! Judge him not too harshly, Madame—until you have proven yourself as he has!" Subsequent issues show both Tigra and Pym could not prove worthy of Avengers material.

Despite Cap's critiquing the team's privacy policies, the Avengers did not change. Van Dyne grew in her dual roles as Wasp and social butterfly, but she acknowledged the roster's solo pursuits—the self-centeredness of the 1980s—tore the team apart. In the end, Pym reaffirmed his individualism through his old nemesis Egghead's demise. The Avengers united to battle the villains no one hero could withstand, but until then, they stood apart. In 1985, both Pym and Iron Man (albeit not Stark) returned to active status in the Avengers' new west coast spinoff. Affectionately dubbed the "Wackos," the West Coasters operated with a looser structure than the main group, although the team had its ups and downs. By issue #16 (Jan. 1987), a depressed Pym tried to commit suicide and Iron Man faced expulsion. Yellowjacket's court-martial continued to cast a shadow over Earth's Mightiest Heroes.

In *The Avengers* #232 (June 1983) James L. Fyre wrote, "When I first started reading his solo adventures as the Ant-Man back in *Tales to Astonish*, I never would've dreamed that he'd go through so many changes." In issue #233 (July 1983), reader Kevin Scott Collier reflected, "There's a lot to learn in comics today. When I was ten years old, they seemed to be no more than very entertaining stories. But now, I can see that they tell you something about society, the world as it is now." Reader Roxanne C. Smith agreed. "Sometimes life is like that, though: sometimes the only breaks are the bad ones, and it seems that the whole world exists only to tear you down." For Pym, rebuilding his manhood reaffirmed America's identity in the Cold War—and provided a rallying point for the Avengers to assemble.

Works Cited

Busiek, Kurt (w), and Carlos Pacheo (a). "Avengers Assemble!" *Avengers Forever* #12 (Feb. 2000). New York: Marvel Comics.

_____. "City at the Heart of Forever." *Avengers Forever* #3 (Feb. 1999). New York: Marvel Comics.

Cannon, Lou. *President Reagan: The Role of a Lifetime*. New York: Public Affairs, 2000.

Daniels, Les. *Marvel: Five Fabulous Decades of the World's Greatest Comics*. New York: Harry N. Abrams, 1995.

DeMatteis, J.M. (w), and Don Perlin (a). "Born Again (and Again and Again…)." *The Avengers* #218 (Apr. 1982). New York: Marvel Comics.

Ehrman, John. *The Eighties: America in the Age of Reagan*. New Haven: Yale University Press, 2006.

Engleheart, Steve (w), and Al Milgrom (a). "The Dive." *West Coast Avengers* #16 (Jan. 1987). New York: Marvel Comics.

Faludi, Susan. *Backlash: The Undeclared War Against American Women*. New York: Crown, 1991.

_____. *Stiffed: The Betrayal of the American Man*. New York: HarperCollins, 2011.

Grant, Steven (w), and Greg LaRocque (a). "An Eye for an Eye." *The Avengers* #226 (Dec. 1982). New York: Marvel Comics.

Kimmel, Michael. *Manhood in America: A Cultural History*, 3d ed. New York: Oxford University Press, 2011.

Latch, Christopher. *The Culture of Narcissism: American Life in an Age of Diminishing Expectations*. New York: W.W. Norton, 1979.

Pustz, Matthew. "'Paralysis and Stagnation and Drift': America's Malaise as Demonstrated in Comic Books of the 1970s." *Comic Books and American Cultural History*, ed. Matthew Pustz. New York: Continuum International, 2011: 136–151.

Shaw, Tony. *Hollywood's Cold War*. Amherst: University of Massachusetts Press, 2007.

Shooter, Jim. "Hank Pym Was Not a Wife-Beater." Jim Shooter. Writer. Creator. Large Mammal. http://www.jimshooter.com/2011/03/hank-pym-was-not-wife-beater.html. 29 March 2011. Accessed June 1, 2013.

Shooter, Jim (w), and Mark Bright (a). "Two from the Heart." *The Avengers* #224 (Oct. 1982). New York: Marvel Comics.

Shooter, Jim (w), and Gene Colan (a). "...By Force of Mind!" *The Avengers* #211 (Sept. 1981). New York: Marvel Comics.

Shooter, Jim (w), and Bob Hall (a). "Court-Martial." *The Avengers* #213 (Nov. 1981). New York: Marvel Comics.

_____, and _____. "Double-Cross!" *The Avengers* #217 (Mar. 1982). New York: Marvel Comics.

_____, and _____. "Three Angels Fallen!" *The Avengers* #214 (Dec. 1981). New York: Marvel Comics.

_____, and _____. "War Against the Gods!" *The Avengers* #220 (June 1982). New York: Marvel Comics.

Shooter, Jim (w), and Alan Kupperberg (a). "Men of Deadly Pride!" *The Avengers* #212 (Oct. 1981). New York: Marvel Comics.

Shooter, Jim (w), and Greg LaRocque (a). "A Gathering of Evil!" *The Avengers* #222 (Aug. 1982). New York: Marvel Comics.

Shooter, Jim (w), and George Perez (a). "Beware the Ant-Man!" *The Avengers* #166 (July 1977). New York: Marvel Comics.

Shooter, Jim (w), and Alan Weiss (a). "All the Ways of Power!" *The Avengers* #215 (Jan. 1982). New York: Marvel Comics.

_____. "...To Avenge the Avengers!" *The Avengers* #216 (Feb. 1982). New York: Marvel Comics.

Stern, Roger (w), and Sal Buscema (a). "Testing ... 1 ... 2 ... 3!" *The Avengers* #227 (Jan. 1983). New York: Marvel Comics.

Stern, Roger (w), and John Byrne (a). "The Annihilation Gambit!" *The Avengers* #233 (July 1983). New York: Marvel Comics.

Stern, Roger (w) and Al Milgrom (a). "And Now ... Starfox!" *The Avengers* #232 (June 1983). New York: Marvel Comics.

_____, and _____. "Final Curtain!" *The Avengers* #229 (Mar. 1983). New York: Marvel Comics.

_____, and _____. "The Last Farewell!" *The Avengers* #230 (Apr. 1983). New York: Marvel Comics.

_____, and _____. "Trial and Error!" *The Avengers* #228 (Feb. 1983). New York: Marvel Comics.

_____, and _____. "Up from the Depths!" *The Avengers* #231 (May 1983). New York: Marvel Comics.

Wolfe, Tom. "The 'Me' Decade and the Third Great Awakening." *New York Magazine* (Aug. 23, 1976): 27–48.

Wright, Bradford. *Comic Book Nation: The Transformation of Youth Culture in America*. Baltimore: Johns Hopkins University Press, 2001.

Zelenetz, Alan (w), and Greg LaRocque (a). "What If Yellowjacket Had Died?" *What If?* #35 (Oct. 1982). New York: Marvel Comics.

Everything Old Is New Again
Figuring Out Who the Enemy Is in the 1980s

Jason LaTouche

The Avengers "Under Siege" storyline of 1986 and 1987 appeared during a time in which the United States was grappling with a series of profound cultural and social changes. Coming after the intense social upheavals sparked by the civil rights movements of the 1960s and 1970s and the political upheavals of the Vietnam War and Watergate, the 1980s was witness to the rise of a social and political backlash against the prominent progressive politics of the previous decades. At the same time, the 1980s confronted the United States with dramatic changes that upended long standing notions of global political power and new technologies that changed the way in which people came to understand their world.

As exemplars of the heroic model in general and as the foremost representation of the Marvel Universe's idea of group heroism, *The Avengers* "Under Siege" storyline of 1986 and 1987 repeatedly confronts these dynamic social and political challenges, intentionally and unintentionally exposing and reflecting the social and political divides that were in such conflict.

The Whole World Is Watching

One of the dramatic changes of the 1980s was the rise of cable television and the creation of dedicated cable news channels. From 1979 to 1985 alone the percent of households in the United States having access to cable television increased from nineteen to forty-one percent (Rust and Donthu 6). Beginning with the foundation of the Cable-Satellite Public Affairs Network (C-SPAN) in 1979 and the CNN cable news channel in 1980, this rising cable television penetration facilitated a dramatic change to more live news coverage and more omnipresent coverage of news stories and political events both big and small.

While C-SPAN was providing live coverage of governmental proceedings, CNN created a model of news programming emphasizing live reporting and twenty-four hour news coverage. This model became increasingly influential as CNN's reach and impact grew dramatically. While initially airing in only two million homes in the United States in 1980, by the end of the decade CNN would be in 58 million U.S. homes and over 140 countries around the world (Flournoy 229). As the C-SPAN and CNN models of live coverage and twenty-four hour reporting became more common, the role of the televised news media became more ubiquitous, no longer constrained to a nightly news report and extreme event special news bulletins.

Along with these new models of televised news coverage came an increase in entertainment-focused televised news coverage. Created in 1981, *Entertainment Tonight* and its numerous imitators placed a new emphasis on televised celebrity news coverage, thereby bolstering the importance of public appearance and image management to public figures.

The importance of these changes are reflected in *The Avengers* "Under Siege" storyline. Throughout the storyline media is a constant presence, attended to by both the heroes and villains. Indeed the storyline opens with the narration of a reporter setting the scene—a common rhetorical device that here serves the dual purpose of reflecting a 'real' news report and providing the narrative scene setting for the storyline (Stern, "Wild" 1). *The Avengers* #275 (Jan. 1987) echoes this framework, also opening with a full page narrative framing device of a television news report (Stern, "Even" 1). This framing device is used in similar smaller ways several other times throughout the story.

It is revealing of the impact of the real world trends towards television journalism that all the various news reporters portrayed within the storyline are television news reporters and not print reporters. Indeed, with one small exception, even all the numerous news reports consumed by the Avengers and their antagonists, the Masters of Evil, are televised journalism.

Reflecting how televised media was changing the nature of the public role of prominent individuals and groups, the Avengers themselves are presented as both the focus and product of this news reporting—as both celebrity image and serious news story in one. In one extended sequence, the Avengers' leader, the Wasp, and her ally the Black Knight attend a charity event that is being covered for television by *Entertainment Tonight* reporters. Acceding to the role of celebrity journalism, the Wasp bolsters her and the Avengers' public image by posing on the red carpet in a designer dress while answering personal questions posed to her by an *Entertainment Tonight* reporter. In the midst of doing this she is suddenly accosted by a CBS News television reporter who begins to probe her on the key political issues surrounding the Avengers thereby forcing her to simultaneously attend to her place as a subject of television news journalism.

This use of televised news media within the narrative serves to give the storyline real-world legitimacy through the use of current forms of reporting emphasizing immediacy and by the continual referencing of actual real-world news agencies. Importantly, it also telegraphs how the Avengers were being positioned in the fictional world as both a political organization and an entertainment product for public consumption, echoing the real world parallels that were being created through the rise of ubiquitous television news media and the crossover of news media with entertainment media in the new models of television based journalism.

All Is Forgiven?

This tension within the Avengers between their political actions and their public image is central to the opening conflict in the series. At the beginning of the storyline there is a massive political protest and counter-protest happening outside the Avengers' mansion due to their recent induction of the Sub-Mariner into the Avengers. This protest is being covered by the news media and is driven by two groups within the public arguing over the nature of the Sub-Mariner. One group of older protestors support the Sub-Mariner, arguing that "Namor was one our greatest allies in World War II" (Stern, "Wild..." 2). Another group of protestors argue that making Namor an Avenger is an outrage due to his more recent history of attacking New York City, with one protestor declaring, "The Russians were our allies back then, too! An' we don't trust them!" (Stern, "Wild..." 2).

This protest reflects the complicated history of the character of the Sub-Mariner within the Marvel Universe. In the stories of the 1940s the Sub-Mariner had largely filled the role of a hero, working alongside Captain America and the Human Torch. With the revival of the character in the 1960s, the Sub-Mariner had often been used as an anti-hero. This version of the Sub-Mariner held deep-seated resentment against the surface dwellers whom he believed responsible for the problems of his undersea realm. As a result, the revived Sub-Mariner had repeatedly been at odds with the surface world and its heroes. By the 1980s, the Sub-Mariner was again being positioned by Marvel as a much more typical heroic character.

The protestors' conflict within the "Under Siege" storyline reflected the battle over which aspect of the Sub-Mariner's history would be pre-eminent in public perception. However, this conflict did not derive solely from the character's fictional history. In fact, this conflict also reflected the larger political reality within the real world.

One of the most profound geo-political changes of the 1980s was the dramatic social realignments that occurred within the Soviet Union over the course of the decade and the subsequent impact this had on U.S.-Soviet relations. At the start of the decade, U.S.-Soviet relations were very frosty, with the United States' President Ronald Reagan repeatedly characterizing the Soviet Union as being an "evil" empire (Halsall). By the mid to late 1980s with the rise of Mikhail Gorbachev to power within the Soviet Union and his implementation of perestroika policies aimed at shifting the political structures of the Soviet Union towards more openness and political freedom, attitudes towards the Soviet Union were shifting within the United States.

Suddenly, the Soviet Union which had been the United States' central Cold War antagonist for almost forty years was undergoing a dramatic reappraisal among much of the general public of the U.S. Surveys showed that at the start of the 1980s almost 80 percent of the people in the United States had a negative image of the Soviet Union. By the time of the publication of *The Avengers* "Under Siege" storyline this percentage had dropped to about 50 percent (Richman 137). Similarly, over the same time span the percentage of adults in the United States who agreed with the statement that "Russia seeks global domination" dropped from the low 70s to the low 50s (Richman 137).

However, while opinions were changing rapidly about the Soviet Union there still remained a predominant number of people who held fast to the traditional beliefs about the Soviet Union as an 'evil' empire as established over almost forty years of Cold War politics and elaborated by Ronald Reagan at the start of the 1980s. This growing divide in opinion provoked controversy about the nature of U.S.-Soviet relations.

The debate over the Sub-Mariner in the "Under Siege" storyline explicitly reflects this tension over changing attitudes towards the Soviet Union. Indeed, the overt referencing of Russia by the protestors depicted in the storyline emphasizes this point. In the character of the Sub-Mariner *The Avengers* storyline is elaborating the larger social conflict between those whose beliefs were rapidly changing to accommodate the new social realities and those who were attempting to preserve and restore their past beliefs in the face of a confusing, shifting world.

This tension is at the heart of both how the media representations within *The Avengers* were reflecting how the role of media was changing in society and how the political debate about the nature of past versus present geo-political reality between the U.S. and the Soviet Union was mirrored in the conflict over the Sub-Mariner membership in the Avengers. In each case, *The Avengers* was reflecting real world conflicts over changing value systems. However, nowhere is this societal conflict over maintaining versus rejecting traditional social arrangements felt more strongly within *The Avengers* "Under Siege" storyline than in the ways in which the conflict between the ideas of the New Right conservative movement and those of the feminist Women's Movement was reflected in the depiction of the role of women within the storyline.

Who's in Charge Here?

The late 1970s and early 1980s saw the rise of the New Right conservative movement. A response to the second wave Women's Movement of the 1960s and 1970s, the New Right movement sought to resist many of the changes being sought by the Women's Movement (Conover 632; Petchesky 208).

The second wave Women's Movement was pressing for equality of treatment and opportunity regardless of sex. Feminist activists sought to challenge traditional gender roles that assigned the economic sphere to men and the home sphere to women. These activists sought to ensure that both women and men had equal ability to work, to parent, and to lead within society.

The work of these activists was bolstered by societal changes within the 1960s and 1970s such as the creation of the birth control pill, increased middle class college access, and the increased awareness of and support for equality campaigns created by the civil rights movements of the 1950s and 1960s.

As a result of these forces, dramatic changes were occurring in the social role of women within the United States. The percentage of college graduates that were women had been steadily increasing and by the mid–1980s women comprised about half of all college graduates (Rosenfeld and Ward 477). Similarly the percent of women in the labor force had been steadily rising. Whereas in 1972 women had comprised 41 percent of the U.S. labor force, by the time of the publication of the "Under Siege" storyline fifteen years later, women made up 52 percent of the labor force ("Women in the Labor Force: A Databook" 11).

These changes were a direct challenge to more traditionalist views of the nuclear family model where men and women married early, the husband worked outside the home, and the wife stayed home taking care of the children and the household responsibilities. Indeed, the labor participation rate of married women and mothers was higher than for women overall. By the mid–1980s, more than 50 percent of all married women, 67 percent of mothers of school-age children, and 53 percent of mothers of pre-school age children were in the labor force (Shehan and Scanzoni 444).

Not surprisingly with increased rates of education and labor force participation, increasing number of women delayed getting married as they pursued educational opportunities and career goals. By 1985 the average age of first marriage for women in the U.S. reached 23.3 years old, at the time the highest age recorded (Shehan and Scanzoni 444).

These changes in social behavior were also linked with changes in social attitudes. During the peak of the Women's Movement in the early to mid 1970s, surveys consistently demonstrated a growing agreement with the Women's Movement's central thesis that women were experiencing inequality. Comparable studies done in 1972 and 1976 showed that in just a four year period the percent of people expressing support for the idea that "men have more of the top jobs because our society discriminates against women" increased from 48 percent to 62 percent (Gurin 155). Similarly, the percent of people expressing positive attitudes towards the Women's Liberation Movement had increased from 36 percent to 46 percent (Gurin 155).

These changes in social attitudes were not just limited to women. While there was a gap in support for feminist women's issues, with generally more women than men in support of women's issues, some studies showed that this gap was shrinking (Shapiro and Mahajan 54).

The New Right arose in response to these trends. A backlash movement, the New Right sought to bolster traditional gender roles and the nuclear family model (Conover 634–635; Shehan and Scanzoni 445).

Central to this movement was the idea that the natural and proper place for men was to be the leaders and doers of society and that the natural and proper place of women was to be self-sacrificing caregivers (Klatch 676–678). Indeed, central to this belief system was the idea that women did not want to be leaders because they did not want to engage in the aggressive, decisive actions necessary to achieve and maintain leadership positions (Klatch 679–680).

In this way the New Right movement arose as a direct response to both the ideas and successes of the Women's Movement. Embodied by the massive electoral college victories of Ronald Reagan in the Presidential elections of 1980 and 1984, the New Right was at the forefront of a conservative political movement that swept the nation in the early to mid 1980s. Indeed, in the congressional elections of 1980 Republicans picked up thirty-four seats in the House of Representatives and twelve seats in the Senate. In fact, the New Right movement successfully targeted six liberal senators for defeat as the Republicans took control of the Senate in the biggest electoral swing in the Senate since 1958 (Conover 632).

The rise of the New Right response to the Women's Movement also began to manifest itself in public attitudes towards the ideas of the Women's Movement. Whereas support for feminist ideas had been growing through the early to mid 1970s, the rise of the New Right movement reflected an increasingly conservative response to these ideas that stagnated or reversed many of the attitude changes the Women's Movement had been targeting.

By the late 1970s and early 1980s the gap between men and women in their support of women's issues was growing wider (Shapiro and Mahajan 54; Twenge 42). Studies conducted in the mid–1980s around the time of *The Avengers* "Under Siege" storyline show that only 25 percent or less of men supported the Women's Movement and equality of the sexes (Burke and Black 936).

In fact, overall attitudes towards traditional gender norms which had been seeing decreasing support during the peak of the Women's Movement were now showing increasing support by the early 1980s. For example, one set of studies conducted in 1972 and again in 1983 showed that support for traditional gender roles had grown significantly. These studies showed that support for the idea that "in general, men are more qualified than women for jobs that have great responsibility" had increased from 24 percent of adults in 1972 to 51 percent of adults in 1983 (Gurin 155). Similarly, the percent of adults supporting the belief that "by nature women are happiest when they are making a home and caring for children" had more than doubled from 12 percent in 1972 to 26 percent in 1983 (Gurin 155).

However, in spite of these more conservative attitudes significant support for feminist ideas remained. Indeed, surveys done in 1983 showed that while only 13 percent of people believed that "women have less opportunity than men to get education for top jobs" 52 percent of people believed "many qualified women can't get good jobs; men with the same skills have much less trouble" (Gurin 155). Similarly, while 37 percent of people believed that "men are born with more drive to be ambitious and successful than women" 43 percent believed "women have 'too little power'" and 46 percent believed "men have 'too much power'" (Gurin 155).

As a genre of literature centrally concerned with issues of power, authority, and leadership, superhero comic books were affected by these debates. *The Avengers* in particular, as a series about the most powerful superhero team in the Marvel Universe, was uniquely situated to reflect the larger cultural debate about the role of women in society.

This was particularly true during the "Under Siege" storyline as the Avengers had historically had a leadership structure under which the group was led by a formally defined chairperson.

Reflecting some of the changes called for by the Women's Movement, at the time of the "Under Siege" storyline the Avengers were being led by the Wasp, a female superhero who was the first female member of the Avengers and who had been associated with the team since its inception in the 1960s. Indeed, having Wasp as the chairperson of the Avengers was a particularly feminist statement as the original incarnation of the Wasp had depicted her as a flighty, weak, vain, romance-obsessed character that was completely subordinate to the male super-heroes around her. To have the Wasp assume the leadership of the Avengers was, on the surface, a direct feminist repudiation of the earlier gender stereotyped depiction of the character.

This feminist interpretation of the character is made explicit throughout the "Under Siege" storyline as the Wasp repeatedly butts heads with Hercules over her position as the leader of the Avengers. It is revealing that Hercules is the only member of the Avengers that overtly challenges Wasp's leadership of the Avengers. Hercules is the literal representation of the Greek god and as such is depicted as a throwback to the sexist attitudes of the ancient past.

As such, Hercules rejects the very idea of being commanded by a woman. From the very first issue of the storyline Hercules is constantly thinking and saying how much he resents and rejects the idea of the Wasp's leadership (Stern, "Wild" 5, 14). In fact, the Avengers antagonists prey upon Hercules' sexism by having a seemingly random human man taunt him in a bar about "takin' orders from a dame" (Stern, "Rites" 3). This so enrages Hercules he throws the human through a plate glass window into the path of an oncoming truck (Stern, "Rites" 4).

Eventually Hercules directly refuses to follow Wasp's orders declaring, "I have humored your commands in weeks past, Wasp ... but no more! ... Fool woman! When this is done, I shall demand new leadership in the Avengers!" (Stern, "Divided" 14). At this point it has been made clear that Hercules' objection to the Wasp's leadership is solely based on her being a women and not on the particular leadership decisions she has made.

In Hercules' traditionalist mindset the Wasp is unfit for leadership because she is a woman and leadership is the role of a man. In this Hercules is being set up as an extreme example of the New Right's backlash against the Women's Movement. Hammering this connection home, Hercules is confronted by Wasp for allowing the Sub-Mariner to go off to face a deadly foe on his own. Wasp is furious that Sub-Mariner would leave on his own without informing her or seeking the team's assistance, a move that Hercules was both aware of and endorsed. Hercules responds to the Wasp's anger by declaring, "twas nothing wrong with the Sub-Mariner's thinking! Facing Attuma alone is a point of honor! But then, I shouldn't expect a woman to understand such things!" (Stern, "Breakaway!" 2). This directly echoes the New Right critique that women both are not naturally predisposed for leadership and lack the desire to embrace the hard decision making leadership requires (Klatch 679–680).

In this depiction *The Avengers* "Under Siege" storyline seems to embrace the Women's Movement feminist critique. Hercules' attitude is not portrayed sympathetically. Indeed, Hercules is depicted as backward and regressive in his attitudes towards Wasp's leadership. All of the other men of the Avengers, including Captain America who had historically been held up as the exemplar of morality both of the Avengers and the Marvel Universe more generally, are depicted as accepting the Wasp's leadership in a perfectly matter-of-fact manner, precisely the equality of treatment being advocated for by the Women's Movement.

In this manner the storyline appears to support the Women's Movement's feminist stance over the backlash politics of the New Right movement. However, a closer examination of the subtext of the storyline reveals a much more complicated story of gender politics.

Who's the Hero and Who's the Villain?

In the "Under Siege" storyline, Baron Zemo, the son of Captain America's arch-nemesis, has gathered together more than a dozen super-villains to enact his master plan to take over Avengers' Mansion and destroy the Avengers. Zemo is an ordinary human without super-powers. However, Zemo is a master planner and strategist and these qualities let him lead a group of super-villains possessed of all manner of superhuman abilities and godlike powers.

Zemo and his team, the Masters of Evil, successfully take over Avengers' Mansion. They beat Hercules and the Avengers' butler Jarvis to near the point of death. They hold Captain America and the Black Knight hostage. All the while, Zemo maintains a firm control over the super powered Masters of Evil, marshaling them to obey him and carry his plans to fruition.

The leadership of the group lies firmly in the hands of a man who possesses the dynamic and assertive qualities the New Right believed were necessary for leadership. However, Zemo's leadership is not without challenge. One of Zemo's recruits is Moonstone, a female super-powered villain. Importantly, Moonstone is depicted as having the same qualities of leadership as Zemo. Indeed, it is made clear throughout the storyline that Moonstone poses a real threat to Zemo's leadership.

In fact, Zemo declares at one point that "of all the super-criminals I have brought together, Moonstone presents the most direct challenge to my leadership" (Stern, "Rites..." 7). The storyline makes it clear that Zemo's belief is correct as Moonstone acts decisively to undercut his leadership. Moonstone is depicted as being just as ruthless and cunning as Zemo. Indeed, Moonstone is the only super villain not afraid to challenge Zemo directly for leadership (Stern, "Rites..." 18). Even after Zemo tricks her and has her restrained she still refuses to accede to his leadership until he explains his plans.

She is able to do this because Zemo's plans for the Masters of Evil depend upon the successful implementation of several complex technological stratagems. These stratagems are led by Moonstone and Yellowjacket, another female member of the Masters of Evil. Indeed, Zemo's entire plan is dependent on these women's intellectual skills in manipulating complex technology and developing new technological solutions to their problems.

Both Moonstone and Yellowjacket are aware of their importance and the irreplaceable value of their skill set. Both women also refuse to surrender to the leadership of men they feel are less competent than them. They demand the positions of power and respect they deserve. Just as Moonstone challenges Zemo for leadership of the team, Yellowjacket refuses to play second fiddle to a man.

When the Fixer, a male supervillain renowned for his technical skill, tries to take over Yellowjacket's assignment to hack into the Avengers' computer database, Yellowjacket puts him in his place. The Fixer tries to push Yellowjacket out saying, "sweetness, why don't you let me give you a hand, hmm?" (Stern, "Divided..." 8). Yellowjacket responds by almost breaking his thumb as she dismissively says, "Keep your hands to yourself" (Stern, "Rites" 8).

Zemo acknowledges the primacy of Yellowjacket's role later in the storyline as he informs the Fixer that he will be *assisting* Yellowjacket in the critical job of removing the Avenger's computers memory circuits (Stern, "Even..." 17). Later as Zemo watches Yellowjacket and the Fixer complete the tasks he warns the Fixer but not Yellowjacket to be careful (Stern, "Revenge" 10).

In all of these interactions, the way the women of the Masters of Evil are depicted closely models the feminist idea. The women are treated as equals by Zemo. Their skills and abilities are acknowledged and they are accorded the respect and position their skills demand. The women expect and demand equal treatment and get it. Zemo even extends such gender attitudes towards the Avengers rationally acknowledging that Captain Marvel, a female, is "the most powerful Avenger of all" and recognizing that his whole plan is predicated first and foremost on stopping her (Stern, "Rites..." 7).

By contrast, the supposedly feminist representation of the Wasp as the chairperson of the Avengers upon further examination actually seems to validate many of the points the New Right was emphasizing about gender roles. On the surface the Wasp appears to be a very feminist portrayal. She is the leader of the Avengers and Hercules' sexist challenging of her leadership is overtly repudiated in the storyline. Wasp also has several moments in the storyline where she is assertive and aggressive. For example, she answers an alarm call at her apartment by herself, rejecting assistance (Stern, "Breakaway" 6). She gives orders to Thor and Captain America and they follow them (Stern, "Revenge" 16). She expresses her steely desire to fight and seek vengeance on the Avengers' enemies (Stern, "Even..." 22).

However, for each portrayal of the Wasp as an assured, competent, respected leader there are numerous examples of her displaying the exact opposite qualities. Indeed, the norm is more for the Wasp to be doubtful, emotional, tentative, and subordinate. In fact, the very first thing Wasp says in the storyline is that it's "all my fault" that the protests are occurring (Stern, "Wild..." 5). She continues this self-negation of her leadership skills throughout the storyline. As Hercules lies in the hospital on the verge of death she fretfully worries about what to do (Stern, "Even..." 5). Later, she cries on Ant-man's shoulder as she blames herself for causing the end of the Avengers (Stern, "Even..." 9–10).

Supporting her self-doubt, the Wasp's leadership is questioned. While Hercules is the most obvious example of her leadership being questions, her orders are not always immediately followed. When she orders an injured Black Knight to stay and guard other injured allies but the Black Knight refuses to comply and the Wasp gives up on trying to command him to do so (Stern, "The Price" 3). Similarly, when the two women Avengers, Captain Marvel and the Wasp, participate in fights with super villains they are not treated as the equals of their male peers. When they do fight against the Masters of Evil, Captain Marvel and Wasp nearly always fight their female counterparts, even though there are significantly more men than women on the super villain team. In fact, both Captain Marvel and the Wasp are largely sidelined in the epic final confrontation of the book, neither participating in the main battle with the most powerful members of the Masters of Evil in spite of the fact that Captain Marvel had earlier been characterized in the book as the most powerful member of the Avengers.

In the same manner, when the Avengers go into battle the Wasp is frequently sidelined despite being their leader. Whereas her male teammates are consistently portrayed as indefatigable and unyielding against their enemies, Wasp is, over the course of the storyline, depicted as too tired to fight (Stern, "Breakaway" 19) or sent away from the battle by the men to get or provide help while the men fight on (Stern, "Divided..." 16; Stern, "The Price..." 5). In this way, the image shown of the Wasp is often that of the New Right's idea of women as lacking the innate qualities and drives necessary for leadership. She is too emotional, too passive, and not naturally suited for the role she is attempting to play because she is a woman.

Even how she is physically depicted reflects this attitude. Whereas Moonstone and Yellowjacket always assume assertive poses and scenes where they are shown as being dynamic and engaged in important activity, the women of the Avengers are often portrayed in sexualized and stereotyped manners. The Wasp appears in the storyline in extended sequences both in a clingy dress low cut to her navel and in a skimpy bikini (Stern, "Rites..." 14; Stern, "Divided" 9). Similarly, Captain Marvel appears in a short dress, drawn from below to emphasize her bare legs and sitting at a café primping her hair and casting a coy glance around her (Stern, "Divided..." 5; Stern, "Rites" 9).

Even the body language used for the Wasp communicates stereotypes of gender. At different points in the storyline, the Wasp is shown curled into herself as she frets, pouting with her hands on her hips while tapping her toe, and crying while being comforted by her male teammate (Stern, "Breakaway" 1, 5; Stern, "Even..." 9–10).

In this way, *The Avengers* "Under Siege" sets up an interesting contrast. The storyline tells the reader that the Wasp is a representation of feminist advancement and poses Hercules as an indictment of the New Right's traditional gender roles. However, the storyline actually presents a much more complicated analysis of gender: for the super villain women are truly represented as the embodiment of the Women's Movement's ideal of gender equality while the superhero Wasp actually depicts many of the New Right's traditional ideas of gender, supporting their argument that leadership is the role of men not women.

Just as with its representations over the conflicts of the new media forms and changing geo-political beliefs systems of the 1980s, *The Avengers* "Under Siege" storyline's treatment of gender shows how the real world fights in the 1980s over changing social values found their way into *The Avengers* in complicated ways. In a fitting dénouement, the writer of *The Avengers* "Under Siege" storyline, Roger Stern, left soon after this storyline ended. He has said that the reason he left was that he had made Captain Marvel the new leader of the Avengers and he was asked by his editors to replace her with Captain America. He refused to do this because he believed that it would "look both racist and sexist" (Krug). Ironically, if he wanted to really resist sexism, he should have broadened his scope. It was not always clear to see in the complicated world of the 1980s, but clearly the most feminist leader was not a superhero but a super villain.

Works Cited

Burke, Ronald, and Susan Black. "Save the Males: Backlash in Organizations." *Journal of Business Ethics* 16.9 (June 1997): 933–942. Print.

Conover, Pamela Johnston. "The Mobilization of the New Right: A Test of Various Explanations." *The Western Political Quarterly* 36.4 (Dec. 1983): 632–649. Print.

Flournoy, Don. Rev. of *CNN World Report. Ted Turner's International News Coup. Academia Research Monograph #9,* by John Libby. *Journal of Peace Research* (May 1993): 229. Print.

Gurin, Patricia. "Women's Gender Consciousness." *The Public Opinion Quarterly* 49.2 (Summer 1985): 143–163. Print.

Halsall, Paul. "Modern History Sourcebook: Ronald Reagan: Evil Empire Speech, June 8, 1982." *Fordham University.* Fordham University, 1998. Web. 3 Sept. 2013.

Klatch, Rebecca. "Coalition and Conflict Among Women of the New Right." *Signs* 13.4 (Summer 1988): 671–694. Print.

Krug, Kurt. "Comic Book Legends: Roger Stern." Mania, 12 August 2009. Web. 2 Sept. 2013.

Petchesky, Rosalind. "Antiabortion, Antifeminism, and the Rise of the New Right." *Feminist Studies* 7.2 (Summer, 1981): 206–246. Print.

Richman, Alvin. "Poll Trends: Changing American Attitudes Toward the Soviet Union." *The Public Opinion Quarterly* 55.1 (Spring 1991): 135–148. Print.

Rosenfeld, Rachel, and Kathryn Ward. "The Contemporary U.S. Women's Movement: An Empirical Example of Competition Theory." *Sociological Forum* 6.3 (Sept. 1991): 471–500. Print.

Rust, Roland, and Naveen Donthu. "A Programming and Positioning Strategy for Cable Television Networks." *Journal of Advertising* 17.4 (1988): 6–13. Print.

Shapiro, Robert, and Harpreet Mahajan. "Gender Differences in Policy Preferences: A Summary of Trends From the 1960s to the 1980s." *The Public Opinion Quarterly* 50.1 (Spring 1986): 42–61. Print.

Shehan, Constance, and John Scanzoni. "Gender Patterns in the United States: Demographic Trends and Policy Prospects." *Family Relations* 37.4 (Oct. 1988): 444–450. Print.

Stern, Roger (w), and John Buscema (a). "Breakaway!" *The Avengers* #271 (Sept. 1986). New York: Marvel Comics. Print.

_____. "Divided ... We Fall!" *The Avengers* #274 (Dec. 1986). New York: Marvel Comics. Print.

_____. "Even a God Can Die." *The Avengers* #275 (Jan. 1987). New York: Marvel Comics. Print.

_____. "The Price of Victory." *The Avengers* #277 (Mar. 1987). New York: Marvel Comics. Print.

_____. "Revenge." *The Avengers* #276 (Feb. 1987). New York: Marvel Comics. Print.

_____. "Rites of Conquest!" *The Avengers* #273 (Nov. 1986). New York: Marvel Comics. Print.

_____. "Wild in the Streets!" *The Avengers* #270 (Aug. 1986). New York: Marvel Comics. Print.

Twenge, Jean. "Attitudes Toward Women, 1970–1995: A Meta-Analysis." *Psychology of Women Quarterly* 21 (1997): 35–51. Print.

"Women in the Labor Force: A Databook." *BLS Reports* 1040 (Feb. 2013): 1–104. Print.

The Earth's Mightiest Heroes
and America's Post–Cold War
Identity Crisis

John Darowski

The early 1990s were a commercially successful time for the comic book industry. Sales were at the highest point in decades thanks to a booming speculator's market. The critical success of mature works such as *Watchmen* and *Maus*, coupled with the 1989 *Batman* movie, brought mainstream attention to the medium. At the same time, reports began to appear about the record-setting prices early and rare issues could fetch at auction. The result was the false assumption that any comic book was an investment commodity which could only go up in value (Rhoades 128). The industry was quick to embrace this attitude by offering a slew of new titles that popularized a hyper-masculine aesthetic featuring large, muscular men with big guns and impossibly-proportioned women, as well as gimmicky variant covers including foil-embossed, hologram, and glow-in-the-dark varieties. Events such as *The Death of Superman*, Batman's *Knightfall*, and Spider-Man's Clone Saga saw traditional heroes replaced by more contemporary versions, often in the mold of violent, "grim 'n' gritty" antiheroes; other titles, like *The Avengers*, had their heroes update their costumes and characterizations in similar fashion. Such stunts, endemic of commercial concerns of quantity over quality, laid the seed for the inevitable bust of the speculation bubble, which occurred in the latter half of the decade. Despite the range of quality in the content, a critical reading of comic books from the early nineties reveals that superheroes were undergoing a crisis of identity which mirrored that of the United States in the post–Cold War era.

With the fall of the Berlin Wall in 1989 and the collapse of the Soviet Union in 1991, the United States had ostensibly won the Cold War. The geopolitical conflict between democracy and capitalism on the one hand and communism on the other had endured for over four decades. Given the bipolar nature of such a war, American society both justified its course of action and sublimated its concerns and anxieties by projecting any negative values onto the external Other. As the Soviet Union was portrayed as oppressive and totalitarian, the United States became enshrined in freedom (York and York 6). One's identity could be determined as much by what one was not, not-the-Soviet-Union or not–Communist, as by what one was, the United States of America or an American (Darowski 171). The use of absolutes to define identity resulted in a consensus ideology that codified what it meant to be American.

Accompanying the Cold War consensus ideology was the formation of a grand narrative that defined the scope and desired outcome of the conflict. This narrative may be summarized as preventing Armageddon with the promised reward of utopia. Armageddon, in this case, could be termed either nuclear annihilation or the destruction of the American way of life. As such, there was a military and a political component to national security. As both sides of the Cold War possessed nuclear weapons, a heated war would have resulted in mutually assured destruction. So instead the two superpowers engaged in a cold war of containment, a zero-sum game wherein a gain for one side was a loss for the other. Security came to be defined as preventing the U.S.S.R. and its allies from expanding their sphere of influence (Costello 34). The promised utopia would come from not merely the defeat of communism, but that subsequently everyone would be able to enjoy the American Dream of life, liberty, and the pursuit of happiness.

Comic book superheroes were an effective medium to tap into these ambient discourses. Cold War propaganda portrayed the U.S. combating a villain with nuclear capabilities in a struggle over the fate of the planet (Johnson 63). The moral certainties of superhero stories, with their stark contrasts between good and evil, easily aligned themselves with the Cold War narratives being expounded by experts and leaders (Costello 63). The grand narrative became a sociopolitical metaphor which formed the subtext of many comic book tales (Howe 358).

Coming out of the Cold War as the world's sole super-power, the United States should have felt confident that the greater narrative that had guided them through the long struggle had been justified and the promised reward was inevitable (Smith 163). Yet without a stable, external Other against which to define itself, America's identity increasingly came under scrutiny. "One thing at least is clear—identity only becomes an issue when it is in crisis, when something assumed to be fixed, coherent, and stable is displaced by the experience of doubt and uncertainty" (Mercer 259). Both external and internal forces formed the crucible of the crisis of national identity.

Internationally, the United States became the leading military and political force on the planet. But what should be its new mission? As the sole remaining super-power, there was pressure for the country to take responsibility as the world's policeman. However, without any checks on this authority, the ability to do the right thing in the name of the greater good could become an exercise in moral relativism. The enforcement of American values on others could cause more harm than good and result in the U.S. becoming as totalitarian as the U.S.S.R. was feared to be (Darowski 172). To counter this would involve acknowledging that the world did not adhere to a singular super-narrative, but was composed of fragmented, often-competing narratives that did not necessarily align with geopolitical boundaries (Smith 164). Terrorist and anarchist groups pledged loyalty to an ideology rather than a nation, resulting in threats from unknown sources for unclear goals (Costello 165). And there was an accompanying anxiety that such terrorists may be able to obtain some of the more destructive armaments of the former Soviet Union.

Nationally, what should have been a triumph of the American Way instead became a questioning of the validity of the American Dream. Reports on crime, drug use and the AIDS epidemic highlighted those citizens who were disenfranchised in many ways from full participation in the American Way due to race, class, or sexuality. And there was little faith in government institutions to be able to provide solutions (Costello 165). After all, as Ronald Reagan stated in his first inaugural address only a decade previously, in 1981: "government is not the solution to our problem; government is the problem." Not enough had been done to change the minds of citizens in regards to this statement.

The consensus ideology of the Cold War had been shattered and no one was sure what should take its place (Howe 165). Traditional values were questioned and new, sometimes radical, options were proposed (Johnson 157). But new ideas had yet to be tested to prove their validity. What path should the nation take?

The superhero genre was facing a similar crisis. As a sociopolitical metaphor, their never-ending battle seemed to have come to an end. While they still had their recurring foes, such enemies became increasingly empty signifiers without the informing subtext. Jeffrey K. Johnson sums up the dilemma:

> Many comic book readers and creators asked if a superhero should be a positive moral and ethical symbol of good citizenship or should the hero adopt a new more relativist ethical viewpoint? Should heroes serve as an example of what readers could strive for or should these supermen and women provide violent wish fulfillment to readers burdened by an often dangerous and discouraging world? [163].

Comic books, with their monthly publication schedule, are an ideal medium to mirror the anxieties and concerns of a contemporary culture. It is necessary for the realities of a society to be reflected in the text for the characters to stay relevant and interesting to a continually developing audience. Superheroes are there to confirm the rightness of our world, said rightness being determined by whoever is writing the series at the time (Freim 174–5). When the very nature of what is right comes into debate, such stories become a way to evaluate societal morals, preserving those which are beneficial, adopting the new as they prove valid, and discarding the old as they become obsolete.

The Avengers proves to be an ideal site for this type of cultural examination. As one of the earliest Marvel Comics titles, beginning publication in September 1963, the series possesses a tradition that could be challenged by the new ideas of the time period, unlike the brand new superhero teams which were introduced in the early nineties. With a team of heroes brought together "to combat those threats which no single hero could stand against" (#343 2), there could be a mixture of established and new characters around which to frame the cultural debate rather than outright replacing a titular character, as was the experiment on many other titles. Additionally, the title benefited from a consistent creative team of writer Bob Harras, penciler Steven Epting, and inker/colorist Tom Palmer. From issues #343 to 375 (Jan. 1992 to June 1994), *The Avengers* crafted a long-form narrative, built around an intergalactic war and its fallout as well as internal strife caused by the villain Proctor, to examine new roles and ideas around the ongoing cultural debate concerning national identity.

The Avengers #343 (Jan. 1992), "First Night," establishes the reorganized membership of the main branch of the team.[1] The new line-up consists of: the World War II super-soldier Captain America (Steve Rogers); former Russian secret agent Black Widow (Natasha Romanov); the Norse god of thunder Thor; the Greek god Hercules; the Vision, a synthetic humanoid with the ability to alter his body's density; the medieval-themed Black Knight (Dane Whitman); Sersi, an Eternal who, like her namesake from *The Odyssey*, could make objects or people change form (though here it is accomplished through re-arranging molecular structures); and the newest recruit, Crystal, an Inhuman who can command the four elements.[2]

The issue of identity is established very quickly in the story when Captain America laments: "Being an Avenger used to mean something! It was a mark of honor, of distinction. We were a fellowship of friends. Now it's ... I don't know ... changed. We've become an ill-defined group of strangers" (17). This was due to not merely the high turnover in membership in recent months, but that even familiar characters had undergone changes to become unfamiliar. The most radical of these was Thor. No longer the Norse god of myth and founding member of the Avengers, the powers and mystic hammer of Thor had been granted to blue-collar construction worker and divorced dad Eric Masterson, turning an old hero into an entirely new character.[3] Additionally, the Vision had changed from his traditional yellow, green, and red appearance with human-like personality to become a ghostly white figure with little personality. Even the Black Knight had upgraded his medieval sword, the cursed Ebony Blade, for a laser sword that looked like something out of *Star Wars*: "A beam of concentrated photonic energy, coupled with neural inhibitors which can stun the nervous system of any opponent" (16).

The last two examples bring up an issue that had become a source of anxiety as it affected almost every American's life: technology. The early nineties was the dawn of the information age as the concept of the World Wide Web was introduced, while simultaneously gadgets and products were shrinking in size (Darowski 171). Personal computers and telephones were becoming more mobile, cheaper, and more pervasive in everyday life. The Avengers seemed to embrace this change. Their previously-destroyed base, a brownstone mansion, had been replaced with a sleek post-modern building filled with rooms crammed with as much technology as possible. But accompanying the convenience of portability arose concerns about the dehumanizing affect this technology could have on people's lives (Darowski 173). New modes of communication increasingly isolated the individual and could result in fragmenting social cohesion (Hammontree 168). How soon before everyone become as impersonal as the Vision?

Not long before the introduction of the new team line-up, the Avengers switched from being a U.S.–backed organization to being sponsored by the U.N., a move reflective of the United States' increased role on the world stage. According to the grand narrative of the Cold War, the dissolution of the Soviet Union should have resulted in world peace. Instead, pockets of religious, ethnic, and politic turmoil, some of which had been held in check by the U.S.S.R., arose which required continual policing by the U.N. and NATO. As the sole superpower, the United States was expected to provide the bulk of the military force and leadership for these operations, requiring the nation to continue in a state of active war in multiple regions around the globe for many years.

These actions included the 1989 invasion of Panama to oust corrupt leader Manuel Noriega; the Persian Gulf War in 1991; sending peacekeeping troops into civil war-torn Somalia from 1992 to 1995; and intervention in the former Soviet state of Yugoslavia from 1992 to 1995 (Johnson 152–5). While most of these operations were able to bring conflict to an end, others, like Somalia, had no resolution. This, as well as the economic expenditure involved, led some citizens to question the purpose and necessity of policing the world.

By far the military action which received the most attention was the Persian Gulf War. In August 1990, the Middle East country of Iraq invaded its neighbor

Kuwait. A multinational coalition, with most of the troops coming from the Unites States, was formed to liberate Kuwait and invade Iraq (Johnson 152). Also known as Operation: Desert Storm, this became the first televised war. Citizens around the world could follow the course of events as news cameras captured the aerial bombardment and subsequent ground invasion that destroyed most of Iraq's infrastructure, in addition to the heavy sanctions the U.N. imposed on the country. The consequences of this conflict would continue to plague the world in the following decades.

"Operation: Galactic Storm," the nineteen-part crossover event that ran in multiple comic book titles from March to May 1992, was obviously titled to echo the Middle East battle. But this really happened in name only. As a commentary on the continuing military actions, this story placed the Avengers in a far different situation. Whereas the U.S. was a super-power attempting to establish peace between or within smaller nations, the Avengers were faced with trying to broker an accord between two galactic empires who possessed far superior technology.

Earth becomes concerned over matters of galactic politics because the empires of the Shi'ar and the Kree make use of a wormhole near the Earth's sun as a shortcut between galaxies. The continued use of the wormhole has a destabilizing effect on the sun that will cause it to go nova. The Avengers intercede between the two empires to help save Earth as well as prevent the use of a doomsday weapon, the nega-bomb. In the end, the leader of the Kree, the Supreme Intelligence, unleashes the nega-bomb on his own people, destroying hundreds of worlds in an attempt to jumpstart Kree evolution.

While "Operation: Galactic Storm" may not have worked as a sociopolitical metaphor for the contemporary U.S. military engagements, what it did effectively was enter into the debate over creeping moral relativism. With traditional codes of conduct and their underlying religious principles called into question in the post–Cold War era, a viable alternative was contemplated—the morality of an action should be based on the situation and not a universal standard. However, this may also imply that there would be less control over the consequences. As Captain America warns towards the beginning of the storyline: "All I'm urging is caution, Wasp. It's a slippery, muddy road once you begin making death threats and incarcerating people ... and I don't want to see the Avengers ... despite the best intentions ... get caught in the muck" (Harras, "Storm..." 19).

After the detonation of the nega-bomb, the Avengers are split on how to proceed. Some want to leave the judgment of the Supreme Intelligence to the surviving Kree while others want to avenge the dead by killing the Kree leader. A group composed of Iron Man, Black Knight, Sersi, Hercules, Thor, Vision and Wonder Man proceed to mete out their own justice, with the Black Knight delivering the killing blow to the Supreme Intelligence. Iron Man later justifies this course of action to Captain America: "It just means that many of us disagree with you as far as what constitutes appropriate conduct in time of war" and "I truly believe that conventional standards of morality are inapplicable in times of war" (Gruenwald 3, 24). Somehow, this is said without a trace of irony that Captain America is the only Avenger to actually have served in the military during wartime.

These actions did indeed prove to be a slippery slope for Sersi. On another alien world, Polemachus, in issues #358–359 (Jan.–Feb. 1993), the Avengers fight against the archaic practices of the inhabitants who wish to sacrifice a girl in order to appease their gods into stabilizing the planet's energy ring. After the Avengers succeed in this task by their own powers, the high priest still kills the girl, claiming the gods must have their gift. Sersi lashes out and kills the priest in retaliation. While some of Sersi's extreme actions are later blamed on the Mahd W'yry, an Eternal affliction wherein the experience of long life wearies the mind and leads to madness, this also illustrates the easiness of justifying a course of action, or worse, once it has proved acceptable in other circumstances. As a later issue asks, "First and foremost in this code of honor is the time-tested commandment, 'Avengers do not kill.' Or do they? What will happen now that the creed has been broken? Will they embrace tactics as brutal as the forces they oppose?" (Harras, "The First...").

Just how brutal their enemies' tactics could be was revealed with the fallout from "Operation: Galactic Storm." A splinter group of Kree fanatics, later named the Lunatic Legion, targets the Avengers for revenge for the execution of the Supreme Intelligence as well as the mistaken belief that the Avengers had unleashed the nega-bomb. First, they send an assassin to kill the Black Knight in #350 (Aug. 1992) and then, when that failed, they attempt to blow up the Earth with their own nega-bomb in #366 (Sept. 1993). This last action illustrated a fear that, without the regulation of the Soviet Union, a former Soviet or an Islamic rogue state or a terrorist group could acquire an atomic bomb and target the United States in the fallout of the Cold War or the Persian Gulf War; a fear highlighted by the 1993 truck bomb attack on the World Trade Center (Johnson 162).

The Lunatic Legion also addressed concerns of identity by appearing as doubles of the Avengers. The leader wields a hammer-like weapon like Thor, one woman has red hair, unique among the blue-skinned Kree, which mirrors the Black Widow, and another possesses long brown hair similar to Black Knight. This doubling may appear superficial, but it allows for the uncanny experience of testing other possible identities at a time when the nation's core identity was unstable. Doubling allows one to help define one's identity by recreating an external Other against which to define oneself. While a core identity may not be stabilized, it is at least possible to say what one is not. The Lunatic Legion could be interpreted as a nineties version of the Avengers; violent, revenge-driven characters with a penchant for large weapons, big shoulder-pads, and lots of pouches on their outfits. This hyper-masculine aesthetic could be read as a reaction to the yuppie trend of the 1980s. The Avengers themselves only flirted with that possibly identity for one issue, #363's "A Gathering of Hate."

Doubling was a theme throughout this two and a half years of the publication of the Avengers. Proctor and his team, the Gatherers, also mirrored the Avengers, being as they were the last surviving Avengers from alternate dimension that had been destroyed by Sersi's counterparts. While it could be argued that the Avengers fought against threats to a potential utopia as they arose, the Gatherers were set on preventing Armageddon by any means necessary. The doubling effect was clear from the onset when the Avengers were attacked by the doppelganger of the Swordsman, a member who had fallen in the line of duty, and continued through the revelation that Proctor was a double of the Black Knight. The idea that the Gatherers were alternate Avengers highlights the division within a group which emphasized the fragmentation that was occurring in American society.

The division is easy to see in politics. Each party sought to present a new dominant vision that would capture the consensus of American citizens (Costello 163). But the polarizing partisanship seemed more concerned with blaming the other party for the country's problems than offering real solutions. The liberal Left characterized the Right as championing business and religious values at the cost of civil liberties and the lower classes, while the neoconservative movement criticized the Left as fostering entitlements while seeking out the interests of lobby groups (Costello 198). The infighting led to an ideological culture war which ignored the centrist positions of most Americans and, coupled with the lack of compromise and accomplishment, served to deepen the loss of faith in government institutions to provide solutions for the nation's domestic issues.

It is easy to understand the mistrust of government institution when contemplating the horrific incident of the Rodney King beating. In March 1991, a group of Los Angeles police officers subdued King, an African American paroled felon, after a high speed chase when King refused to pull over at a traffic stop. A videotape of the police tasering and then kicking King in the head and beating him with batons as he tried to crawl away soon became a national sensation. When a criminal trial jury failed to convict the officers for assault and excessive force, riots broke out in South Central Los Angeles, which lasted for days. Fifty people died and over 2,000 were injured as rioters, mostly black, destroyed more than 1,500 buildings and caused an estimated one billion dollars in damages (Johnson 155). These incidents highlighted those who felt marginalized from the American Dream, and violence became one way for those excluded to make their voice heard (Mercer 6).

While most superhero stories construct sociopolitical realities in an informing metaphor, sometimes the subtext becomes the text. Such is the case for the young Avenger Rage, an African American whose very name may be an expression of a minority attitude towards the establishment. In *The Avengers* #341–342 (Nov.–Dec. 1991), "Rage of Angels" and "By Reason of Insanity?," guest writer Fabian Nicieza tackled the issue of race head on, opening with a full-page spread of a handcuffed Latino, Carmello Martinez, being beaten by white police officers. The resultant protests are exacerbated by the white supremacists group the Sons of the Serpent until Rage intervenes. When Rage asks the Avengers why they aren't doing anything about this, the Falcon, also African American, explains: "The Avengers, as a concept, aren't about dealing with problems of this kind" (10).

It is later revealed that a being known as the Hater Monger, who feeds off hate, had been sponsoring the Sons of the Serpents and manipulating events to produce more conflict between the races. Though the Hate Monger is defeated, a pessimistic Rage leaves the Avengers feeling that nothing has been resolved, a sentiment which the reader should share. Addressing racism both validates the problem and underscores its immensity as something that cannot be solved in a single issue of a comic book (Freim 181). As Black Widow points out: "You can't eliminate hatred and poverty through physical violence" (9).

The L.A. riots continued to cement an association between race and crime (Mercer 6). As the national identity was in crisis, there came a strong message of the need to protect society from moral decay. But this threat had an unsubtle identity subtext of stereotyping. As blacks were linked to violent crime, the poor were identified with the rising drug epidemic and homosexuals with sexually transmitted diseases such as HIV (Costello 163). Underlining this message of moral decay was that these things were a threat to the American family, which itself had become a site of uncertainty.

During the Cold War, the nuclear family came to be viewed as the fulfillment of the American Way. With the development of a powerful consensus beginning in the 1950s, citizens were cautioned against any abnormal behavior that could indicate foreign conspirators. The stability of traditional roles became a matter of political security. The epitome of this tradition and normalcy became enshrined in the nuclear family, consisting of a father, a mother and children acting within their assigned spheres (Getner 957). By the early nineties, the increased mainstream attention given to homosexuality coupled with a rising divorce rate and revelations of scandalous affairs among politicians and civic leaders, created the perception that the traditional family was under threat. What had once been offered as a means of achieving progress and virtue was becoming as fragmented as the rest of society (Costello 170).

Family is not a common topic in the superhero genre as most heroes are not married or even in a stable relationship. Teams can form ersatz family units, with the members filling in the traditional roles as needed. This run of the Avengers is a bit of an exception as it did feature a married member, though the storyline addresses the anxieties of the period. Crystal is married to the mutant speedster Quicksilver and they have a human daughter, Luna. However, the couple is estranged, living in separate cities despite a proclaimed desire to try and make the marriage work. Throughout this, Crystal also struggles with a mutual attraction to the Black Knight, though Sersi also tries to claim the Knight's affection. The challenges to Crystal's martial relationship are not fully resolved in this story, as the definition of family continues to be an immediate societal concern.

The conclusion to the Proctor saga occurs in *The Avengers* #375 (June 1994), "The Last Gathering." After trying to kill Sersi by collapsing all realities, Proctor is instead beheaded with his own sword by Sersi. Black Knight and Sersi, the two Avengers who had broken the code against killing, choose self-imposed exile in an alternate dimension, thereby expunging the more radical members of the band. However, traditional forms are also restored: the Vision returns to his yellow, green, and red form and began to explore emotions again; and the Avengers Mansion is mystically transformed back into the original brownstone.

These symbolic changes mirror the prevailing attitude of the United States as it approached the midpoint of the decade. While numerous changes had been contemplated, few had taken root in society and many ideas were instead marginalized or discarded in favor of a return of traditional practices that had already proven their ability to stand the test of time (Johnson 157, 160). There was some adaptation of these morals to new circumstances, such as the digital revolution. Yet the return to core values did not signal an end to the ongoing national identity crisis. No new narrative had been agreed upon by consensus. But a turn to previous norms provided stability to help carry America forward into a new millennium.

Notes

1. There was a concurrent West Coast branch based in California.

2. Eternals and Inhumans are offshoots of humanity created by alien intervention in ancient times. The Eternals were created by the Celestials and, as the name implies, had very long lives, so that Sersi was the Circe from *The Odyssey*. The Inhumans were created through the genetic manipulation of the Kree.

3. Thor would later reclaim his power and identity and Masterson would receive an enchanted mallet and become the hero Thunderstrike.

Works Cited

Costello, Matthew J. *Secret Identity Crisis: Comic Books and the Unmasking of Cold War America.* New York: Continuum, 2009.

Darowski, Joseph J. "Searching for Meaning in 'The Death of Superman.'" In Joseph J. Darowski, ed., *The Ages of Superman: Essays on the Man of Steel in Changing Times.* Jefferson, NC: McFarland, 2012.

Freim, Nicole. "The Dark Amazon Saga: Diana Meets the Iron Age." In Joseph J. Darowski, ed., *The Ages of Wonder Woman: Essays on the Amazon Princess in Changing Times.* Jefferson, NC: McFarland, 2014.

Getner, Robert. "'With Great Power Comes Great Responsibility': Cold War Culture and the Birth of Marvel Comics." *The Journal of Popular Culture* 40.6 (2007): 953–978.

Gruenwald, Mark (w), Rik Levins (p), and Danny Bulandi (i). "After the Storm." *Captain America* #401 (June 1992). New York: Marvel Comics, 1992.

Hammontree, D.R. "Backlash and Bracelets: The Patriarch's World, 1986–1992." In Joseph J. Darowski, ed., *The Ages of Wonder Woman: Essays on the Amazon Princess in Changing Times.* Jefferson, NC: McFarland, 2014.

Harras, Bob (w), Steven Epting (p), and Tom Palmer (i). "Arkon's Asylum." *The Avengers* #358 (Jan. 1993). New York: Marvel Comics, 1993.

_____, _____, and _____. "Empire's End." *The Avengers* #347 (May 1992). New York: Marvel Comics, 1992.

_____, _____, and _____. "First Night." *The Avengers* #343 (Jan. 1992). New York: Marvel Comics, 1992.

_____, _____, and _____. "The First Rule." *The Avengers* #366 (Sept. 1993). New York: Marvel Comics, 1993.

_____, _____, and _____. "A Gathering of Hate." *The Avengers* #363 (June 1993). New York: Marvel Comics, 1993.

_____, _____, and _____. "Gift of the Gods." *The Avengers* #359 (Feb. 1993). New York: Marvel Comics, 1993.

_____, _____, and _____. "The Last Gathering." *The Avengers* #375 (June 1994). New York: Marvel Comics, 1994.

_____, _____, and _____. "Repercussions." *The Avengers* #350 (Aug. 1992). New York: Marvel Comics, 1993.

_____, _____, and _____. "Storm Gatherings." *The Avengers* #345 (Mar. 1992). New York: Marvel Comics, 1992.

Howe, Sean. *Marvel Comics: The Untold Story.* New York: Harper Perennial, 2012.

Johnson, Jeffery K. *Super-History: Comic Book Superheroes and American Society.* Jefferson, NC: McFarland, 2012.

Mercer, Kobena. *Welcome to the Jungle: New Positions in Black Cultural Studies.* New York: Routledge, 1994.

Nicieza, Fabian (w), Steven Epting (p), and Tom Palmer (i). "By Reason of Insanity?" *The Avengers* #342 (Dec. 1991). New York: Marvel Comics, 1991.

_____, and _____. "Rage of Angels." *The Avengers* #341 (Nov. 1991). New York: Marvel Comics, 1991.

Rhoades, Shirrel. *A Complete History of American Comic Books.* New York: Peter Lang, 2008.

Smith, Matthew J. "The 'Triangle Era' of Superman: Continuity, Marketing and Grand Narratives in the 1990s." In Joseph J. Darowski, ed., *The Ages of Superman: Essays on the Man of Steel in Changing Time.* Jefferson, NC: McFarland, 2012.

York, Chris, and Rafiel York. "Introduction: Fredric Wertham, Containment and Comic Books." In Chris York and Rafiel York, eds., *Comic Books and the Cold War, 1946–1962: Essays on Graphic Treatment of Communism, the Code and Social Concerns.* Jefferson, NC: McFarland, 2012.

The Spy King

*How Christopher Priest's Version of
the Black Panther Shook Up
Earth's Mightiest Heroes*

Todd Steven Burroughs

Put the Panther down, Alkema—NOW! And tell us where Hank
Pym is—or we'll make you wish you had!"—Busiek/Perez,
"Renewed" 15

This reader couldn't hide his disappointment. The Avengers had returned
from the "Heroes Reborn" universe in 1998 with a brand new book, written,
drawn, and co-plotted by fan favorite Kurt Busiek and comic book superhero
artist legend George Perez. The first 57 issues (including a #0 issue) of the third
volume of the comic, all written by Busiek, combined the best of the old and
the new: Wonder Man returned from the dead, but as a being of ionic energy;
the Scarlet Witch was more powerful, more confident and more comfortable
with her sexual nature and—having been separated from her husband, the
Vision—her feelings for Wonder Man; Captain America was back, leading the
team, but he wielded an electronic shield that could turn into a staff; Justice
and Firestar, fresh from the New Warriors, joined the team as reservists; and
T'Challa, the Black Panther ... well, in the "Ultron Unlimited" storyline which
featured the long-awaited return of the Avengers' greatest foe, the sentient robot
Ultron, the Wakandan King got captured in the first three pages of Part One
(Vol. 1, #19), and got thrown around by "Alkema–2," the second version of
Alkema, a third-rate West Coast Avengers android villain.

"OOOH, Cap! Such fire, such steel!" Alkema–2 responds to Captain
America. "I've positively got CHILLS! So you've mislaid an Avenger, eh? I call
that CARELESSNESS! But here—let me give you a REPLACEMENT!"

(*ibid.*). As she says this, she blasts them while throwing Panther back at the team, causing all of them to get knocked off of their feet.

Even though the Panther played (barely) more than a token part in the storyline, that first scene with Alkema had negative historical resonance that was particularly frustrating for those readers who followed T'Challa in his own brand-new, extraordinary book. This was because in 1998, the same year the Avengers returned from the "Reborn" universe, *The Black Panther* title had been creatively, and radically, resuscitated by Joe Quesada and Jimmy Palmiotti, two artists who had proven themselves in the industry. Marvel contracted the duo to revamp four third-tier concepts: The Inhumans (a family of powerful beings who are best known through their guest-starring appearances in *The Fantastic Four*), Daredevil (which had hit its stride with writer-artist Frank Miller in the early 1980s but had fallen in popularity after Miller left to create the classic Batman storyline *The Dark Knight Returns* for arch-rival DC Comics), The Punisher (a character that had been so overexposed by 1998, it had a crossover storyline with Archie Andrews of Archie Comics) and Black Panther, a third-tier African superhero that hadn't had an ongoing series since the 1970s.

Quesada and Palmiotti had given the *Panther* title to Christopher Priest, who, born James Owsley, had been one of the first black writers and editors at Marvel Comics. Priest turned the Black Panther into essentially a truly "Dark Knight" who, with his advanced African technology and his honed fighting skills, took down Mephisto (a demon who would often battle powerful adversaries such as the Silver Surfer) in "The Client," T'Challa's debut "Marvel Knights" story arc. In issue #4 of "The Client," Everett K. Ross, T'Challa's State Department attaché, is understandably scared to death of Mephisto.

> **Ross:** KILL HIM! KILL HIM! You want me to call the Avengers?
> **T'Challa:** Why?
> **Ross:** Why? WHY? Are you seeing what I'M seeing—? [Priest and Texeira 89].

T'Challa then gives Mephisto a strong right hook—*BAAPP!*—and the demon goes down for the count (*ibid.*).

So, in his own title, he can defeat a version of the Devil without help from outsiders, but in *The Avengers*, he gets taken out by one of Ultron's underlings and needs the help of Captain America, Thor and Iron Man?[1]

Thankfully for this reader, Priest had his own Avengers story that pre-dated "Ultron Unlimited." The one-issue story was called "That Business with the Avengers," and it made a major retroactive continuity change in Avengers history. In that storyline, it was revealed that T'Challa joined the Avengers in 1968 to spy on the team!

This essay examines both *The Avengers'* "Ultron Unlimited" and *Black Pan-*

ther's "That Business with the Avengers" storylines from the point of view of the history of the Black Panther as a solo character versus as an Avengers character. It is done in the larger context of T'Challa's historical positioning as a fantasy African creation of white American liberals in the 1960s, and to what degree Christopher Priest's portrayal changed this. The argument made is that when T'Challa is on his own, he is a fully realized character, with his non–Western cultural and socio-political viewpoint intact, but when he is in the Avengers, he is made to fit a politically and culturally assimilationist mode. Priest's portrayal in 1998 broke this dichotomy, forcing Avengers creators, as well as the rest of Marvel Comics, to permanently portray him as the unassimilated former.

The Black Panther: A Super-Symbol of an Anticolonial Africa

The Black Panther's first appearance was in *The Fantastic Four Vol. 1*, #52–53. "The Black Panther!" and "The Way It Began!" Until the end of the first issue, he seemed like the FF's new villain. He lured the team to Wakanda, and battled all four. If it wasn't for a little help from Wyatt Wingfoot, Johnny Storm's college roommate and a sleeping passenger on the trip, the Panther would have beaten one of comics' foremost superteams. In pure Machiavellian fashion, T'Challa revealed after his defeat that the team was lured to Wakanda just to test his skills to see if he was ready to take on Ulysses Klaw, the invader of Wakanda who had killed his father, T'Chaka. Klaw had used the technology he developed to create creatures of "solidified sound" and to recreate himself as a master of sound waves. T'Challa, with some help from the Fantastic Four, defeats Klaw and his sound creations (Lee/Kirby 1966).

With that storyline, the first black superhero in American mainstream comic books was born. Not only was he black, but he was an African. Not only was he an African, but the king of an African nation that had never been colonized and had its own mineral that the West craved, vibranium. During the same year, in the real world, civil rights organizers in Alabama started a political party, the Lowndes County Freedom Organization, and chose as its visual mascot a drawing of a black panther. (It was during this organizing that one of the Civil Rights Movement leaders, Stokely Carmichael, would publicly coin the phrase "Black Power!") This same symbol would be used by black Marxists in Oakland, California later that year when they formed a radical political organization, The Black Panther Party for Self-Defense. One scholar on black superheroes wrote that Panther's appearance around the same time as the formation of the LCFO and the BPP was "synchronicity" (Nama 42). He explained that T'Challa's first appearance had larger socio-political significance not only outside of comics, but even outside America.

> [T'Challa] was an idealized composite of third-world black revolutionaries and the anti-colonialist movement of the 1950s that they represented. The cresting geopolitical waves of the anticolonialist movement thrust to the surface figures such as Jomo Kenyatta, Patrice Lumumba, and Kwame Nkrumah, third-world revolutionaries and leaders of the African push for independence. These African leaders embodied the best hopes of their people and captured the imagination of the anticolonialist movement with their charisma and promise to free Africa from European imperialism. Unfortunately, these and other African leaders were unable to completely fulfill their mission to make their peoples' lives fundamentally better, due to a combination of economic turmoil, internal and external forces, and decades of political deceit. As a result, many African leaders found themselves deposed by a coup d'état, assassinated, forced to live in exile, or incrementally transformed into despicable dictators. Against this tattered backdrop, T'Challa performs exemplary symbolic work as a recuperative figure and majestic signifier of the best of the black anticolonialist movement [43].

Panther Power vs. the Sidney Poitier of Superheroes: Solo Black Panther vs. Team Member Black Panther, 1968–1997

With such a strong outline of the character, the beginning of the Black Panther as a Western team player seemed like a great example of positive race relations and geo-political relations in 1968, almost a year after the race-based urban disturbances in several major American cities in 1967 and hitting the stands just two to three months before Martin Luther King's assassination. In the first issue of *Captain America, Vol. 1*, #100 (it continued the numbering, and its story arc, from *Tales of Suspense*, the title Cap shared with Iron Man), Cap, SHIELD agent Sharon Carter (who, was, of course, undercover and, in true superhero comic book fashion, wore glasses as her disguise), and T'Challa, the Black Panther, defeated an imposter Baron Zemo and his men in Africa, stopping a deadly solar ray from obliterating the Earth. Nick Fury, director of SHIELD, joined on panel by Dum Dum Dugan, destroy the ray. The trio heads to America in the last three panels of the last page, using T'Challa's Magna-ship, apparently the same ship in which he lured the Fantastic Four.

> **Cap:** It's indeed an HONOR to have a KING for a pilot! Does this mean you accept my offer, T'Challa?
> **T'Challa:** I wish to CONSIDER it, my friend!

Cap: Since I am no longer on active duty with the AVENGERS, they have a VACANCY in their roster—one which I hope will be filled by—the PANTHER!!

T'Challa: But what does the future hold for YOU?

Cap: So long as FREEDOM may be threatened—CAPTAIN AMERICA must follow his destiny—WHEREVER it may lead! [Lee and Kirby, "This Monster Unmasked!" 20].

T'Challa does indeed accept Captain America's offer. In *The Avengers* #52 (May 1968), the Black Panther visits Avengers mansion for the first time.[2] It is bad timing, however, because a villain named the Grim Reaper had just left for dead Avengers members Wasp, Hawkeye and Goliath. Jasper Sitwell of SHIELD discovers the African king and mistakenly thinks T'Challa is the would-be murderer. T'Challa, eventually understanding that he has been framed, allows himself to be taken into custody by the New York City Police Department. Having failed to prove the Panther's identity and status as the king of an independent nation, T'Challa breaks out a window at police headquarters, finds the Reaper in Avengers headquarters, and defeats him in battle. The fallen Avengers revive themselves, the police clear T'Challa, and T'Challa officially becomes an Avenger, abandoning his throne, apparently, for no good reason but to keep him in New York City and in a regular book:

T'Challa: Then, let the word go forth ... that today, you have gained a new ALLY—one who has given up a THRONE, that he may better serve a GREATER kingdom ... the whole of mankind itself! For now, the PANTHER is truly an AVENGER!!! [Thomas and Buscema, "Death Calls for the Arch-Heroes" 20].

T'Challa is spotlighted several times in the Avengers for the rest of the decade. In *The Avengers* #61, Black Knight, Hawkeye and the Vision join him in returning to Wakanda to fight Man-Ape, the anti-technologist, anti–Western tribal leader who has taken over Wakanda. In that fight, the other Avengers are knocked out cold, leaving T'Challa to fight and defeat the villain himself. In *The Avengers* #73–74, T'Challa takes on the Sons of the Serpent, a kind of supervillian Ku Klux Klan who have pitted white racist demagogues versus black demagogues on television in order to start a race war, with a black singer named Monica Lynne caught in the middle and eventually being rescued by T'Challa. The shock ending is that the two broadcast demagogues were the leaders of the group, seeking only "power for ourselves" (Thomas/Buscema, 1970, 20).[3] *The Avengers* #87, by writer Roy Thomas and artist Frank Giacoia, "Look Homeward, Avenger," is an expanded origin story of T'Challa, fleshing out the details given in his *Fantastic Four* debut and adding in a childhood friend of T'Challa's who became a traitor, working for AIM (Advanced Idea Mechanics), a technological terrorist organization.

In these late 1960s early 1970s Avengers stories, T'Challa is a king who has abdicated his throne. He assumes a secret identity, "Luke Charles," and becomes an inner city teacher in New York City. These moves essentially take away all the power, prestige and mystery—all of the *Non-Western African royal-ness*, the anticolonial symbolism, from the almost amoral character introduced in *Fantastic Four* #52. Under Roy Thomas, who replaces Stan Lee as the company's main writer and editor when Lee eventually becomes Marvel's publisher, T'Challa—The Black Panther, Lumumba as superhero—becomes an African costumed version of Sidney Poitier, a noble Negro who, in popular 1960s Hollywood films, puts his own concerns aside for German nuns ("Lilies in the Field") or working-class white British students ("To Sir with Love"). Poitier was portrayed in his films as a proud man who, confusingly, serviced the problems, goals and concerns of his white co-stars and not his, or his communities, own. The characters Poitier played fought on-screen for whites while, in the real world, Africans were fighting white colonials for independence and African Americans were fighting America's white social and political structures to obtain civil rights and black political, social and economic self-determination in black communities.

The original characterization of T'Challa returned with a vengeance when The Black Panther was given his own strip in 1973 in a title called *Jungle Action*, originally a 1950s reprint comic filled with white Tarzan-like heroes. The first issue featuring T'Challa (#5) was a reprint of *The Avengers* #61, the Man-Ape story, but the following issue started a new series by writer Don McGregor. McGregor's Panther has moved back to Wakanda, and Monica Lynne (from *The Avengers* #73–74), has joined him as a temporary resident and love interest. Although Stan Lee and Jack Kirby created T'Challa and Wakanda, McGregor expanded T'Challa's fictional universe greatly, giving Wakanda a distinct look and culture, a geography, religious rituals, tribal rivalries and, perhaps most importantly, a royal court for King T'Challa. With McGregor's Panther, you could read a comic about a universe that, up until 1973, was unthought-of: one starring an African king in an African land, separate from the Avengers. (This team-book/solo book disparity is not that unusual from, say, Thor, or Sub-Mariner, or other kings or princes of specific nations/cultural environments, but the Panther's background and significance in the real world makes this dichotomy a unique discussion, since there are no actual Asgardians or Atlantians that those respective characters represent.) The only thing that McGregor dismissed was the element that, under Priest and later Panther writer Reginald Hudlin, would make T'Challa one of the most formidable characters in comics (and Batman and Iron Man among the most formidable movie superheroes): his technological advances.

Jungle Action was cancelled when the character's co-creator, Jack Kirby, returned to Marvel in the mid–1970s, and took over the reins of a new *Black Panther* (*Vol. 1*, #1, January, 1977) comic book as writer, penciler and editor, with inking done by Mike Royer. Under Kirby's tenure, that comic was a sci-fi adventure book that had nothing to do with the Avengers (and barely with Wakanda, for that matter, since Kirby ignored all of McGregor's innovations). The Black Panther continued to make guest appearances in *The Avengers* and The *Fantastic Four* in the 1970s and 1980s, and had a mini-series set in Wakanda and in 1988 and a multi-part strip by a returning McGregor in the anthology series *Marvel Comics Presents* in 1989. (Both those temporary comic book series dealt with apartheid and were set in the African continent.) But he remained a guest star in *The Fantastic Four* and a background player in *The Avengers*—until 1998.

Priest Power: "The Client" Deals with "That Business with the Avengers," 1998, and Busiek's "Ultron Unlimited," 1999

Christopher Priest was "a little horrified" that he was given the Black Panther assignment by Joe Quesada and Jimmy Palmiotti in 1998. He wasn't in love with the character, even though he would be the first African American writer to write the character in an on-going series:

> I mean, Black Panther? Who reads Black Panther? Black Panther?! The guy with no powers? The guy in back of the Avengers class photo, whose main job was to point and cry out, "Look—A BIG, SCALY MONSTER! THOR—GO GET HIM! That guy?!" [Priest and Texeira, Introduction].

He complained that Marvel would never let him write the book he'd have to write if Panther would be taken seriously: one in which he'd be like Ra's al Ghul, the mysterious Batman villain now popularized by acclaimed actor Liam Neeson in Christopher Nolan's "Dark Knight" film trilogy. Priest's Panther would combine al Ghul and Batman, and be a silent, threatening "night creature, a fearsome African warrior, a manner of black man most blacks in Brooklyn had never seen" (*ibid.*). Priest said that if his character was going to be operating like a real character in the real world, there would be repercussions for the established structure of the Marvel universe: "It's a violation of the Fantasy Land Nice-Nice Accords, signed by both DC and Marvel, that says the U.S. government is always good all of the time, everyone accepts Panther, and the Avengers hold hands and sing and what have you" (*ibid.*).

Priest even makes fun of how Marvel Comics readers regard the Black Panther, if they regard him at all. On Page 7 of the trade paperback collection of "The Client," the first appearance of T'Challa in his new series, Panther and the Dora Milaje (which Ross says means "adored ones" in Hausa), his wives-in-training and bodyguards, leave Wakanda for Brooklyn to deal with a scandal involving the death of a young African American girl who was the beneficiary of Wakandan charity in New York City. The trio meets a Brooklyn drug dealer, Manuel Ramos. Panther is dressed in a sharp suit and bald head, looks like a "Godfather"-like Don, or the literary character Hawk, made popular by Avery Brooks in the 1980s "Spenser: For Hire" and "A Man Called Hawk" television series. The Dora Milaje are at his side, looking both like deadly bodyguards and supermodels. In a car with his friends, Ramos, like Ross, mirrors the first impressions of the comic book audience:

> **Ramos:** I hear you a PUNK, yo. Be carryin' the OTHER Avengers' BAGS and what not. "The Black Panther." SHEE-RIGHT [Priest and Texerira 8].

After warning Ramos, Panther uses his technology to knock him out. He then proceeds to rough him up, creating the fear he needs in his new informant. The Dora Milaje quickly and brutally subdue the other gang members in Ramos's car. Priest had this Panther act decisively, and violently, in his first few pages, letting Marvel fans immediately know that this was not the almost-genteel Panther they had read in those Avengers comics of decades ago.

Priest took the Marvel ethos—the idea that its characters are in the same "real" world as the reader—seriously in *Black Panther*. He gave T'Challa a permanent State Department attaché, Everett K. Ross. To fight perceptions it was a "black" superhero comic (meaning an all-black one, for black audiences), Priest made Ross, a young white man, the book's narrator. He also gave T'Challa a white half-brother and political rival, the Wakandan nationalist zealot White Wolf, and Nikki, a white former love interest who happened to be Ross's boss and current girlfriend. This Panther did not fight the Ku Klux Klan or racist white South Africans, as did McGregor's and the 1988 mini-series character did; this Panther took on international conspiracies created by Wakanda's enemies, within and outside the African nation. Priest's Panther was a post-modern satire of superhero comics, black-white race relations, pre–911 geo-politics and 1990s popular culture, using Eddie Murphy's comedic film "Coming To America" as an inspiration (Priest and Texeira, *ibid.*).

Black Panther Vol. 2, #9: "That Business with the Avengers"

When Priest dealt with the Panther's status in the Avengers, he decided to retroactively change the 1960s continuity, a process known in comics circles as a "ret-con." He had to answer a serious and obvious question for sophisticated, post-modern comics readers in the 1990s—ones for whom the Black Power versus American integration/assimilation issues of the 1960s were by then in history textbooks. *Why would an African king leave his country to join a superhero group in the West?* He chose to retcon the sacred Lee-Kirby text of *Captain America Vol. 1, #100*, putting realpolitik motives in the mind of a non–Western king concerned about a new group of superpowered Westerners.

In *Black Panther, Vol. 2, #9* (which begins, by the way, with a homage/"faux reprint" of *Captain America, Vol. 1, #100*, complete with Stan Lee–type narration and Jack Kirby–ish art), the dialogue from the end of Cap 100 is repeated with some important additions: T'Challa is either looking down with his eyes closed, flying the ship while Cap speaks. Priest lets T'Challa answer Cap's request for Avengers membership nomination with a little more detail:

> **T'Challa:** I wish to consider it, my friend—
>   T'Challa's eyes are open, looking seriously at the reader:
> **T'Challa:**—consider it VERY carefully ... [Priest and Jusko 50].

The books' main villain, is Achebe, a crazy dictator who has taken over Wakanda and is attempting to destroy the Black Panther's reputation by hiding a bomb in a predominately African American crowd wanting to pay tribute to T'Challa while he was in New York City being feted by the Presidential administration at a dinner at the New York Hilton Hotel. To the throngs of African Americans gathered on the streets of Manhattan, T'Challa is a kind of a superhero Nelson Mandela. This mirrors the iconic image The Black Panther has to blacks in the real world who grew up on superhero comics.

In issue #9, T'Challa reveals the real reason he joined the Avengers. Achebe wonders out loud why T'Challa left his throne to join the Avengers, a group who always has him in the back of the Avengers photos (apparently a running gag in Priest's early issues). Achebe also points out that the team's members never address him as king.

> **T'Challa:** I HARDLY owe ANSWERS to the USURPER of my rightful THRONE—But the AVENGERS are my FRIENDS, among whom there can be NO issues of PROTOCOL. And as for WHY—

While T'Challa is talking and untying a kidnapped, and now rescued, Monica Lynne (his now-former love interest from the McGregor issues), the Avengers start to rescue the crowd.

> **T'Challa:**—it seemed the PRUDENT and REASONABLE thing to DO—given the potential THREAT these people posed to the KINGDOM—ACCEPTING their invitation afforded me the chance to thoroughly INVESTIGATE their claims—[Priest and Jusko 63–64].

With the exception of newbie Firestar reacting, the Avengers teammates keep their minds on the task at hand. And then, at the end, after Panther implores the crowd to go home, Firestar speaks up:

> **Firestar:** Wow ... that was AMAZING, Panther. And what a GREAT BLUFF—telling that Achebe guy you only JOINED the Avengers to SPY on them...
> **T'Challa:** —?! Bluff?!
> **Firestar** (realizing she was wrong): You ... said you thought the Avengers might be a THREAT—so you JOINED—to investigate them ... or ... maybe I mishear you...
> **Captain America:** DID she—? Did we ALL mishear you—?
> In the last panel, The Black Panther walks away from the Avengers, all characters in silhouette.
> **T'Challa:** No. You did NOT [Priest and Jusko 67].

In the next issue, #10, Ross narrates the situation this way, as Steve Rogers, Captain America's civilian alter ego, is seen working out on a punching bag.

> **Ross:** Lots of people do lots of things in the name of national security. And Wakanda, always a prime target for invasion or outside confluence—survived as an independent state ONLY by being one step ahead of the BAD GUYS. And, in those early days, who could know if the Avengers were TRULY the flag-waving eagle scouts they said they were—or if they were ENEMIES of the Wakandan STATE. There was only one way the client could find out: Shake the hand of the one man the client implicitly trusted—take that bond of TRUST—and EXPLOIT it [Priest and Jusko 85].

The reader now gets to see the problem with the Avengers escalating a few pages later, when Iron Man, talking to T'Challa, refers to "disturbing reports" coming in about violent moves. The king is making to secure Wakandan sovereignty from U.S. government forces.

> **T'Challa:** The reports are true. These are matters of national security.
> **Iron Man:** And—that's it?
> **T'Challa:** For now.
> **Iron Man:** Panther—the AVENGERS—your teammates—are due some explanation.
> **Scarlet Witch:** I think what he's saying is we should trust him.
> **T'Challa:** Your TRUST is irrelevant to me—and I am not ASKING you for ANYTHING. Factions of your government have committed an ACT OF WAR against my throne. I cannot PROVE it—and so I MUST NOT ask for your help. Your charter represents a contumacious conflict of interest. And, my friends, I PROMISE you—things will get MUCH WORSE before they get any better. To live, to die, to rule again—the PANTHER must walk ALONE [Priest and Jusko 89].

Ultron Unlimited

The "Ultron Unlimited" storyline was the first Avengers story that featured the "all-new, all-different" T'Challa. After getting captured and thrown around by Alkema, he rescues Firestar from sacrificing herself by blasting the villain android with all her microwave heat power. The focus of the first issue is the fight with Alkhema. It's the second issue, #20,[4] however, that deals, directly albeit briefly, with the fallout of Priest's "That Business with the Avengers."

The issue of Panther's spying is confronted immediately, and then discarded as quickly. The second issue of the storyline begins with members of the Avengers—Captain America, Black Panther, Iron Man, Thor, Firestar and Justice—arrive at the Pentagon at the request of the military. While Captain America, who is in front of the line inside the Pentagon, is talking with the military brass, Justice and Firestar, in the back of the line, gossip about T'Challa's revelation.

> **Justice:** I don't get it, Angel. I can see why we were working with Panther BEFORE—he was there on the scene when ALKHEMA attacked the quinjet plant, and it's a WAKANDAN plant anyway—

Panther pretends not to overhear, but Captain America does, and begins to look back at them.

> **Justice:**—but why'd Cap invite him along on THIS mission, too? After we found out he only joined the Avengers in the FIRST place so he could SPY on us, you'd think—
> **Firestar:** Vance, SHH! His enhanced senses—he can HEAR y—

Captain America, who has gone back to the end of the line to confront Firestar and Justice, does so.

> **Captain America:** Justice. Firestar. Let me make something CLEAR. Whatever REASONS the Black Panther may have had for joining the Avengers originally—he's since proven his bravery and his loyalty OVER and OVER, and the Avengers are PROUD to have him in their ranks.

Justice and Firestar look embarrassed.

> **Justice:** Uh—of course. I didn't MEAN—

Firestar glares at Justice. Captain America turns away. Panther is walking forward, while Thor turns back to the young pair.

> **Justice:** Huh? I wasn't knocking the Panther's RECORD—I just thought, well, that Cap was STEAMED at the Panther over this. He's the one who put him up for MEMBERSHIP way back wh—
> **Firestar:** Vance, you're sweet and you mean well and I love you madly—but this isn't really the t—

Thor interrupts by putting himself in front of the young reservists. Firestar bumps into him.

Thor: If thou wilt PERMIT me, my young friends?
Firestar:—TUHH! THOR!
Thor: Think on THIS, young Vance. If THOU hadst quarreled with one that had been like a BROTHER to these—quarreled most DEEPLY—

The military is escorting Captain America and the Avengers into its command center.

Thor:—wouldst thou afterward easily countenance DISPARAGING words said of thy brother by ANOTHER...?
Justice: Point TAKEN, Thor.

And just like that, the personal/political conflict is over, because as a general tells the Avengers in the next panel, a splash page and a quarter:

General: Ah, there you are! We don't have time for pleasantries, Avengers—so let's get right down to business! [Busiek and Perez, "Unfolding" 1–3].

Panther is silent for the rest of issue #20. In issue #21, he is front in center on the cover, in front of the "big three" (Iron Man, Captain America and Thor). He is also a lead character is the title/credits splash page, with the big three and again, and Firestar in the rear.

Captain America tasks Panther to find Ultron's command center. The Panther shows Firestar his tracking skills, which really impresses her. Ultron 16 spots them, and puts together his aircraft from the surrounding environment. The renegade robot that has kidnapped several Avengers is ready for battle. Firestar is knocked aside, but manages to follow Panther's instructions for shooting up a signal flare for the rest of the Avengers.

Later in the battle, Ultron appears to have defeated the team with an "ionic shock blast."

Ultron: You never LEARN. You cannot HARM me—cannot damage one made of indestructible ADAMANTIUM. All you can do—is CEASE your struggling—and DIE! [Busiek and Perez, "Unveiled," 14–15].

Here's where Busiek adapts Priest's Panther. Panther is in the background, in silhouette, his new energy daggers drawn. Because Priest has him quiet and unknowable, with any thought balloons permanently banished, Busiek works around these new restrictions, putting his (murmured) thoughts in the third-person narration.

Narration: "No, Ultron," murmurs the Black Panther, so softly only he can hear. "The Avengers NEVER give up" (*ibid.*).

Black Panther strikes Ultron 16 with the energy daggers. Ultron 16 slams him back, out of the rest of the story for a few pages. Later, Panther picks up a scent, and bids the Avengers to follow him through some tunnels. Panther is leading. Panther discovers the rest of the kidnapped Avengers—and Ultron 17 (*ibid.*, 20)!

In issue #22, Panther, Cap, Thor, Iron Man and Firestar square off against an army of Ultrons. With the exception of the one of the Ultron's copies mentioning Panther's new "hi-tech, vibranium-weave suit" (created by Priest for the solo series) there was nothing of detail about Panther (Busiek and Perez, "Triumphant!" 16).

In following Priest's lead, Panther was a *slightly* different character in the Busiek/Perez Avengers. During a significant, character-crowded Avengers storyline, Busiek adopted Priest's version of the character, in ways small and not so small: the Black Panther: (a) was in the foreground, not in the background; (b) used his new technology; and, most importantly, (c) was acknowledged as an Avenger who was also the calculating king of his own nation—a team player who respected his superhero colleagues, but didn't necessarily have to answer to them. Priest's changes had been incorporated into the Marvel Universe narrative, for other creators to reference and use.

Panther and the Avengers, Post-Priest, 1999–2013

Priest's portrayal of the Black Panther in his Marvel Knights imprint forever changed how he was viewed as an Avenger. From Priest (and Busiek) onward, the Panther was rendered in the remainder of *The Avengers* Volume 3—and beyond, up through 2013—as a mysterious figure who was loyal to the team—unless his own agenda, often unknown, was as stake. He was not a fulltime member of the group, and has not been through 2013. Banished forever was the outdated 1960s Sidney Poitier figure; Priest's African version of Ra's al Ghul-meets-"Dark Knight" had been imprinted on Marvel creators. But perhaps old racial patterns re-exert themselves in new ways: interestingly enough, when the Avengers dissembled to make way for The New Avengers in 2004, the "black token"[5] position was taken by a hip-hop-styled Luke Cage who, although thug-like tough and smart, was very loyal to Captain America and the Avengers.[6]

The Black Panther ongoing series, meanwhile, was cancelled in 2003. However, it was rebooted in 2005 by Hollywood director Reginald Hudlin, who, politically and culturally, went much further than Priest did. Under Hudlin, the second African American to write the ongoing series, Panther was an African defending his homeland from Marvel supervillains who notably represented white, Christian, imperialist, Western powers that, in the real world, had colonized Africa. In Hudlin's first issue, arguably a "Year One" soft-reboot of the character's entire history, T'Challa defeats a young, inexperienced Captain America. Even more significantly and symbolically in that first issue, the Panther's nation, its African-based religious systems and its geo-global politics were viewed from the culturally hostile viewpoint of the 2005 "War On Terror" Bush administration-era. As Hudlin's series progresses, T'Challa marries Ororo Munroe, a.k.a. Storm of the X-Men, in 2006 and the duo becomes an African superhero "power couple." This storyline took place around the same time, in the real world, world-famous hiphop artist and music mogul Sean Carter ("Jay-Z") was publicly dating his future wife, equally world-famous R&B singing star Beyoncé Knowles and America and the world was getting to know a U.S. senator from Illinois named Barack Obama and his wife, Michelle Obama. With the notable exception of the company-wide "Civil War" crossover event in 2006–2007, the Avengers were not regulars in Hudlin's *Black Panther* ongoing series. It got cancelled in 2008, then rebooted in 2009 with a female Black Panther, T'Challa's sister Shuri, a creation of Hudlin's.

Although the Black Panther character, T'Challa and/or Shuri, struggles to keep an ongoing comic book in the 21st century, Priest's portrayal of T'Challa even influenced the 2010–2013 animated series, "The Avengers: Earth's Mightiest Heroes," although not totally. Panther is shown in the series spying on the Avengers prior to his meeting, and fighting, the team in "Panther's Quest." In that episode, he asks the Avengers to help in regaining his kingdom (!) from Man-Ape, a plot the openly Afrocentric Hudlin (and not a Man-Ape fan) probably chuckled and sighed over. Again, the old patterns repeat: no matter how mysterious he acted earlier in the animated series, T'Challa reverts to his "old" 1960s Avengers comic book identity at the end of the episode, thanking Earth's Mightiest Heroes for helping him and joining the team to, somewhat illogically, better serve his now-damaged Wakanda (Giacoppo)! During the 52 episodes of the animated series, the Panther, a recurring character, rarely speaks (another Priest innovation or just an example of being an updated "token?"), but has little problem putting the needs of Wakanda above the needs of the group. But, again, old patterns seem to have a hegemonic hold: when "The Avengers: Earth's Mightiest Heroes" was updated in 2013 as a new animated series, "Avengers Assemble," the token black character is the Falcon, who is portrayed as a young, inexperienced hero grateful to be an Avenger and working with Captain America, Thor and Iron Man. Panther has yet to been seen or referenced in "Avengers Assemble" Season One as of this writing in late 2013. To show how the established dichotomist pattern discussed here in comics extends into animation, Hudlin's first "Year One" *Black Panther* storyline, "Who Is the Black Panther?," was adapted into *Marvel Knights Animation: Black Panther*, a six-episode, limited animation "digital comic" in 2010 and broadcast on Black Entertainment Television in 2011, becoming easily the most Afrocentric product to bear the Marvel Comics brand name in the company's almost 80-year history.

As Marvel Comics' answer to DC's Justice League, a group of comparatively bland superheroes who had no discernible personality conflicts for the first decade of their existence, the Avengers attempted to show "real" relations within a superhero team.[7] Because of both the racial upheavals of the 1960s, and the bland way T'Challa was portrayed in *The Avengers* comics in the 1970s and 1980s, any Avengers turmoil did not extend to him, the noble African token, because Marvel had made a historic integrationist point with its/the first black comic book superhero. In a post-modern way, Priest wanted to make a point, too: he wanted to show that it was time for The Black Panther to be portrayed, and accepted (by the Avengers and by the reader), the way he would be if he were created in the late 20th, or early 21st century, using post-modern sensibilities, a more cynical and accurate view of world geo-politics, and just plain logic. Using the base of Stan Lee and Jack Kirby's first Black Panther story arc in those now-collector's item pair of 1966 *Fantastic Four* issues, Priest, ironically, *re-created the Panther by reviving his original characterization.*

> I'm sure Black Panther was *somebody's* favorite character as they grew up, but the hero's legacy is one of an also-ran whose Big Talk African aristocracy rather prohibits much in the way of snappy dialogue. Readers want to identify with their heroic fantasy, and a great many fans want to read about fantastic adventures set in what Stan Lee once called, "The World Outside Our Window." Wakanda, a technologically advanced African nation steeped in tribal tradition, hardly qualifies, and, the race of the character notwithstanding, the cool aloofness and formal Big Talk successive writers created for him inspired less curiosity as disinterest. As often as not, The Black Panther came off more boring than mysterious.
>
> It seemed to me, as a reader, the writers simply didn't know what to do with this man who had no super-powers, no snappy dialog, no berserker rage and no obvious character faults to capitalize on. Over the years, Panther became a sideshow. Stripped of his advanced tech, that Reed Richards marveled at in Panther's first appearance in FANTASTIC FOUR #52, a mindset evolved that Panther, for some odd reason, created incredible advanced technology while eschewing the use of the same. I believe someone explained it to me that Panther feels a true warrior doesn't need bullet-proof costumes or global positioning communicards. That, to prove himself a man and a true warrior, Panther would go into battle side by side with the likes of Thor and Iron Man, and not take so much as a flashlight.
>
> What was even odder, for me, was the uproar of fans outraged by our evolution of the character into an extremely capable and not always clearly heroic figure, a man of uncertainty and mystery who used all of the vast resources at his disposal to accomplish his goals. Cries of heresy went forth from readers who hadn't ever read our book and, more to the point, who likely didn't support BLACK PANTHER in any of the several incarnations of ongoing adventures Marvel has attempted. Expletive-laden rants came in from people who know nothing about Panther, never really bought Panther on any regular basis, and who, frankly, think Panther is lame but who have bought into the severely errant illogic of the day—the de-evolution of a very clever and very unique character created by Stan Lee and Jack Kirby. Again and again I was asked, "How dare you change Panther!", to which I replied, "I didn't change Pan-

ther—other writers over the years changed Panther, losing sight of FF #52. *I* changed him *back* [Priest, "Adventures"].

Christopher Priest's version—his *vision*—of the Black Panther forced the Avengers team, *The Avengers* title, and, ultimately, the readers, to finally take him seriously, 30 years later after his first appearance with the team. With Priest's (and later Hudlin's) interpretation, the Black Panther in the 21st century is now considered to be a powerful character who can go toe-toe with anyone, even the Silver Surfer.[8] This is not just because the character evolved; it was because black comic book creators believed American society evolved to the point where mainstream superhero comic book audiences could see a powerful, potentially dangerous African king as both a loyal Avenger and his own man.

Notes

1. In the history of American superhero comics, there are literally thousands of examples of how superheroes have more ability and power in their own solo titles compared with when they are part of a team book, where they have to share the space and story with other characters. As someone who has read superhero comics for at least 30 years, I freely admit this. However, I think this example is still relevant to this particular discussion.
2. It's interesting to point out that, in this particular appearance of the character, the Panther wears a cowl that leaves the bottom of his face visible. Was this a huge mistake Marvel's ace artist John Buscema made, or did Marvel want to drive home the point in the real-world Black Power era that the character was indeed a *Black* Panther, and not a white man with a colorful, fearsome name? With the racially based turmoil in America in 1967 and 1968, with hundreds of cities having racial-based disturbances, and with mass media attempting to respond (for example, Bill Cosby on television as the first black person to co-star in a television series, NBC's *I Spy*), it seems like the latter.
3. Historically, in my causal examination of 20th century white liberal media portrayals of American black-white race conflict, white and black demagogues are portrayed as equally poisonousness—equally *wrong*—ignoring the structures of white institutional racism and the concept of white privilege, which together solidify the position of power whites have over blacks in a white supremacist culture. For more on the idea that white racism is an ingrained part of American society, see scholar Derrick Bell's works using Critical Race Theory.
4. There was a #0 issue that was just a prelude. I've decided not to count that here.
5. A separate topic would be a scholarly interpretation of the "black Avenger Token" experiences of The Falcon in *The Avengers Vol. 1* in the late 1970s and early 1980s and Triathlon in Vol. 3 in the early 2000s. Both characters were separately shoehorned into the Avengers by respective U.S. government liaisons Henry Peter Gyrich and Dwayne Freeman (the latter an African American) because of federal equal opportunity requirements. Neither stayed with the team for any length of time, partly because of how they joined and the conflicts that surrounded their joining created. With the Falcon, the issue was racial quotas, while with Triathlon, the issue was both racial quotas and religious tolerance/tokenism.
6. "Luke Cage: Hero For Hire," later renamed "Power Man" and now returning to just Luke Cage, was a superhero inspired by John Shaft in the "Shaft" 1970s movie trilogy. In 1972, he was the Marvel's first black character to have his own 20-page title, unlike T'Challa, who had a 15-page strip in *Jungle Action*. Cage has had a variety of characterizations over the four decades since his creation, ranging from 1970s-era Shaft-like private eye to 1990s and 2000s hip-hop-era "gangsta" thug.

7. In response to the Marvel style of increased characterization and more internal melo-drama, DC Comics quickly followed suit in the 1970s, with a Justice League that saw Hawkman bickering with Green Arrow, and a more feminist Wonder Woman leaving the team. Arguably, this presentation of conflict within the Justice League would culminate in the very controversial 2004 Justice League miniseries, *Identity Crisis*. The series shows, among other disturbing scenes, Leaguers agreeing to let the League magician, Zatanna, "mind-wipe" Batman because he had attempted to stop Zatanna from lobotomizing the villain Dr. Light. Both extreme measures were taken by Zatanna and the rest of the League because Light had broken into the League's orbiting satellite and sodomized Sue Dibny, the wife of League mainstay Elongated Man. In 2013, some DC fans are relieved that this story was "ret-conned" out of existence in 2011, when DC re-booted its entire universe.

8. See McDuffie Dwayne (w) and Paul Pelletier (a), *The New Fantastic Four* trade paperback (New York: Marvel Comics), 2008, for the cosmic adventures of T'Challa and Storm when the couple is asked by departing Fantastic Four leader Reed Richards and his wife, Susan Storm Richards, to lead the team after the events of the "Civil War" company-wide crossover.

Works Cited

Busiek, Kurt (w), and George Perez (a). "Ultron Unlimited, Part One: This Evil Renewed." *The Avengers*, v. 3, #19, August 1999. New York: Marvel Comics. Print.

_____, and _____. "Ultron Unlimited, Part Two: This Evil Unfolding." *The Avengers*, v. 3, #20, September 1999. New York: Marvel Comics. Print.

_____, and _____. "Ultron Unlimited, Part Three: This Evil Unveiled." *The Avengers*, v. 3, #21, October 1999. New York: Marvel Comics. Print.

_____, and _____. "Ultron Unlimited, Part Four: This Evil Triumphant!" *The Avengers*, v. 3, #22, December 1999. New York: Marvel Comics. Print.

Giacoppo, Paul (w), and Sebastian Montes (dir.) "Panther's Quest." *The Avengers: Earth's Mightiest Heroes*, Season One, Ep. 11. Airdate: November 17, 2010. Television.

Lee, Stan (w), and Jack Kirby (a). "The Black Panther!" *The Fantastic Four*, v. 1, #52, July 1966. New York: Marvel Comics. Print.

_____, and _____. "This Monster Unmasked!" *Captain America*, v. 1, #100, April, 1968. New York: Marvel Comics. Print.

_____, and _____. "The Way It Began!" *The Fantastic Four*, v. 1, #53, August 1966. New York: Marvel Comics. Print.

Nama, Adilifu. *Super Black: American Pop Culture and Black Superheroes*. Austin: University of Texas Press, 2011. Print.

Priest, Christopher. "Adventures in the Funnybook Game, Chapter 16: The Death of the Black Panther: Quesada's Bitch Survives the Mean Season," *digital-priest.com, The Official Website of Christopher J. Priest*, April 20, 2002. http://digitalpriest.com/legacy/comics/adventures/frames/panther_death.htm. Retrieved October 8, 2013. Web.

Priest, Christopher (w), and Joe Jusko, et al. (a). *Black Panther: Enemy of the State* trade paperback. New York: Marvel Comics, 2001. Reprints *Black Panther*, vol. 2, #6–12 from 1998, 1999. Print.

Priest, Christopher (w), and Mark Texeria (a). *Black Panther: The Client* trade paperback. New York: Marvel Comics, 2001. Reprints *Black Panther*, vol. 2, #1–5 from 1998. Print.

Thomas, Roy (w), and John Buscema (a). "Death Calls for the Arch-Heroes!" *The Avengers*, v. 1, #52, May 1968. New York: Marvel Comics.

_____, and _____. "Pursue the Panther." *The Avengers*, v. 1, #74, March 1970. New York: Marvel Comics. Print.

The *Ultimates* as Superheroes in the Age of Social Media and Celebrity

MORGAN B. O'ROURKE

Perhaps more than ever, today is the age of superheroes. They not only appear in comic books but also in television shows like *Smallville* and *Arrow*, video games such as *Injustice: Gods Among Us* and *Marvel: Ultimate Alliance*, and films like *Spider-Man* and *The Avengers*. In the summer of 2013 alone, *The Avengers* earned over $600 million domestically and over $1 billion internationally, quickly putting it near the top of the all-time box office list ("All-Time USA Box Office."). But the heroes that companies like DC and Marvel present us with today are different from the original heroes introduced several decades ago. When Marvel launched the *Iron Man* movie franchise, it updated the hero's origin story to fit today's market. Originally Tony Stark created the Iron Man suit when he was captured by enemy forces in Vietnam and then subsequently used it to escape ("Iron Man (Anthony Stark)"). In the new movies, Tony is captured by the enemy of today, a band of terrorists who wants him to build weapons. The character in the movies is still unquestionably Iron Man; he still builds the Iron Man suit and escapes captivity, ultimately becoming a hero. The overall story and character are the same, with some details adapted for new audiences.

The comic books where today's cinematic superheroes began are no different. Over the years as society and comic book readers have changed, the comic books have adjusted accordingly. Recently DC Comics launched the new "52," restarting all of its comic books at issue number one, changing origin stories, altering existing timelines, and reshaping the characters in an effort to appeal more to today's audiences (Steinberg 1).

Marvel, another industry giant, had previously "relaunched" its characters,

120

albeit in a different fashion, by creating an alternate universe—the "Ultimate Universe"—with new versions of mainstream heroes who were just beginning their careers. This strategy allowed Marvel to explore how today's morals, culture, and technology would shape superheroes. For example, back in 2000, Marvel issued *Ultimate Spider-Man*. This comic book told the story of a contemporary Peter Parker, drawing on many aspects of Spider-Man from the original story, but changing some elements as well, such as making Peter a web designer rather than a photographer. Later in 2002, Marvel relaunched its flagship team the Avengers in this new universe as *The Ultimates* (Millar, Hitch, and Currie). This publication—even more than the other Ultimate Universe comic books that Marvel released—redefined the modern superhero.

The Ultimates highlighted the flaws inherent in superheroes, putting equal focus on what made them human and what made them super. In its pages, Tony Stark—better known as Iron Man—has a brain tumor and is a borderline alcoholic. Hank Pym, aka "Giant Man," has an inferiority complex, suffers from depression, and beats his wife. In his desperation to feel powerful and important, Bruce Banner willingly becomes the monstrous Hulk. The Wasp is a closet mutant with dangerously low self-esteem. Thor is a pacifist with the powers of a god, but is also possibly psychotic. A man out of time, Captain America views the world through a lens of black and white morals (Millar, Hitch, and Currie). Both the choice to reinvent some of Marvel's most well-known characters as deeply-troubled individuals in *The Ultimates* and the subsequent popularity of the comic book reveal aspects modern conceptions of heroes, celebrity, and power. The first three issues of *The Ultimates* all sold over a hundred thousand copies and were some of the top comic books in their month of publication, ranking fourth, second, and third respectively (*ICv2: Inside Pop Culture*).

This, of course, raises the question of why such deeply flawed characters resonate with readers. The answer would seem to be, in part, that readers like the heroes *because* they are so flawed. The Ultimates represent a new type of hero, part superhero and part celebrity, who struggles to find a balance between humble service and selfish grabs for attention. In *The Ultimates,* superheroes are not always pure, and sometimes are not even all that good. They struggle with the same very human problems that many of us suffer. At the end of day, though, they are more than their collective flaws and foibles: they are heroes, and that is something that most readers can appreciate.

This essay's analysis of how *The Ultimates* reformulates the hero is important for two main reasons. First, while numerous studies have looked at the significance of superheroes, no one has examined this series specifically and how they have contributed to the medium. Previous scholars have analyzed superhero movies (e.g., Terrill, "Put On a Happy Face"), cartoons (e.g., Baker and Raney), graphic novels (e.g., Doyle), and even other superhero comics (e.g., Baker and Raney; Davidson; Doyle; Goffe; Hoppenstand; McAllister; Pearson; Shugart; and Terrill "Spectacular Repression"), but not *The Ultimates*. Several of these studies have looked at how the qualities, characters, and ideals of the presented superheroes relate to the audience that comic books address (Davidson, Goffe, Hoppenstand, and Pearson). Thus, this study extends past research by analyzing *The Ultimates* as a contemporary reimagining of old heroes that reflects a change in societal views and values.

Secondly, this study uses *The Ultimates* to extend examination of the distinction between celebrity and hero in today's media age. In the abstract, society seems to have clear distinctions between heroes and celebrities, but in the social media age those boundaries are becoming increasingly blurred. We have more access to both heroes and celebrities than ever before, and the more we learn about them the harder they become to differentiate. Heroes are thought of as having done something meaningful or important, but does that mean celebrities cannot? If a movie star tweets about AIDS in Africa, or gives money to start a school, is she still a celebrity or is she a hero? Several scholars have looked at the differences between what constitutes a hero and what constitutes a celebrity (e.g., Javors; North, Bland, and Ellis; Schickel) and the role of the media in branding these individuals (North, Bland, and Ellis; Schickel). *The Ultimates* provides an ideal fictionalized medium for looking at this issue further for it depicts superheroes in the media age—the Ultimates even have their own PR representative—and also imagines what would happen if existing celebrities, like fictional billionaire Tony Stark, were to become superheroes.

The Characteristics of Superheroes and Their Post–9/11 Evolution

The superhero, put simply, is an individual with some kind of fantastic power, be it from technology, biology, magic, or intense physical training, who rises above his or her fears and limitations to achieve something extraordinary (Fingeroth 14–17; Davidson 19–20; Ford 5–6). It is this power or ability that sets them apart from other heroes like the police and enables the superhero to face threats that ordinary humans never could.

Within the American superhero genre, most superheroes are orphans, whether in the literal sense of losing their parents at a young age, or in the figurative sense, with their parents cutting off ties or being otherwise removed from the picture (e.g., appearing in the comic book's first issue and then never being referred to again) (Fingeroth 66). Even heroes who are not orphans are almost always outsiders, somehow cut off from society, whether because of their powers, their appearance, or their actions (Shugart 98; Ruzicka 47–48; Ford 8).

Another superhero trademark is the mask. Many heroes wear masks to conceal their identities, thereby allowing them to lead otherwise normal lives separate from their super lives and also keeping any non-powered friends and family out of the limelight and away from harm (Fingeroth 49). Of course, some heroes choose not to wear masks. These heroes typically lack close family or friends who would be endangered if their identity became public knowledge, or if they do have close family and friends, they are also superheroes and able to protect themselves. Even in these situations though (e.g., the Fantastic Four or the X-Men), the heroes still use code names to protect their civilian identities to a degree and to sequester themselves from the public. Besides protection, heroes use masks and code names for anonymity; they do not want or need to be thanked for their efforts (Fingeroth 49).

Superheroes are further defined by their morality. Although the hero may struggle with issues of morality on the course of his or her journey, the hero almost universally does right. Superheroes always possess some strength of character, often buried and needing to be found, and have a positive value system, which they are dedicated to protecting (Fingeroth 17). On the rare occasions when the hero makes a mistake or a bad decision, it is always in the vein of character growth, ensuring that next time the hero will make the right call. For example, when Spider-Man chooses not to stop a criminal running by him, the criminal later kills Spider-Man's uncle, driving the superhero to use his power[s] to help others and never to forget that "with great power come great responsibility." The typical superhero reflects the best values and morals of society, even when society itself can be divided or unsure (Fingeroth 14–17; Pearson 11–13; Ružička 46–48).

In addition, the superhero is slow to change. Characters hardly—if ever—age. Superman, for instance, has been around for over 75 years and is still a thirtyish young reporter at *The Daily Planet*. Superheroes also rarely die. Because the good guys almost always win, heroes are seemingly safe. If one is killed, the death typically does not last (resurrection is almost as common a trope in the superhero genre as death).

Superheroes are also the perfect embodiment of what Lawrence and Jewett call the American monomyth, which describes what drives most heroic narratives. First, some evil, either external or internal in origin, threatens a harmonious community. Normal institutions—such as the police—fail to stop the threat, causing a selfless hero to emerge. The hero must renounce temptation to defeat the evil. In the process, the hero is aided by fate or, if one prefers, luck. After a decisive victory and harmonious restoration of the community, the monomyth narrative concludes with the hero receding into obscurity (qtd. in Ford 8).

The superhero narratives of comic books meet all but the last criterion of the American Monomyth: superheroes do not fade away into the night. Indeed, some superhero series have run successfully for over 75 years (e.g., Superman) and show no signs of stopping. In comic books, the monomyth is a cycle. When one adventure is done, the heroes may step back with every intention of leaving their super heroics behind them, but some new evil always arises to disturb the community that the heroes have sworn to protect, forcing them to step up again and perpetually deferring their fade into obscurity.

For years, superheroes embodied these characteristics and the monomyth and generated successful comic books easily selling over a million copies, but over time the markets changed. Today a successful comic book is lucky to sell a hundred thousand copies (Rhoades). Comic books have always had to adapt to changing markets, whether that meant adding sidekicks like Robin to appeal to younger readers, or changing villains to reflect new evils.

In a post–9/11 world, however, the need to evolve was greater than ever. With the 2001 attacks, the moral and cultural landscape in American society underwent great change. First, the Bush administration's response to 9/11 painted the world in black and white terms. A fervor of nationalism swept across the country. In his rhetoric pursing the "war on terror," Bush mirrored the sentiments of a World War II-era America, where comic books heroes like Captain America first took off (Pearson 22). All too quickly, however, this illusion of moral clarity gave way to a world more complicated than ever. The villains and even heroes were not who we thought they were. Saddam Hussein had no weapons of mass destruction. Meanwhile, our own government was spying on us under the Patriot Act and torturing prisoners at Guantanamo Bay. Suddenly the black and white morality that was conjured by the war on terror began falling apart. People started questioning the government and its agenda, and rightly so (Rich 153–176). Heroes' morality was not automatic anymore. In this new world, it seemed that no one could know with certainty what was truly right. As the times changed, comic books could no longer market good and evil the same way.

This was not the first time that comic books had to adapt to changing social views. During the Vietnam era, when opinions of our government were at an all-time low, villains took on new shapes. In Watchmen the government disbands superheroes after winning the war in Vietnam, leading to a dystopian society on the brink of nuclear extinction (Davidson 19–21). The '60s also saw Captain America, a superhero originally created in World War II to serve his government, expose evil in that very body ("Captain America [Steve Rogers]"). But years later during the Reagan administration, confidence in the America we felt we once knew was restored. When John Byrne was tasked with relaunching

Superman in 1986, he drew on that national spirit and crafted an optimistic and uplifting story of the ultimate immigrant, who came across the galaxy to a better place in America (O'Rourke and O'Rourke 121–122). Superheroes were pure again, at least until the 1990s, when the grim n' gritty aesthetic became the dominant tone in comic books.

Following the Bush era and faced with a more complicated and perhaps more cynical world, the comic book industry looked for ways to evolve yet again. In a world obsessed with reality television, Facebook, Twitter, and the latest bit of celebrity gossip, Marvel launched *The Ultimates*, a fresh look at Marvel's flagship team the Avengers, in a newly-crafted "Ultimate Universe" (Sargent 1–2). In launching *The Ultimates,* Marvel was looking for a new take on the hero. Rather than have the characters assume the role of heroes automatically, the comic books explored what having powers in the 21st century would be like and, in doing so, how fame and celebrity culture might impact the world of superheroes.

Most heroes could be said to have some degree of celebrity, but not all celebrities are heroes. Society views heroes as individuals who have accomplished something significant or meaningful, whereas celebrities are more often famous simply for being famous. While people see heroes as role models and examples to aspire to, they usually consider celebrities as less serious, such as actors, models, and media stars (North, Bland, and Ellis 40). Not all heroes are famous or well known. A hero could just as easily be a great teacher in an inner-city school, a doctor who saves lives in the local hospital, or a volunteer at a homeless shelter (Javors 1). Indeed even within the heroic framework of the monomyth, the superhero recedes into obscurity in the end. Celebrities, on the hand, thrive on publicity. Whether it is an actor who wants to promote a new film or a model trying to sell a clothing line, celebrities want the public's attention so they can sell their product, or in the case of some reality television stars, sell themselves.

Overall, then, society tends to make clear distinctions between heroes and celebrities. In a survey comparing heroes and celebrities, for instance, North, Bland, and Ellis asked participants to list their favorite heroes and celebrities. The top five heroes were Winston Churchill, Nelson Mandela, Martin Luther King, Jr., Princess Diana, and Jesus, while the top celebrities were David Beckham, Billy Connolly, Michael Jackson, Sean Connery, and Robbie Williams. When asked if they would rather meet their favorite hero or their favorite celebrity, the majority of these people said they would rather meet their top hero (North, Bland, and Ellis 44). As much as we might like reading about celebrities and their various eccentricities and problems, we would rather interact with heroes. In the Ultimate Universe, Marvel explored these notions of heroism and celebrity for a post-modern age.

An aspect of contemporary culture clearly linked to celebrity is omnipresence of media like television, Facebook, and Twitter. We see celebrities using media to their advantage all the time, whether for advertising, activism, or self-promotion. In fact, many celebrity endorsement deals now even come with a rider that requires celebrities to use social media to promote the product (Hampp 1–2). But social media also covers celebrity sex scandals, drunken brawls, and verbal gaffes (Schickel 522–523). How, then, would social media affect superheroes? In the past, Marvel has tried to examine superheroes from the perspectives of ordinary citizens such as Aunt May ("Parker, May (Aunt May)") and even from the vantage points of reporters as in *Civil War: Front Line* (Jenkins, Leiber, Bachs, and Kobayashi), but the Ultimates allowed Marvel to explore a more contemporary approach, where heroes are aware of the media, interact with reporters, and at times try to control or "spin" the story.

The Analysis of Celebrity and Social Media in the Ultimate Universe

The Ultimates begins in the middle of a battle in World War II, quickly introducing readers to Captain America, the world's first superhero. Captain America successfully stops a missile aimed at the United States, but seemingly sacrifices himself in the process. Years later Nick Fury, new head of SHIELD (Strategic Hazard Intervention Espionage Logistics Directorate) prioritizes research into the Super-Soldier program that created Captain America in an attempt to create a state-sponsored superhero team to respond to new global threats for the Bush administration.

Tony Stark quickly joins the team as Iron Man, soon followed by super-soldier scientists Hank and Janet Pym, Giant Man and the Wasp respectively. When Captain America is discovered alive in the Atlantic Ocean, he becomes the leader of the new team of super soldiers: The Ultimates. Bruce Banner, a scientist who is working on the super-soldier serum, mixes Captain America's blood with his existing Hulk serum in an attempt to become the next Captain America, and instead permanently bonds the Hulk formula to his DNA. The Hulk's ensuing rampage in New York City kills hundreds, but gives the Ultimates their first real super villain to fight. During the battle, Thor comes to help stop the Hulk, thereby unofficially joining the team. When the Hulk is finally defeated, the Ultimates decide to cover up the fact that the Hulk is actually Bruce Banner, allowing the team to take credit for saving the city. After the battle Cap, Tony, and Thor celebrate the Ultimates' first big win, while Hank violently assaults his wife Janet and flees (Millar, Hitch, and Currie).

As news of Hank's attack on Janet spreads, Black Widow, Hawkeye, Quicksilver, and the Scarlet Witch— all black ops members of SHIELD—are taking out an infestation of shape-shifting aliens. The team soon discovers that the alien invasion is much more widespread than initially believed. The Ultimates are eventually able to repel the invasion, thanks mostly to Thor, who decimates the enemy fleet, and the Hulk, who Captain America manages to manipulate into working with the Ultimates (Millar, Hitch, Neary, and Currie).

One year passes between the alien invasion and the beginning of volume two of the Ultimates. The Ultimates are much more military oriented now, as they are rescuing hostages in foreign countries, working more and more with the mainstream U.S. armed forces, and all in all living up to name "super soldiers." Thor, objecting to the team's new militaristic focus, is no longer working with the Ultimates. Thor's criticism of the team and the team's increasingly drastic actions cause public opinion of the Ultimates to drop significantly. The team's initial cover-up of Bruce Banner's responsibility for the Hulk's earlier destruction of New York City also comes to light, further hurting the public's faith in them. Later when Thor believes that his brother Loki, god of mischief, is manipulating reality, the rest of the team believes Thor is just crazy, and in the end the team, with the help of the new European Union super soldiers, attack and capture Thor (Millar, Hitch, and Neary).

On the surface, the Ultimates appear to resemble their mainstream counterparts from earlier comic books very closely, but upon further examination, one can see that these heroes are quite different. The Ultimates are petty, self-obsessed, and flawed. They enjoy being heroes as much for the fame as for actually doing good and constantly try to control their image in the media. Hero vs. celebrity is a false dichotomy for the Ultimates, they exhibit traits of both superheroes and celebrities. They possess aspects of both a secret identity and a super identity, they are sometimes selfless, and other times selfish.

Secret Identity vs. Super Identity

Most American comic book superheroes do everything in their power to hide their true identity. They do this, as mentioned earlier, through the use of code names and masks. By keeping their identity a secret, superheroes hope to ensure both their own safety and the safety of their friends and families (Fingeroth 49). The Ultimates, true to the form, all use code names: Captain America, Iron Man, Thor, the Wasp, Giant Man, Hawkeye, Black Widow, Quicksilver, the Scarlet Witch, and even the Hulk. Technically, Captain America and Iron Man even wear masks; Cap wears a modified version of his original World War

II uniform, and Tony's Iron Man visor obscures his face (Millar, Hitch, and Currie). Most of the Ultimates also lack any close personal ties to mainstream society, as they are either literal or figurative orphans (See Fingeroth 49). All of Captain America's family is dead, and the few friends he has left are old enough to be his grandparents. Iron Man is an eccentric billionaire, out of touch with the common people, while the Pyms are both scientists for a top-secret government program. Indeed, the only member of the team who has any real connection to society outside the team is Hawkeye, who even then keeps his family in the dark about the majority of what his job entails (Millar, Hitch, Neary and Currie; Millar, Hitch, and Currie). Despite all this, however, the Ultimates never really embrace the idea of having a secret identity.

Celebrities thrive on public attention. They build their careers on getting people to notice them. Whether promoting a movie or a new book, launching a television show, or creating their own fragrance line, celebrities depend on fame to make a living (see Hampp). For celebrities, almost all press is good press. Even negative coverage of celebrities—like drug addictions, on-going feuds, and verbal gaffes—keeps the celebrity's name in the public's mind. When Lindsay Lohan, or more recently Amanda Bynes, started their downward spirals, there were headlines everywhere. Lohan is now even exploiting her former problems for a new TV special with Oprah (Fung). The constant attention of the media can also be a burden, however. In today's world, it is harder and harder for celebrities to maintain any kind of privacy. While celebrities may at times exploit their private lives for personal gain, selling wedding videos, baby pictures, and the like, celebrities also have to deal with the constant media surveillance by tabloids and entertainment news outlets that make their money by revealing less positive aspects of the celebrity's life, such as drug addictions, nasty divorces, and sex tapes.

The Ultimates, while having code names and even in some cases masks, use the media in the same way as celebrities. They publicize who they are, as opposed to hiding their identities. In the Ultimate Universe, everyone knows that Captain America is also Steve Rogers and that Tony Stark, billionaire CEO, is Iron Man. Thor is completely open about his powers and his belief that he is a Norse god. To be fair, characters like Steve Rogers, and Tony Stark lack true secret identities in Marvel's mainstream universe as well—Cap because of the press surrounding his supposed death following World War II and Tony because his identity has previously been exposed—but they are certainly the exception to the rule. All of the Ultimates are completely open about their identities as superheroes in ways most superhero teams are not. They openly broadcast their superhero status to the world, ensuring their civilian names and superhero identities are synonymous.

The reasons behind the Ultimates' openness become clearer if one looks at their military origins. When Nick Fury and Bruce Banner conceptualize the idea of a team of "state sponsored super people," it is in place of a fully-staffed military; the idea is, in Banner's words, "downsizing conventional numbers and reinvesting in a small superhuman unit for 21st century problems" (Millar, Hitch, and Currie). The Ultimates are construed as a military deterrent, a new force to handle super crime and to prevent attacks on the United States. For this idea to work, the Ultimates have to be visible. The original idea of mutually assured destruction or "MAD" in the cold war would never have worked if the United States and the Soviet Union did not know they both had nuclear weapons. For the Ultimates to deter an attack, potential attackers have to know the Ultimates exist. This also explains why the Ultimates are given a new state of the art base highly visible in the middle of the Manhattan Bay (Millar, Hitch, and Currie). Moreover, public knowledge of this superhero team seems to reassure American citizens about the government's new approach to national security.

Given all of the persuasive needs, the Ultimates have their own public relations department, headed by Betty Ross, a name that brings to mind Betsy Ross, who made the first American flag. Unlike this revered figure from American history, Betty Ross's job is to create a new symbol of American strength through carefully orchestrated press work, press work that is at odds with the traditional superhero's desire for anonymity. One of her first tasks is to organize the televised launch party for the Ultimates, which is broadcast in 42 different languages worldwide, calling attention to and glorifying America's new superhuman deterrent. Betty is also very adept at spinning the media to present the best possible image of the team. At the launch party, she and Nick Fury have a disagreement over Betty hiring male models to wave flags on camera, whereupon she coldly replies that "the last thing the world wants to see is a bunch of pimple faced fatties cheering on their favorite superhero team" (Millar, Hitch, and Currie). She wants media coverage of the team to portray supporters as attractive, thereby encouraging viewers to identify with the Ultimates and their cause. Betty also organizes a televised training exercise for the press to observe so they can fawn over the new superhero team. Later when Fury is at a loss as to how the Ultimates will not look completely incompetent after Bruce Banner becomes the Hulk and attacks New York City, Betty provides the answer: "[J]ust hush up the Bruce Banner connection and all of your little super people here go down in history as the heroes who saved Manhattan." While this cover up does briefly establish a secret identity for the Hulk, Banner's name is eventually leaked to the press, and the backlash over his crimes and the Ultimates' public lies greatly hurts their reputation (Millar, Hitch, and Currie). In other words, the one instance of a real secret identity being used in the Ultimates is a PR ploy to look good in the press that, in the end, significantly harms the Ultimate's public image.

While Betty handles the media coverage for the team as a whole, the individuals on the team are all frequently featured in the press. In volume one alone, members of the team are interviewed by Larry King, Howard Stern, Oprah, and various news affiliates after the Hulk attack. The team greatly enjoys the attention and, despite the Hulk's three-figure death toll, are celebrating at the end of volume one. Tony even toasts Banner "without whom I think it's safe to say [we] wouldn't be standing here this evening." Earlier, Fury mentions a possible movie deal about the Ultimates. The team members are thrilled at the idea and begin imagining who the perfect the actors to play them would be (Millar, Hitch, and Currie).

This scene is very indicative of the Ultimates' overall behavior in volume one: while they want to be superheroes, they love the celebrity attention they garner and continually crave it, despite not having done anything super heroic to deserve it. In volume two when the Ultimates eventually stop the alien invasion, the Wasp remarks that she "think[s] we're finally super heroes" referring to the team's seemingly clearcut defeat of the evil aliens (Millar, Hitch, Neary, and Currie). After the invasion, public opinion of the Ultimates soars despite a small portion of the population who believes the attack was faked. The media are covering every angle of the story, and when Janet's stylist asks if she ever reads the articles people are writing about her, Jan happily replies that she has piles of papers at her house waiting to become clippings and that even Thor—easily the least attention-obsessed member of the team—had been googling himself to see what people were saying about him (Millar, Hitch, Neary, and Currie). The lure of a public, super-identity draws the entire team in and, at least temporarily, makes them happy.

Selflessness vs. Selfishness

Superheroes are often defined by their selflessness and willingness to serve (Ford 8), their ability to give up something of themselves to serve a greater purpose. The Ultimates are, to some degree, selfless. They do put themselves in harm's way to help others. They use their extraordinary powers for good, for both the monumental challenges like stopping an alien invasion and for smaller, but no less heroic tasks like rescuing people from burning buildings (Millar, Hitch, Neary, and Currie).

Celebrities on the other hand, are typically defined as being selfish (see North, Bland, and Ellis 40). They put themselves and their image and efforts to accrue personal wealth above others. The Ultimates are paid to be superheroes. Because the super-soldier project falls under SHIELD jurisdiction, the Ultimates are paid members of the U.S. military, much in the way any other soldier might be. For comic book superheroes, this is highly unusual. With the notable exception of Luke Cage's original "Heroes for Hire" business, where anyone could buy his services ("Cage, Luke"), superheroes are rarely paid. In the mainstream Marvel Universe during the Civil War storyline, the government wanted heroes to register and become paid employees of the United States, something the heroes objected to ("Civil War"). By being paid, the Ultimates' supposed selflessness in risking their lives to help others is cast in a different light. The Ultimates' actions are a job requirement, not some greater moral imperative or sacrifice.

In addition to being paid to take risks most heroes take for free, the Ultimates work with trained military personnel from SHIELD, thereby mitigating the risks to the team. These regular soldiers often wind up serving as cannon fodder for the Ultimates. For example, when Hawkeye and the Black Widow begin cleaning out two office buildings full of aliens, they take several squads of soldiers with them. After a bomb goes off, all but one of the soldiers that Hawkeye is with are killed, yet in the end Hawkeye and Black Widow come out virtually unscathed and apparently unconcerned over the loss of life (Millar, Hitch, Neary, and Currie). Hawkeye, Black Widow, and the rest of the team simply accept these losses as part of the job, and never really express any sadness or grief over losing so many soldiers who are supposed to be their comrades in arms. The Ultimates' job is certainly dangerous, but the parameters in which they work greatly reduce the risk to the team. The only instances of major injury to the team come when the Hulk and Thor are hurt fighting against the team, when Hank beats Jan, and when Captain America assaults Hank for his attack on his wife (Millar, Hitch, and Currie).

The Ultimates also lie to the public on a regular basis to preserve their image. As mentioned earlier, when the Hulk attacks New York City and kills hundreds of people, the Ultimates hide Banner's name from the press to prevent anyone from uncovering his connection to the Ultimates. This is pure selfishness. The Ultimates spin the story so they become the daring heroes who saved New York and avoid any real culpability for their part in the massacre. While it could be argued that the Ultimates' actions were taken in part to protect Banner, this argument quickly falls apart. When the team captures Banner, they are angry and disrespectful towards him for his actions, with Captain America going so far as to kick him in the face (Millar, Hitch, and Currie). Banner's choice to become the Hulk again was an act of selfishness in and of itself; he knew full well the devastation his previous Hulk episodes caused but he chose to inject himself with the Hulk serum anyway in a desperate bid to feel important (Millar, Hitch, and Currie) The team's decision to cover up Banner's connection to the Hulk is no less selfish; the conversation between Betty and Nick Fury makes it perfectly clear the cover up is motivated entirely by the need to preserve the Ultimates' positive image. With the cover up in place, the public heaps the heroes with praise for their actions, and any animosity the team has for Banner or for his actions seems to evaporate almost instantly. By the end of the first volume, Captain America, Tony, and Thor are all toasting Banner, celebrating his role in making them heroes (Millar, Hitch, and Currie).

When the truth about Banner being the Hulk eventually comes out, the team's selfishness becomes even clearer. The team's first reaction to the news is anger over the public backlash, not guilt. Indeed the only hero to express any guilt at all is Captain America, and even he quickly moves on. The Ultimates know full well that Banner will be found guilty of murder and executed, but only the Wasp briefly expresses sympathy for Banner. Even Betty Ross, Banner's on again and off again girlfriend, accepts Banner's fate, refusing to spend time with Banner when there is a PR crisis to handle. Later at the actual execution she, Tony, and Nick are all remorseful, but none of them feels strongly enough to try to stop the execution (Millar, Hitch, and Neary). When Captain America confronts Thor about possibly being the source of the leak, he tells Thor that his actions have likely killed Banner, but only after berating Thor for making the team "look like liars." While Cap may seem angry because of Banner's situation, Cap's actions show he is more angry over no longer feeling like a hero and over what he believes is Thor's betrayal of the team (Millar, Hitch, Neary and Currie). Given the heroes' reactions and their willingness to let Banner be executed if it buys them back even a small amount of public good will, the selfish motives of the initial cover up become clear. The team takes similar actions again and again, covering up the alien invasion until it is almost too late, lying about plans to send the Ultimates into the Middle East, and using whatever they can to spin their public image in a positive light (Millar, Hitch, Neary and Currie; Millar Hitch, and Neary). Other superheroes who interact with the media deal with bad press all the time (e.g., Spider-Man, the X-Men, and the Fantastic Four), but the Ultimates are uniquely selfish in their desire to want to look good and their willingness to get their hands dirty to do it.

The Ultimates believe themselves to be heroes. They see themselves as repeatedly trying to do what is best for society only to have society turn against them. The Ultimates would almost certainly believe they are selfless. But in reality any good intentions and selflessness the Ultimates had, vanishes when they get their first real taste of fame. Following the Hulk disaster the team was faced with a choice, tell the truth and likely have the team be shut down, or lie and continue to be praised as heroes. The Ultimates' choice to selfishly cling to fame changes them both as a team and as individuals, and starts their decent from heroes to celebrities.

Role Models vs. Terrible Examples

Superheroes are typically seen as positive role models, whose good behavior is worthy of emulation, whereas celebrities are often viewed as bad examples, whose actions show us what *not* to do (North, Bland, and Ellis 40). This is not to say that all superheroes make good role models or that all celebrities exhibit bad behavior, but simply, that most often heroes are viewed as positive examples and celebrities as negative ones.

In many ways, the Ultimates are good role models. Every member of the team joins because he or she wants to be a superhero; they want to do good, and in some ways they do. The Ultimates stop the Hulk, end an alien invasion, rescue kids from burning buildings, and save a sunken submarine (Millar, Hitch, Neary, and Currie; Millar, Hitch, and Neary). The Ultimates have no obligation to become heroes, or even to try, but they still choose to use their powers for the greater good. In the case of Captain America, Giant-Man, and even the Hulk, who despite his failure and the destruction he brings wants nothing more than to be a hero, they originally received their powers from the government sponsored super-soldier program because they wanted to serve and help people. Thor, the Wasp, and Iron Man develop their abilities apart from the government program, but still choose to use them to help others. Cap, Tony, Thor, Janet, Hank, and Bruce all came to the Ultimates with the best of intentions, and that willingness to help others is admirable.

Unfortunately, as the saying goes, the road to hell is paved with good intentions. Despite their noble beginnings, many of the actions the Ultimates take are far from laudable. The team repeatedly lies to the public to protect its own interests. Beyond covering up the Hulk's true identity, team members keep the alien invasion a secret until it is almost too late, hide the Scarlet Witch and Quicksilver's involvement with the team, and create false backgrounds for former black ops members Hawkeye and Black Widow (Millar, Hitch, Neary, and Currie). These lies both endanger the public and hide the truth to preserve the team's image. The Scarlet Witch and Quicksilver are both former terrorists, and their presence on the team is kept secret precisely because Fury worries about how the public would react (Millar, Hitch, Neary, and Currie). The team's repeated lies and the huge damage these lies do are by no means exemplary.

The Ultimates are also deeply flawed individuals, exhibiting many traits that role models should not have. Tony Stark is constantly drinking, including several times before flying the Iron Man suit. While the word "alcoholic" is never used, it would certainly seem appropriate. Giant-Man, aka Hank Pym, physically assaults the Wasp in a brutal attempt to defend his bruised ego. The Wasp has dangerously low self-esteem, having stayed with Hank up to this point, despite his history of abusing her. Bruce Banner is incredibly needy, and knowing full well the death and destruction the Hulk has caused previously, still chooses to become the Hulk again in an attempt to feel important. Moreover, volumes two and three imply that Quicksilver and the Scarlet Witch's relationship is incestuous, an implication later confirmed in volume five. Thor is believed to be psychotic, yet is allowed to wield a nearly all-powerful hammer and serve on the team. Captain America is reckless and violent, beating up Giant-Man after his attack on the Wasp and nearly attacking Thor when he thinks Thor has betrayed the team (Millar, Hitch, Neary, and Currie).

At the end of volume three, Hank, after being kicked out of the Ultimates, winds up joining a new team of young people trying to be superheroes. Calling themselves "The Defenders," the group members styles themselves after the Ultimates. Hank soon learns, however, that none of the Defenders have powers of any kind. Between their over-eager attitudes and their reckless actions, it becomes clear that they crave attention and celebrity more than they actually want to do good. When the Defenders learn of a robbery that is going to happen, rather than call the police they call the press, hoping to stop the robbery themselves and become famous. The attempt fails miserably, nearly getting one member of the team killed (Millar, Hitch, and Neary). These youths, who clearly idolize the Ultimates, are one of the best examples of why the Ultimates are terrible role models. The Ultimates are able to ignore a lot of the risks of being superheroes thanks to their powers and the support of SHIELD. That fact, coupled with their lies and media manipulation, makes being a superhero seem like all fun and games from an outside perspective. The Defenders want to be idolized like the Ultimates, but are ignorant of the dangers that come with their actions. They associate being superheroes with easy fame and fortune, more than they do actual acts of heroism. At one point in the comic book, the Defenders try to hail a cab to go stop a fire when Iron Man shows up and extinguishes it. A member of the Defenders callously remarks on how "Iron Man's just going to waltz in there and grab all the glory" before being reminded that heroes are supposed to care about helping people rather than fame (Millar, Hitch, and Neary). Using the Ultimates as role models endangered these young people and misinformed them about what being a superhero really means.

The Ultimates do have some admirable qualities, but their deep-seated flaws and sheer number of mistakes prevent them from being real role models. In volumes one and two, most of the public adore the Ultimates. After the Hulk attack, even the naysayers acknowledge the good that the Ultimates are doing. People see the Ultimates as role models, especially compared to other heroes in the Ultimate Universe. At one point, Gail, Captain America's former fiancée, says to him, "It's just nice to see [her grandkids] watching somebody decent for a change, after Spider-Man or one of those horrible X-Men" (Millar, Hitch, Neary, and Currie). As more and more of the Ultimates' flaws and secrets come to light, however, public opinion of the team dips. The Ultimates perform positive acts, but the good the team does is viewed within the context of their flaws and lies. Positive opinions of the Ultimates are less universal, with individuals weighing the team's merits on individual own terms.

Conclusion

The Ultimates do not fit traditional definitions of either heroes or celebrities. They have a secret identity and a super identity, are simultaneously selfless and selfish, and display qualities of both role models and horrible examples. The Ultimates represent a fusion of the concepts of hero and celebrity, a new look at super humans in a media age. With Twitter, Facebook, Google, and the like, we now are immersed in a culture built on fame and have access to almost any information or misinformation at the click of a button; the Ultimates examine how this celebrity and media culture would challenge the supposed purity of the superhero and the superhero narrative.

The Ultimates raise three key points about heroism today. First, *The Ultimates* serves as a warning to would-be heroes about just how easy is to be led astray by fame. All of the members of the Ultimates joined with the best of intentions—they wanted to do good—but all too quickly they fell victim to fame and fortune. They started to care more about looking heroic than actually being heroic. Sadly, real-life public figures are not immune to this hunger for recognition. People like Lance Armstrong, become so enamored with celebrity that they are willing to cheat and lie to hold onto it. *The Ultimates* also calls to mind the emerging movement of real-life superheroes, people who don costumes and go on patrol, whether that means breaking up a mugging or taking pictures of a meth lab. While these real-life superheroes are trying to do good, one must question their methods. Is wearing a costume and roaming the streets looking for trouble really the best course of action, or would it be easier and more effective simply to report crimes to the police? By wearing costumes and giving interviews, these people are attracting a great deal attention, more so than the typical Good Samaritan. Their need to be recognized detracts from their heroism and leads them down a dangerous path.

Secondly, *The Ultimates* reminds us not to accept everything at face value. By giving us a peek behind the curtain, *The Ultimates* reveals all of the superheroes' lies and manipulations, and how the public accepts them. If not for the leak on the team, the information about the Hulk cover up may never have come to light, and society would have gone on believing that the Ultimates saved New York. This serves to remind readers to question what they see and hear. Blindly accepting the information we are given may lead to negative, even catastrophic outcomes. Given *The Ultimates'* publication during the Bush administration's war in Iraq and the choice to have the Ultimates working for the Bush White House, the authors' message seems very deliberate and timely.

Lastly, *The Ultimates* highlights how we hold heroes to impossible standards. At first glance the Ultimates appear to be perfect, but as we get to know them better we see that flaws and doubts plague every character. None of the Ultimates are perfect. Just like in *The Ultimates*, the media-saturated world we live in loves to build heroes and celebrities up, and then turn just as quickly to tear them down the moment they display weakness. It is unrealistic and naïve to think that just because individuals become heroes or celebrities that they are somehow made of sterner stuff than the rest of us. We all have secrets, we all have flaws, and we all have doubts. Yet on a daily basis we see reports tearing into celebrities, heroes, and public figures for the very same issues we face in our own lives. At a time when we need heroes more than ever, such harsh criticism may discourage people from even trying to step up and become heroes

The Ultimates are an entirely new breed of superhero, built upon notions of heroes and celebrities in today's culture. This union created a hero more flawed than ever, but a realistic one, reflective of the struggles that real-life public figures face. Comic books had to evolve to meet changing societal values, and the huge sales of *The Ultimates* show just how receptive society is to this new contemporary hero.

Works Cited

"All-Time USA Box Office." *IMDb*. IMDb.com, n.d. Web. 22 Aug. 2013. http://www.imdb.com/boxoffice/alltimegross.

Baker, Kaysee, and Arthur A. Raney. "Equally Super? Gender-Role Stereotyping of Superheroes in Children's Animated Programs." *Mass Communication & Society* 10.1 (2007): 25–41. *Communication & Mass Media Complete*. Web. 5 June 2013.

Bendis, Brian M. (w), Mark Millar (w), Adam Kubert (p), Danny Miki (i), and John Dell (i). *Ultimate Fantastic Four "The Fantastic"* New York: Marvel, 2004. Print.

"Cage, Luke." *Marvel Universe Wiki RSS*. Marvel, n.d. Web. 10 Oct. 2013.

"Captain America (Steve Rogers)." *Marvel Universe Wiki RSS*. Marvel Comics, n.d. Web. 8 Oct. 2013.

"Civil War." *Marvel Universe Wiki RSS*. Marvel, n.d. Web. 10 Oct. 2013.

Claremont, Chirs (w). *X-Men: The Dark Phoenix Saga*. New York: Marvel, 1980. Print.

Davidson, Rjurick. "Fighting the Good Fight?: Watching *Watchmen*." *Screen Education* 54 (2009): 18–23. *Communication & Mass Media Complete*. Web. 2 June 2013.

Doyle, Andrew. "Mice in Masks and Ageing Superheroes: Using Graphic Novels in the Media Classroom." *Screen Education* 51 (2008): 68–74. *Communication & Mass Media Complete*. Web. 1 June 2013.

Fingeroth, Danny. *Superman on the Couch.* New York: Continuum International, 2004. Print.

Ford, Cody. "Behind the Mask: A Search for Mythic Constructs in *'V for Vendetta.'"* Conference Papers—*National Communication Association* (2009): *Communication & Mass Media Complete.* Web. 4 June 2013.

Fung, Katherine. "Oprah Is Lindsay Lohan's New 'Mentor,' Says Actress' Mother." *The Huffington Post.* TheHuffingtonPost.com, 16 July 2013. Web. 01 Oct. 2013.

Goffe, Leslie. "Is It a Plane? No, It's the First Arab American Super Hero." *Middle East* 439 (2013): 62–63. *Academic Search Complete.* Web. 7 June 2013.

Hampp, Andrew. "For Today's Celeb, Social Status Takes on a New Meaning." *Advertising Age* 82.33 (2011): 76. *Communication & Mass Media Complete.* Web. 3 June 2013.

Hoppenstand, Gary. "Editorial: Not Your Parents' Comics; or Maybe They Are." *Journal of Popular Culture* 39.4 (2006): 521–522. *Communication & Mass Media Complete.* Web. 3 June 2013.

ICv2: Inside Pop Culture. Web. 22 Aug. 2013. http://www.icv2.com/.

"Iron Man (Anthony Stark)." *Marvel Universe Wiki RSS.* Marvel Comics, n.d. Web. 8 Oct. 2013.

Jenkins, Paul, Steve Leiber, Ramon Bachs, and Kee Kobayashi. *Civil War: Front Line* #1. New York: Marvel, 2006. Print.

Millar, Mark (w), Adam Kubent (p), and Art Thibert (i). *Ultimate X-Men "Return to Weapon X."* New York: Marvel, 2002. Print.

Millar, Mark (w), Adam Kubent (p), Andy Kubent (p), and Art Thibert (i). *Ultimate X-Men "The Tomorrow People"* New York: Marvel, 2001. Print.

Millar, Mark (w), Bryan Hitch (p), and Andrew Currie (i). *The Ultimates Volume One: Super-Human,* 5th ed. New York: Marvel, 2005. Print.

Millar, Mark (w), Bryan Hitch (p), and Paul Neary (i). *The Ultimates 2 Volume One: Gods and Monsters.* New York: Marvel, 2005. Print.

Millar, Mark (w), Bryan Hitch (p), Paul Neary (i), and Andrew Currie (i). *The Ultimates Volume Two: Homeland Security,* 2d ed. New York: Marvel, 2004. Print.

North, Adrian C., Victoria Bland, and Nicky Ellis. "Distinguishing Heroes from Celebrities." *British Journal of Psychology* 96.1 (2005): 39–52. *Academic Search Complete.* Web. 3 June 2013.

O'Rourke, Daniel J., and Morgan B. O'Rourke. "'It's Morning Again in America': John Byrne's Re-Imaging of the Man of Steel." *The Ages of Superman: Essays of the Man of Steel in Changing Times.* Ed. Joseph J. Darowski. Jefferson, NC: McFarland, 2012. 115–24. Print.

"Parker, May (Aunt May)." *Marvel Universe Wiki RSS.* Marvel Comics, n.d. Web. 8 Oct. 2013.

Pearson, Jacob. "Commies, Khrushchev and Captain America: The Cold War According to Captain America, Commie Smasher!" Conference Paper. National Communication Association. Nov. 2009. *Communication & Mass Media Complete.* Web. 10 June 2013.

Rhoades, Shirrel. *Comic Books: How the Industry Works.* New York: Peter Lang, 2008. Print.

Rich, Frank. *The Greatest Story Ever Sold: The Decline and Fall of Truth from 9/11 to Katrina.* New York: Penguin, 2006. Print.

Rosenberg-Javors, Irene. "Redefining Heroes." *Annals of the American Psychotherapy Association* (2008): 35. *Academic Search Complete.* Web. 1 June 2013.

Ružička, Jiří G. "American Superheroes and the Politics of Good and Evil." *New Presence: The Prague Journal of Central European Affairs* 12.2 (2010): 46–48. *Academic Search Complete.* Web. 2 June 2013.

Sargent, J. F. "Comic Book Superheroes Face Their Greatest Challenge!" *Extra!* 26.5 (2013): 14–15. *Communication & Mass Media Complete.* Web. 5 June 2013.

Schickel, Richard. "I Blog Therefore I Am." *Society* 47.6 (2010): 521–524. *Academic Search Complete.* Web. 29 May 2013.

Shugart, Helene. "Supermarginal." *Communication & Critical/Cultural Studies* 6.1 (2009): 98–102. *Communication & Mass Media Complete.* Web. 6 June 2013.

Steinberg, Brian. "DC Comics." *Advertising Age* 82.42 (2011): 48. *Communication & Mass Media Complete.* Web. 5 June 2013.

Terrill, Robert E. "Put on a Happy Face: Batman as a Schizophrenic Savior." *Quarterly Journal of Speech* 79.3 (1993): 319. *Communication & Mass Media Complete*. Web. 10 June 2013.
_____. "Spectacular Repression: Sanitizing the Batman." *Critical Studies in Media Communication* 17.4 (2000): 493–509. *Communication & Mass Media Complete*. Web. 10 June 2013.
Treat, Shaun. "How America Learned to Stop Worrying and Cynically Enjoy! The Post–9/11 Superhero Zeitgeist." *Communication & Critical/Cultural Studies* 6.1 (2009): 103–109. *Communication & Mass Media Complete*. Web. 7 June 2013.
Wanzo, Rebecca. "The Superhero: Meditations on Surveillance, Salvation, and Desire." *Communication & Critical/Cultural Studies* 6.1 (2009): 93–97. *Communication & Mass Media Complete*. Web. 6 June 2013.

"No!"
Great Lakes Avengers *and* *the Uses of Enfreakment*

José Alaniz

In the second issue of the 2005 Marvel mini-series *Great Lakes Avengers: Misassembled,* two members of the Wisconsin-based team of oddball heroes, Flatman and Doorman, go on a recruitment drive in New York City. (The group's ranks have been depleted by death, apathy and the profound depression, exacerbated by alcoholism, of leader Mr. Immortal.)

Things don't go so well: over the course of six pages, the duo is turned down by all the superheroes they solicit, either with patient explanations or, increasingly, rude brush-offs. The scene ends with 24 costumed crime fighters, arranged in two 12-panel-grids on two pages, curtly declaring "No" in direct address. (Some gaze with utter disdain, others simply laugh.) To make our protagonists' humiliation complete, a local TV news program broadcasts amateur footage of Doorman on a New York street, tugging on Captain Ultra's cape, begging him to sign up with—as the wry newscaster calls them—"our very own Milwaukee misfits." The flustered Captain responds, "Geez! How many times do I have to tell you? *Get lost!"* for all the world to see (III: 6, emphasis in original).[1]

The scenario's humor derives partly from its parody-by-reversal of a recurring Avengers motif: the need to trim the team's ever-expanding and unwieldy membership rolls,[2] as well as from the fact that most of the waylaid heroes are "C-list" denizens of the Marvel Universe (Brother Voodoo, Paladin, Justice, Firestar, Araña, etc.).[3] The clear implication: everyone wants to join the gold-standard, urban Avengers, but no one wants to belong to a club of third-rate heartland losers like the GLA. But what precisely makes the GLA such an unappealing prospect, even for fellow "joke" superheroes like Captain Ultra (originally a supervillain useless in battle due to his pyrophobia)?[4] What preoccupies

139

me here is the sort of identities, geographic origins and bodies that prompt such scorn and rejection—even after our heroes go on to the save the universe itself from nihilist supervillain Maelstrom. What precedents of human disqualification does writer Dan Slott and artist Paul Pelletier's satirical vision of superheroics evoke?

This essay mines *GLA: Misassembled* for one particularly salient precedent linking figures such as Mr. Immortal, Doorman, Big Bertha, Dinah Soar, Flatman and Squirrel Girl to ethically-fraught practices of display traceable to the early 19th-century USA: the freak show. Indeed, we can read Slott/Pelletier's miniseries as exhibit A for how, over a decade after congressional passage of the Americans With Disabilities Act in 1990, at the dawn of the politically-correct 21st century, "freak discourses" lived on.

Freaks

Among the more bizarre, disconcerting—some would simply say shameful—aspects of 19th-century U.S. visual culture, the freak show (aka sideshow, aka ten-in-one) by the 1840s had institutionalized the exhibition of people with physical differences for entertainment and big business. In traveling tours, as part of carnivals and fairs, and in P.T. Barnum's "infotainment" American Museum (progenitor of dime museums throughout the Victorian USA), albinos, fat ladies, skeleton men, conjoined twins, "armless wonders," dwarfs and countless other "human curiosities" (aka "human oddities") appeared before paying, gawking, astonished, bemused crowds. Plainly exploitative and dehumanizing, the practice nonetheless brought economic opportunity to the performers, making some of them quite rich, and even produced some of the era's best-known celebrities: Jo-Jo the Dog-Faced Boy (Fyodor Jeftichew), Tom Thumb (Charles Stratton), Chang and Eng the Siamese Twins, etc.[5]

Some historians and Disabilities Studies scholars, such as Robert Bogdan, have emphasized the freak show's social construction, given that "[i]n a strict sense of the word, every exhibit was a fraud" (25) made up largely of hype, exaggerated back-stories for the performers and marketing—crucial elements of show business even today. Others speak of the practice's quasi-psychological uses for the ableist masses; David Hevey's opinion of modern attitudes to physical difference and what he calls its "enfreakment" seems appropriate to the freak show: "The use of disabled people is the anchor of the weird, that is, the fear of within. They are used as the symbol of enfreakment or the surrealism of all society" (345).[6] Rosemarie Garland-Thomson, in turn, sees in them a catalyst for the democratic ethos of the 19th-century USA—built on the backs of the disabled:

A freak show's cultural work is to make the physical particularity of the freak into a hypervisible text against which the viewer's indistinguishable body fades into a seemingly neutral, tractable, and invulnerable instrument of the autonomous will, suitable to the uniform abstract citizenry democracy institutes [10].

Leslie Fiedler, in his landmark *Freaks: Myths and Images of the Secret Self* (1978), links the institution to pre-modern enchantment. Writing of the pitiful remnants of the freak show clinging to carnivals, boardwalks and "shoddy storefronts" in his own time, Fiedler noted their enduring fascination:

Even now if the spell works, if we are lucky or stoned or drunk or blessedly simple, we see what we are supposed to see: not some poor unfortunate approximately embodying the myth after which his affliction is named, but the myth itself—the animal hybrid skulking at the edge of the jungle, the Giant taller than the Ogre whom Jack cheated of his harp and hen, the Midget smaller than a mustard seed [283].

Even if such ways of thinking endured into the 20th century, the freak show as site of mainstream entertainment and profit did not. By the 1890s, the increasing medicalization of disabilities, among other factors, led to new attitudes—such as revulsion, pity, and bourgeois disengagement with the practice as a "low culture" form. As Bogdan put it, "human differences are now framed in other modes and by different institutions" (35). So much so that by the early sound era Hollywood would produce a horror movie on the theme: Tod Browning's notorious *Freaks* (1932), about a troupe of freak show performers (played by real disabled people). Garland-Thomson summed up the freak's historical trajectory in this period: "[W]hat aroused awe now inspires horror; what was taken as a portent shifts to a site of progress. In brief, wonder becomes error" (3).

Nonetheless, the freak show did not disappear; it mutated, exhibiting a "restless plasticity" and "determined evolution and reinvention that is almost always coupled with nostalgia for more prosperous times" (Adams 211). "Freak discourse" spread into new media, "proliferat[ing] into a variety of contemporary discourses" (Garland-Thomson 13)—none more so than the sort of daytime television talk show popularized by such figures as Jerry Springer, Maury Povitch and Ricki Lake in the 1990s.[7] Beetlejuice (Lester Napoleon Green, a dwarf with microcephaly) and the late Hank the Angry Drunken Dwarf (Henry Joseph Nasiff) became fixtures of *The Howard Stern Show* in this era. Such fare made it a core premise to place racial, sexual and physical others on stage for public scrutiny—appealing, in the words of Andrea Dennet, to "pure voyeurism" (321). She goes on:

The television talk show is undeniably a late-twentieth-century freak show that uses many of the same conventions established more than a hundred and fifty years ago by the dime museums. The freak show was—and is—about spectacle: it is a place where human deviance is enhanced, dressed, coiffed and propped up for the entertainment of a paying audience. The freak show is about relationships: *us* versus *them,* the normal versus the freaks [325, emphasis in original].[8]

In the new century, reality TV also turned to disabled bodies as spectacle; even more progressive shows (some with disabled producers) such as *Little People, Big World* (TLC, premiered 2006) and *Push Girls* (Sundance Channel, premiered 2012), at times evoked "freak discourse"—*Freakshow* (AMC, premiered 2013) in the most direct sense: the series chronicles a music producer recruiting disabled people for a modern freak show in Venice Beach, California. As Laura Backstrom wrote: "In both freak shows and reality shows, disabled people purportedly chose to display their bodies through media that is more or less exploitative" (684). Non-fiction programs too, like *Carnivàle* (HBO, 2003–2005), made their allusions to the freak show tradition quite explicit in this period.

Finally, the 1990s saw a resurgence in the live sideshow, in which "self-made freaks" and "geeks" performed such age-old carny tricks as sword-swallowing, pounding nails into their noses ("human pincushion"), displaying copious body alterations, biting the heads off live chickens, and so on, as seen in the Jim Rose Circus Sideshow, the Happy Sideshow, Kamikaze Freakshow and Tokyo Shock Boys (Stephens). Still more "downscale" practices, such as dwarf tossing competitions, came into national prominence at about this time as well (Backstrom: 689). In short, as Laura Backstrom argued, by the 1990s "[t]he disability rights movement was able to transform institutional access, legal rights and terminology for some groups, but it fell short of eliminating the freak discourse that surrounds certain extreme bodies" (683).

Comics, too, partook of the freak show's legacy for some of their visual strategies, through—controversially—resorting to a typology of physical and racial differences. Villains in particular owed much of their look to "freak aesthetics," as seen most starkly in the gallery of deformed evil-doers from Chester Gould's *Dick Tracy* strip (debuted 1931). David Mitchell and Sharon Snyder link such techniques to the Gothic, whereby the artist "yok[es] their unnatural visage with an analysis of individual pathology" (144). As inheritors of those traditions, the pioneers of the superhero's Golden Age did not hesitate to create nemeses—e.g., the Joker, Two-Face, the Claw—whose physical ugliness mirrored their disfigured souls, a satisfying contrast to the costumed crime fighters' anatomical idealization. As I have written elsewhere, a major aspect of the Silver Age's decisive break from the genre's first phase involved introducing physical imperfections (and accompanying angst) to the heroes themselves.[9]

As Fiedler noted, Marvel Comics (which innovated the approach) in fact wove terror itself "into the fabric of their fantasy, and their super-heroes are as often hideous Freaks as handsome defenders of the status quo" (307). DC Comics, in cracking open its competitor's playbook, would even refer to the Doom Patrol in their own series as "those fabulous freaks"[10] and similar epithets (among other things a nod to the 1960s counter culture).[11] The foregoing helps, I hope, to situate in time and culture the late 20th and early 21st century superhero iterations to which we now turn—a little less "fabulous," perhaps, but decidedly still partaking of the "freak discourses" (occluded and overt) we have traced now to *GLA: Misassembled.*

Super-Freaks (Mis-)Assemble!

Debuting in *West Coast Avengers*[12] Vol. 2, #46 (July 1989) under artist-scribe John Byrne, the Great Lakes Avengers parodied superhero conventions with a mid–Western, post–Steve Gerber wit. Based in Milwaukee, Wisconsin, the misfit team's original line-up included Flatman (Al Ventura), "the 2-D defender"; Doorman (Demarr Davis), capable of transforming himself into a short-range teleportation device; Big Bertha (Ashley Crawford), fashion-model in civilian life, morbidly-obese strongwoman in battle[13]; Dinah Soar,[14] alien pterodactyl-like female whose language is understood by almost no human; Mr. Immortal (Craig Hollis), the only human to understand Dinah Soar, routinely killed (gruesomely) only to come back to life. In *Misassembled,* the team's ranks are augmented by Squirrel Girl and her squirrel sidekick Monkey Joe (created by, of all people, Steve Ditko—much more famous for his co-creations Dr. Strange and Spider-Man). Initially taken under the wing of Hawkeye (Clint Barton), himself recently fired from the West Coast team, the "bush league" heroes, as the archer called them (Byrne, Oct. 1989: 3) bounced between various titles[15] throughout the 1990s and early 2000s, only occasionally rising above the status of punchline.

Fan reception proved mixed to unmoved, but over the years the "knock-off" Avengers gained a cult following and critical regard as a fine blend of humor and heroism. Matthew Derman of the *Comics Matter* blog saw much to like in the "at least amusing if not endearing" GLA, which he considered "such an indulgently goofy team" that "str[uck] the perfect balance between ludicrous, likeable, and interesting."[16]

The GLA belong to a tradition of superhero parodies or quasi-parodies stretching back at least to Jerry Siegel and Joe Shuster's *Funny Man* (launched 1948), whose zaniness crescendoed with Harvey Kurtzman and Wally Wood's *Superderman* (*MAD* Vol. 1, #4, April-May, 1953), *Batboy and Rubin* (*Mad* Vol. 1, #8, Dec. 1953-Jan. 1954) and similar works. Later series featuring "low-powered" or "quirky" heroes include DC's *The Inferior Five* (debuted in *Showcase* Vol. 1, #62, June 1966) and Marvel's *Howard the Duck* (launched 1976).[17] Having first appeared in an *Avengers* series, the GLA sets itself apart by mocking tropes, situations and continuity particular to that team.

Not unlike in *Howard the Duck's* "man on the street" skewerings of super-heroes, or *Mystery Men's* "ordinary Joe" deflations, *GLA: Misassembled* presupposes a jaded reader who has absorbed the post–Silver Age critique of the genre's pretentions so as to laugh at them, but still appreciates its power to comment on changing mores. The miniseries' title itself satirizes the *Avengers Disassembled* storyline (2004–5),[18] with its evocation of the famous "Avengers Assemble!" rallying cry—while alluding to the freakish corporeal "misassembly" of the GLA's members.

The plot details the team's woes: ongoing humiliations gaining acceptance from the public and other, more "legitimate" superheroes; as well as the steady attrition of their ranks; "cease and desist" orders from the Maria Stark Foundation. The team leader, Mr. Immortal, in particular, suffers loss after loss: not only his own repeated deaths and resurrections,[19] but (through flashbacks) those of his loved ones, each punctuated by the appearance of Deathurge, a black-and-white-garbed angel of death on skis. The killing of his romantic partner Dinah Soar (I: 19) plunges "Mr. I" into full-blown suicidal depression—especially grievous for someone who cannot die.[20] The series culminates with the "ragtag squad of unsanctioned knock-off Avengers" (Derman) rallying to foil Maelstrom's plot to end the universe by accelerating its collapse.

As mentioned, *GLA: Misassembled* pokes fun at the conventions of super-hero comics, especially the Avengers, as seen in the team's use of a "Quin-jetta" car (I:14 and passim). Unlike the East Coasters' hi-tech flying quinjets, the GLA's vehicle gets stuck in traffic, making them arrive late as the "real" Avengers (Captain America, Thor, Scarlet Witch, etc.) dispatch the Animen (I: 15). As Mr. Immortal puts it, "even when we're the home team, we get benched" (I: 16). More pointedly, the mini-series—through its high body count, among other things—skewers the fetishistic, misogynist death and violence that swept the industry in the 1990s/2000s. For example, the scene in which the team discovers the mangled corpse of Monkey Joe (slain by Leather Boy) closely adheres to the storytelling and mise-en-scène of the notorious *Identity Crisis*[21] sequence in which the Elongated Man (Randolph Dibny) finds his dead wife Sue (see Cronin).

The self-reflexive, postmodern touches don't end there: in several (pre- and posthumous) "pop-up" narrations, Monkey Joe breaks the fourth wall to mock fanboy sensitivities ("Write an angry letter to Marvel *today!*" [I:1, emphasis in original]), bad writing ("A flashback within a flashback is *sloppy* storytelling!"

[III: 16. emphasis in original]) and superhero clichés ("A vigilante operating as an urban myth only works for his first year of continuity. Tops." [II: 11]). Finally, *GLA: Misassembled's* provincial setting takes up the postmodernist attack on grand narratives by boldly engaging the often-elided issues of center vs. periphery and class in superhero comics, through a focus on ridiculously "downscale" champions from the heartland. As the blog *Wit War* archly puts it, "Who will protect the Midwest from bank robbers and Z-list villains?"[22]

Most unsettling and radical, however, is the way the Great Lakes Avengers channel "freak discourses" into the superhero genre, recalling strategies whereby "[p]ostmodernist writers have tended to take up inherited tropes such as the grotesque from their predecessors and interrogate the very nature of their historical and artistic allure" (Mitchell and Snyder: 142). The GLA's "freak superhero" model does just that: revive and to a degree rehabilitate the past's dehumanizing representations of physical others so as to re-enflesh, re-inhabit and re-invent them.

In this process, laughter helps. Not because, as Bogdan reports, "by the turn of the century humor and mockery became stronger element [*sic*] of the freak show" (33), linking the GLA to previous (anti-humanist) traditions of disability display—but rather, because laughter can ultimately serve as a catalyst for dissolving borders between "us" and "them." In discussing Salman Rushdie's problematic 1981 novel *Midnight's Children,* with its differently-abled protagonists, Clare Barker rejects concerns that "Freak Studies" authorizes oppression and grotesque-centric modes of analysis, arguing that "Rushdie's levity allows disability to participate aesthetically in the full range of human experience and perception, including humour and the bizarre—like any other aspect of life" (133).

This despite a state of affairs in which, as Mitchell and Snyder note, "the physical 'fact' of disability inevitably overrides the personal coordinates of the autobiographical subject" (160), and as Garland-Thomson maintains:

> Enfreakment emerges from cultural rituals that stylize, silence, differentiate, and distance the persons whose bodies the freak-hunters or showmen colonize and commercialize. Paradoxically, however, at the same time that enfreakment elaborately foregrounds specific bodily eccentricities, it also collapses all those differences into a "freakery," a single amorphous category of corporeal otherness [10].

We are left with an axis of the freakish, the ludicrous, the human: blatant as they are, the GLA's revival of debasing tropes for disability—which the creators then re-dress[23] with new progressive "content" via characterization—participates in the postmodern project of destabilizing identity, of "re-branding" the derogated into the disarming, the monstrous into the amusing, the sadistic into the tragic. We laugh at them and laugh with them. (Sometimes we even cry with them.) In what follows I want to briefly catalog some of the GLA's "freak" inheritance, arguing such evocations of precedent serve not only to proliferate "freak discourse" in the 21st century, but—unlike in other such recent media depictions—to redeem it.

To begin with, the miniseries' romantic relationship between the blond, blue-eyed "all-American" Mr. Immortal and the alien Dinah Soar (some scenes depict them in bed together) recalls the lurid attention paid to the sex life of the freak in previous eras. "Incongruous" pairings between conjoined twins and their spouses, dwarves and giants, and the like, "readily inspired images of transgressive sex" in the 19th century, and became a hallmark of the more permissive TV talk shows (Dennett: 322). As Fiedler observes,

> In a time of kinky sex and compulsory candor, it is precisely such revelations about Freaks that we demand of those who reimagine them. What do they do on the stool? in bed? in all those private moments once considered out of bounds to public curiosity? There have always been some who suspected that the appeal of the Freak was not unlike that of pornography, and in the age of the explicit, the secret is out [335].

More provocatively, in this context the coming out of Flatman/Ventura as a gay man (IV: 6) flirts with homophobia,[24] just as the darkening of Doorman/Davis' skin since his first appearance courts racism[25] and Squirrel Girl's anatomy evokes the freakshow's degrading hyperbole about human/animal hybrids.[26] That each of these potential slips into the dehumanizing tropes of the past is largely sidestepped through acceptance, lack of commentary, humor and superhero "business as usual" tells us much about the very different, post-ADA era in which said tropes now operate.

A similar approach governs the depiction of Big Bertha/Crawford, who of all the GLA most conspicuously recalls a freakshow staple: the fat lady. And, indeed, if "fat people" of the sideshow, especially women, "were among the most openly mocked performers" (Backstrom: 703), with stage names such as Ima Wadler, Jolly Irene, Big Winnie Johnson and Baby Ruth, Bertha suffers her share of verbal abuse: in an early adventure, a mind-controlled She-Hulk calls her "tubbs" and "lard butt" (Byrne, "Baptism of Fire!" 22 and 27).[27]

But again, a significant inversion of the classic freak model takes place: in her Ashley Crawford identity, Bertha finances the team with her earnings as a top fashion model. (She in fact mulls leaving the team for what she deems its toll on her career.) Fully independent, with seemingly no desire to marry, the post-feminist Bertha—not unlike Squirrel Girl—relishes both her multiple identities: "With my powers, I can shape the fat on my body however I like. Without any effort, I can have the ultimate figure, *be* every man's fantasy. Or I can push my gifts to the limit ... and *do* fantastic things! Be a hero. Save the world" (III: 14, emphasis and ellipsis in original).

If modern "fatsploitation" reality shows such as *The Biggest Loser* (NBC, premiered 2004) and *Ruby* (Style Network, premiered 2008) traffic in "cultural moralizing and stigmatizing of fatness, the medicalization of an 'obesity epidemic,' and the increased modern emphasis on the body as a site of control and expression of identity" which "all lead to the dominant cultural representation of obesity through the lens of a body project based on a weight loss imperative" (Backstrom 692), Crawford feels at ease—even complacent—in both her physiques, whether faulting a misogynist photographer for his "tacky" comments (III: 5) or stopping traffic (literally) with her massive girth (III: 3). The traditional mockery of the fat lady is rechanneled into parodying superhero tropes: if in the old days Clark Kent changed into his Superman costume in phone booths, Crawford demolishes one as she transforms into Bertha (I: 14).[28] Or, more edgily, into satirizing bulimia in the fashion industry: Bertha can only change back to Crawford through *mass regurgitation* (III: 4).

For all that, Bertha's "intragender" status as the GLA's "really, really big guy" (usually a male role)[29] makes her too imposing a figure for some: even as she saves a child, her mother denounces the "ample amazon" as a "freak" (I: 11). As Dennet writes about corporeal others in the modern media freakshow, "The Fat Lady still evokes horror" (323), reflecting the stubborn endurance of "a perceived tension between the medicalization and theatricalization of anatomically different bodies" (Stephens).

Such dichotomous, shifting modes of identity return us to the postmodernist aspects of Slott and Pelletier's freak superhero paradigm: self-reflexive, self-parodic—yet empowering; feared, grotesque, laughable—yet embracing of such "archetypal" views of the freak so as to reshape them. The GLA, in the words of Jason Bainbridge, "navigat[e] a 'postmodern' relationship to modernity, 'postmodern' in the sense that they ... advance different ways of resolving the contradictions and problems with modernity" (80).

Disabled figures avidly disrupting stable identities, demolishing grand narratives of the body, and achieving a level of comfort with that instability, recalls Lennard Davis' concept of dismodernism, which perpetually reminds us that "the body is never a single physical thing so much as a series of attitudes toward it," casting disability itself as "an unstable category" (22–23).[30] Garland-Thomson, as noted, sees this "hyper-individualism" of the freak's body in nationalist terms, arguing that for 19th-century audiences it represented "at once boundless liberty and appalling disorder, the former the promise and the latter the threat of democracy" (12).

As it happens, similar discourses of "boundlessness" and "appalling disorder" have commonly adhered to the final critical facet of the GLA's identity that I want to examine: their geographic origins. For their freakishness, so structured by time (the past), is likewise shaped by a very particular place in the U.S. imaginary.

Conclusion: Flyover Freaks

Maelstrom: Unbelievable! I've done it! One of my plans has *finally* borne fruit! And look—there are no hex bolts or magic hammers to thwart me! No quantum force to bar my way! All this time, the solution was so simple! Don't strike at the heart of Manhattan! Or the fabled city of Olympia! When *destroying the universe ...* start in *Milwaukee! Ha ha ha!* [IV: 13, emphasis and ellipsis in original].

Scott Bukatman, more elegantly than most, has linked the costumed crime fighter to urbanity: "Superhero comics embody the grace of the city; superheroes are graced by the city" (188); "Superhero narratives are sagas of propulsion, thrust, and movement through the city" (189)[31]; Superman is "a monument to the modern city" (197). Flatman concurs: "New York City: it's like a superhero nexus.... Doesn't matter if someone's from an underwater kingdom, a Russian super-spy program, or a galaxy far, far away ... they *all* end up in New York" (II: 8, emphasis and ellipses in original). And no less than the other "positive" ideals interrogated in this essay (physical normalcy, democracy, the superhero), the city, too, must have its defining shadowy Other.

In the U.S. cultural imagination—perhaps no more so than in a popular genre synonymous with industrial modernity—one topos in particular emerged to embody the role of anti–Gotham, negative–Metropolis, bizarro–New York: the Midwest. Indeed, at least since Fitzgerald's Nick Caraway the literary image of this region has been of the place *to escape from.* Spurred on by the centripetal force of the center, with its gravity-defying skyscrapers, its sheer verticality, the hero quits (or tries to quit) the great plains: vast, horizontal, prone, passive. Limned as backward, flat, "empty," the middle–American provinciality of a Peoria is what one abandons in search of reinvention in the big city. Hence nothing else figures the finality of Caraway's failure at the end of *The Great Gatsby* quite like his return to the Midwest (see Jacobson 235).

For American Studies scholar Kent Ryden, the north-central swathe from Ohio to the Dakotas denotes "a landscape of absence" (114) which we find "difficult to see ... not because of too much evident history, but because of too little ... it is defined by the absence of a past, a sort of temporal emptiness" (107). He concludes: "The landscape of the rural and small-town Midwest is a historic document, yet it bespeaks not a self-consciously preserved history of national origins but an unremarkable and largely unrecorded history of railroad building, town founding, and generations of work" (115).

Those regional disparities, especially of class, contribute to the Midwest's "ongoing image problem" (116)[32] which renders the land itself a purgatory of displacement and alienation, ripe for ridicule.[33] As captured by Michael Martone:

> [T]he people who know the place only by driving through it know the flatness. They skim along a grade of least resistance. The interstate defeats their best intentions. I see them staring out, big-hearted and romantic, from the density and the variety of the East to see how big this country is. They are well-read, and they have a vision as they come out of the green hills and the vista opens up, a true vision so vast that at night as they drive there are only the farmyard lights that demonstrate plane geometry by their rearranging patterns. And, in the dawn around Sandusky, they have had enough, and they hunker down and drive, looking for the mountains that they know are ahead somewhere [29].

Such dispiriting visions of the heartland underscore what ultimately makes Mr. Immortal, Flatman, Big Bertha and the others so "grotesque": not just their bodies, but their zip code. When the "big apple's" heroes decline the GLA's offer to join up (with varying degrees of disdain), their "no!" signals a rejection of "Smallville" values (and of genre founders Siegel and Shusters' roots in Cleveland, Ohio) no less than an affirmation of their "democratic" corporeal solidarity in Garland-Thomson's terms. As in the funhouse-mirror TV talk shows, the banality of middle America—especially the underclass—exists to be mocked, othered, dehumanized, freaked. We come to an odd place: the periphery (i.e., working/middle class "normality" as experienced by millions of Midwesterners) defined by the center as abnormal—an innate "flyover freakishness."[34]

Such a view—the normal as monstrous, aberrant—plainly reflects the quasi-fascist logic of the superhero, with its veneration of physical and chronotopal paragons: the perfect body in the perfect place at the perfect time. (Of course, it represents a familiar big-city hubris as well.) Leave it, then, to those freakish geographic others, the GLA, to stand up for the sticks—as they do with Maelstrom, a world-class supervillain who (as quoted in the epigraph) believes he has found the ideal site from which to destroy the universe (after all, who would defend Milwaukee?). Just as the GLA defeats him with pluck and "street smarts," by duping him into committing suicide, so too do they resist corporeal/urban homogenization with all the kookiness of the Midwest supercrip.[35]

This explains Doorman's first impression of New York, the city that rebuffs him: "smells like pee" (II: 10); why Crawford, despite innumerable offers to "set up in Rome" and other supermodel-friendly locales, always refuses (III:14); and why Squirrel Girl cheerfully—"Okey-dokey. Why not?"—abandons NYC for Wisconsin to join the team (II: 17). Such deflations of the center show that, for all their chafing, the GLA holds home near and dear to their hearts, and their identities. Hence, too, the local flavor: instead of the Empire State Building, we have Milwaukee's Germania Building (Byrne, "Franchise" 19); the I-94 replaces the Lincoln Tunnel (I: 15), etc. Not "empty" at all, the periphery's quirky specificity defies the center's sameness. *Vive la différence!*

The group's oxymoronic name, too, connotes something more than just pathetic "also-rans"; it redefines the term "Avengers," democratizing it beyond its bi-coastal roots. Such expansive revisionism dovetails with recent sociocultural changes, including as I've argued the revival of the freak in the U.S. visualscape. As Elizabeth Stephens writes:

> 21st-century freak shows can best be understood as both the latest in a long history of public exhibitions of bodies identified as anatomically unusual and, simultaneously, as active agents in the recent transformation of the popular understanding of the freak show ... [they] represent not only a re-emergence but also a reinvention of the traditional freak shows they reference.

Thus, through their "postmodern" engagement with the stigmatizing "modern" tropes they've inherited, contemporary freaks such as the GLA reassess, reinvent, redeem, and celebrate them—in the process doing the same for the "freakish" other of the superhero city, the Midwest. "Okay, so maybe we weren't anything to write home about," concedes Mr. Immortal, "but we had *heart!*" (I: 12, emphasis in original). Having "heart"—along with amusing, vital imperfections—makes the GLA heroes first and foremost of the crudely, awkwardly *normal.*

After all, what could be more "American" than this reality-TV variant of Warhol's 15 minutes of fame: the idea that anybody—*anybody*—can be an Avenger?

Notes

1. The *Great Lakes Avengers: Misassembled* trade paperback contains no page numbers. The count is my own; roman numerals refer to chapter corresponding to original issue publication.

2. As well known, the team's membership has rarely remained stable for long. In "The Space Phantom," in only the series' second issue, the volatile Hulk quits the team (Lee/Kirby, *The Avengers* Vol. 1, #2, Nov. 1963). "The order changeth" issues, in which a new roster emerges (along with a view into the politics of such determinations), became a hallmark of the series. To take only two more recent examples, in "On the Matter of Heroes!" (Michelinie and Byrne, *The Avengers* Vol. 1, #181, Mar. 1979), government liaison Henry Peter Gyrich confronts a room packed with over two dozen Avengers: "[T]here are just too blasted *many* of you! The national security council can't even keep track of who's coming and going!" (11, emphasis

in original). Gyrich would establish the team's roster at seven. But by the time of "Too Many Avengers!" (Busiek and Pérez, *The Avengers* Vol. 3, #3, May 1998), the team's ranks had swollen to 39.

3. Pelletier's page design emphasizes the "disposability" of these lesser stars; while "marquee" heroes like Wolverine and Spider-Man appear in large, oblong frames, the "second-stringers" merit only the 12-panel grid treatment. Ironically, Justice and Firestar were former members of the "real" Avengers, who joined during writer Kurt Busiek and artist George Pérez's run of the late 1990s and early 2000s.

4. See "Look Out for the Frightful Four" (Thomas and Pérez, *Fantastic Four* Vol. 1, #177, Dec. 1976).

5. See Fiedler, chapter 11 and Adams, Bogdan and Garland-Thomson for overviews of the freak show. Bogdan's seminal history *Freak Show: Presenting Human Oddities for Amusement and Profit* (Chicago: University of Chicago Press, 1988) remains the most thorough source on the subject.

6. Mitchell and Snyder link the dehumanizing representation of disability and physical difference to "literature's dependency upon idiosyncratic, scandalous subject matter" (148).

7. Among the talk shows' conventions harking back to the historical freak show, Backstrom includes "the host as lecturer, the lineup of guests who have unusual personal issues, and the highlighting of transgressive sex and incongruous couples" (683).

8. The cultural historian Rachel Adams adds, "Times have changed, and TV talk shows, reality programs, late-night pornography, and science fiction have claimed the cultural position once occupied by freak shows" (210).

9. See Alaniz, chapter 1.

10. See my discussion of freak discourse and imagery in the original Arnold Drake/Bruno Premiani run of *Doom Patrol* in Alaniz, chapter 5.

11. See Fiedler, chapter 12 on the word and its use in the counter culture and underground comix, including Gilbert Shelton's *The Fabulous Furry Freak Brothers*. Garland-Thomson traces the etymology of "freak" in greater detail (3–4).

12. One might call the GLA a third-rate Avengers, given that they debuted in a series that sought to expand the Avengers franchise to the West, yet was itself seen by some in the fan community as overly derivative of the "real thing." *West Coast Avengers* (renamed *Avengers West Coast*, as it happened, around the time of the GLA's first appearance) ran in two volumes from 1984 to 1994.

13. As pointed out by Derman, the team trafficked in "stolen" character designs: Big Bertha recalls the X-Men villain the Blob (who worked for the Circus of Crime); Doorman resembles Spider-Man in his symbiote phase; while Flatman clearly brings to mind the Fantastic Four's Mr. Fantastic—all of which demonstrates how altering one element of a costume or power (gender for the Blob, three-dimensionality for Mr. Fantastic) renders an otherwise familiar character "ridiculous").

14. The name references the entertainer and television host Dinah Shore (1916–1994).

15. See for example *The Thunderbolts* Vol. 1, #15–17 (1998).

16. Likeable enough, in fact, to garner coverage in the local Milwaukee press; see Weiland.

17. A more complete list of superhero parodies would include Marvel's humor series *Not Brand Echh* (1967–1969) and *What the_?!* (1988–1993), *The Sensational She-Hulk* (1989–1993), as well as much of Grant Morrison's run on DC's *Doom Patrol* Vol. 2 (1989–1993). Other publishers and imprints have produced similar material in the post-revisionist era, such as *Flaming Carrot, The Tick, The Boys, Kick-Ass* and *Freshmen*. Discourses on so-called "real-life superheroes" (RLSH), such as the documentary *Superheroes* (d. Mike Barnett, 2011), often cast them as "oddball" working class types, a theme I pick up in my conclusion.

18. Three of the miniseries' covers parody the "noirish," "grim and gritty" aesthetics of the post–*Civil War* era, advanced by such artists as Mike Deodato, and which peaked in *Dark Avengers* (launched 2009).

19. The reader may construe these repetitive, gory deaths as Mr. Immortal's "perfor-

mances," of the sort freaks like Charles Tripp, the "armless wonder" who could write with his feet, would put on for sideshow audiences.

20. While parodying the "revolving door of death" superhero convention, Mr. Immortal's ability to die and come back is given a metaphysical gloss in the series. Moreover, it subverts the genre's death-denying logic by "programming" mortality into each issue (both through his and that of several others throughout the storyline), reflecting a new openness in U.S. culture to discuss the topic after the Death with Dignity and hospice movements of the 1970s/80s. In fact, writes the blog *Wit War*, death in *GLA: Misassembled* is handled with sensitivity for grief over loss despite the comedic approach—quite a rare blend. This double-voicedness on death precedes Slott; in the Byrne-scripted "Baptism of Fire!," Mr. Immortal dies nobly from radiation poisoning to save the team, in what amounts all the same to a spoof of Mr. Spock's "death" in the resolution of *Star Trek II: The Wrath of Khan* (1982).

21. The *Identity Crisis* miniseries and "mega-event" ran from June to December 2004.

22. For more on literary parody's functions, including its resonances with postmodernism, see Morson, Chapter 4, Part I.

23. Literally re-dress, since at the end of *Misassembled* the team gives up the Avengers identity, takes the name GLX, and dons white, black and yellow leather à la Morrison-era X-Men (IV: 23). The group's many aliases over the years—Great Lakes Champions, Great Lakes Defenders, Lightning Rods, Great Lakes Initiative—underscores their "postmodern" destabilization of identity.

24. Although the representation of Ventura's homosexuality in fact flouts the historical reputation of "Skeletal Men" as "anaphrodisiac"; see Fiedler's comments on the career of the 19th-century freakshow performer Claude Seurat (133–134).

25. As a comparison of the relevant panel from "Franchise's" original publication (Byrne, "Franchise" 29) and its reprint in the *GLA: Misassembled* trade paperback plainly shows. Davis' identity as an African American, though seemingly retconned after his debut, goes unremarked in a later story, "Working Holiday" (Slott and Grist). The "post-racial" tale, in fact, focuses much more attention on his role as the new angel of death after Deathurge's "demotion."

26. Bogdan reports that "pre- and post–Darwinian discussions about the place of human beings in the great order of things and the relationships of the various kinds of humans to each other and to baboons, chimps and gorillas" (29) led to the freakshow's promotion of congenitally-deformed performers such as Seal-Boy, Alligator Boy and Grace McDaniels the Mule Woman (see also Fiedler, chapter 6). Still the most famous in our own time is the Victorian-era Elephant Man, Englishman Joseph Merrick. For more on freaks as sexually and biologically "ambiguous," see Grosz.

27. The choice of She-Hulk here is significant; on this figure as an assimilationist, hypersexualized model of what I call the "borderline" case of disabled superhero, see Alaniz, chapter 4.

28. She even says, "This is a job for..." as she does it. Big Bertha's depiction coincides with the rise of civil rights organizations such as the National Association to Advance Fat Acceptance (founded 1969). On the fraught relationship between the fat community and disability rights movements, especially as it pertains to women, see Backstrom 691.

29. Scott Bukatman, who coined the term, sees such figures as "the most explicitly monstrous bodies in the superhero canon" and "often objects of self-pity" (64). Alternatively, these body types tend to skew villainous, e.g., the Kingpin, the Blob, Mongul.

30. For much more on dismodernism applied to superhero comics, see Alaniz, chapter 5.

31. The issue of propulsion, in fact, fuels Hawkeye's frustration with the GLA's lear jet when, in the middle of the group's first major adventure, he rails: "Can't you get this crate to go any *faster*?" (Byrne, "Baptism of Fire!" 3, emphasis in original). For a "real" superhero from New York City, it goes too slow.

32. As essayist C.J. Hribal describes the region, "in the middle of the middle of nowhere, at least as far as the rest of the country's concerned. Flyover country, as we're known to the coasts. You say to someone you're from Wisconsin and their eyes glaze over. And even if you

never leave the state, you know what they're saying about you. But it's not that so much as the feeling of insignificance that gnaws at you…" (quoted in Ryden 104).

33. *GLA: Misassembled* abounds in such put-downs, e.g., the description of Crawford's photographer: "that man's a legend … *in Milwaukee"* (III: 5, emphasis and ellipsis in original). The critique of the Midwest blurs into that of the suburbs in postwar U.S. literary culture.

34. Literalizing the trope, the 2002 miniseries *The Thing: Freakshow,* depicts a small town in the rural Midwest as inhabited by alien Kree, Skrulls and sideshow freaks—likening the disabled to extraterrestrials in problematic fashion, to say the least. At the end, an Interstate 80 sign reads "New York 568 miles" (Johns and Kolins, "It's Clobberin' Time!" 22).

35. In their reaction against the hyper-urban ethos of the superhero, in fact, we may recognize the vestiges of Greil Marcus' rural portrait of the "old Weird America."

Works Cited

Adams, Rachel. *Sideshow U.S.A: Freaks and the American Cultural Imagination.* Chicago: University of Chicago Press, 2001.

Alaniz, José. *Death, Disability and the Superhero: The Silver Age and Beyond.* Jackson: University Press of Mississippi, 2014.

Backstrom, Laura. "From the Freak Show to the Living Room: Cultural Representations of Dwarfism and Obesity." *Sociological Forum,* 27, #3 (2012): 682–707.

Bainbridge, Jason. "'Worlds Within Worlds': The Role of Superheroes in the Marvel and DC Universes." *The Contemporary Comic Book Superhero.* Ed. Angela Ndalianis. New York: Routledge, 2009: 64–85.

Barker, Clare. *Postcolonial Fiction and Disability: Exceptional Children, Metaphor and Materiality.* Houndmills, Basingstoke, Hampshire: Palgrave Macmillan, 2011.

Benfield, John. "Comics: John Reviews *Great Lakes Avengers: Misassembled* By Dan Slott and Paul Pelletier." *Wit War.com* (Apr. 21, 2009). http://witwar.wordpress.com/2009/04/21/comics-john-reviews-great-lakes-avengers-misassembled-by-dan-slott-and-paul-pelletier/.

Bogdan, Robert. "The Social Construction of Freaks." *Freakery: Cultural Spectacles of the Extraordinary Body.* Ed. Rosemarie Garland-Thomson. New York: New York University Press, 1996: 23–37.

Bukatman, Scott. *Matters of Gravity: Special Effects and Supermen in the 20th Century.* Durham: Duke University Press, 2003.

Byrne, John. "Baptism of Fire!" *Avengers West Coast,* Vol. 2, #48 (Oct. 1989).

_____. "Franchise." *West Coast Avengers,* Vol. 2, #46 (July 1989).

Cronin, Brian. "Meta-Messages—The Great Lakes Avengers Poke Some Fun at *Identity Crisis.*" Comic bookResources.com (July 14, 2013). http://goodcomics.comic bookresources.com/2013/07/14/meta-messages-the-great-lakes-avengers-poke-some-fun-at-identity-crisis/.

Davis, Lennard J. *Bending Over Backwards: Disability, Dismodernism, and Other Difficult Positions.* New York: New York University Press, 2002.

Dennett, Andrea Stulman. "The Dime Museum Freak Show Reconfigured as Talk Show." *Freakery: Cultural Spectacles of the Extraordinary Body.* Ed. Rosemarie Garland-Thomson. New York: New York University Press, 1996: 315–326.

Derman, Matthew. "John Byrne's *West Coast Avengers* Part 2: Great Lakes Avengers." *Comics Matter* (Nov. 2013). http://comicsmatter.blogspot.com/2013/11/john-byrnes-west-coast-avengers-part-2.html.

Fiedler, Leslie A. *Freaks: Myths and Images of the Secret Self.* New York: Simon & Schuster, 1978.

Garland-Thomson, Rosemarie. "Introduction: From Wonder to Error—A Genealogy of Freak Discourse in Modernity." *Freakery: Cultural Spectacles of the Extraordinary Body.* Ed. Rosemarie Garland-Thomson. New York: New York University Press, 1996: 1–19.

Grosz, Elizabeth. "Intolerable Ambiguity: Freaks as/at the Limit." *Freakery: Cultural Spectacles of the Extraordinary Body*. Ed. Rosemarie Garland-Thomson. New York: New York University Press, 1996: 55–66.

Hevey, David. "The Enfreakment of Photography." *The Disability Studies Reader*. Ed. Lennard Davis. New York: Routledge, 1997: 332–347.

Jacobson, Joanne. "The Idea of the Midwest." *Revue Française D'études Américaines* #48/49: La Terre Américaine (Apr.–July 1991): 235–245.

Johns, Geoff, and Scott Kolins. "It's Clobberin' Time!" *The Thing: Freakshow*, Vol. 1, #4 (Nov. 2002).

_____, and _____. "Old Friends." *The Thing: Freakshow*, Vol. 1, #2 (Sept. 2002).

_____, and _____. "Rock Bottom." *The Thing: Freakshow*, Vol. 1, #1 (Aug. 2002).

_____, and _____. "Strange Things." *The Thing: Freakshow*, Vol. 1, #3 (Oct. 2002).

Martone, Michael. "The Flatness." *A Place of Sense: Essays in Search of the Midwest*. Iowa City: University of Iowa Press for the Iowa Humanities Board, 1988: 29–33.

Mitchell, David T., and Sharon L. Snyder. *Narrative Prosthesis: Disability and the Dependencies of Discourse*. Ann Arbor: University of Michigan Press, 2001.

Morson, Gary S. *The Boundaries of Genre: Dostoevsky's Diary of a Writer and the Traditions of Literary Utopia*. Austin: University of Texas Press, 1981.

Ryden, Kent C. *Sum of the Parts: The Mathematics and Politics of Region, Place, and Writing*. Iowa City: University of Iowa Press, 2011.

Slott, Dan, and Paul Grist. "Working Holiday." *GLX-Mas Special* 1, #1 (Feb. 2006): n.p.

Slott, Dan and Paul Pelletier. *Great Lakes Avengers: Misassembled*. New York: Marvel, 2005.

Stephens, Elizabeth. "Twenty-First Century Freak Show: Recent Transformations in the Exhibition of Non-Normative Bodies." *Disability Studies Quarterly* 25, #3 (Summer 2005). http://dsq-sds.org/article/view/580/757.

Weiland, Rob. "Hales Corners, Meet Squirrel Girl: Getting to Know Milwaukee's Own Great Lakes Avengers." Avclubwww (May 10, 2012). http://www.avclub.com/milwaukee/articles/hales-corners-meet-squirrel-girl-getting-to-know-m,73677/.

The Uncivil Debate Within Marvel's *Civil War*

MARK EDLITZ

"Civil blood makes civil hands unclean."—William Shakespeare

The notion of heroes fighting against each other is a fairly well-worn trope of the superhero genre. What distinguishes Marvel's *Civil War* (which began in the summer of 2006 and ran for seven installments) from the many other examples published by Marvel and DC Comics is that the conflict is instigated by a significant dispute rather than by a mere gimmick or misunderstanding that's contrived to get caped crusaders fighting each other. *Civil War*, written by comic book Mark Millar and illustrated by Steve McNiven, is a polemical allegory that explores a vital question relating to civil liberties and national security that has perplexed and divided post–9/11 America: Are there times when national security trumps constitutionally protected civil liberties?

The story begins when the New Warriors, a team of rash and inexperienced superheroes, attempts to capture a group of deadly supervillains, including Nitro, who are on the FBI's most wanted list. The New Warriors' imprudent attack doesn't go to plan and in the chaos Nitro escapes. Namorita, a D-level superhero, chases the evildoer to an elementary school and body checks him into a school bus. Refusing to be imprisoned, Nitro lives up to his name and detonates himself. Not only does he successfully eliminate his would-be captor but he also devastates the entire school. Hundreds of people, mostly children and teachers, are killed in the explosion. As a result of this tragedy and decades of superhero vigilantism, the government implements the Superhuman Registration Act (SHRA), legislation that requires all superheroes to register with the government and to reveal their secret identities.

Whose Side Are You On?

The SHRA ruptures ideological solidarity among superheroes, and many super friends become super enemies. The promotional materials for *Civil War* asked: "Whose Side Are You On?"—encouraging readers to engage in the debate and pick a group for which to root. The Avengers are divided regarding the SHRA. Iron Man and Hank Pym, two founding members of the Avengers, along with such Marvel heavy hitters as Mister Fantastic, She-Hulk and The Thing favor the legislation. Captain America becomes the leader of those who oppose it, and he is joined by Falcon, Punisher, and Daredevil. It's fitting that Iron Man and Captain America would serve as the figureheads for the opposing viewpoints. As Millar said, "[T]hese guys always seemed like the big ones to me. They also perfectly summed up the argument between rational pragmatism and traditionalist idealism" ("Mark Millar's Civil War Post-Game Show").

As a senior member of the Avengers, Iron Man quickly becomes the leader of the pro-legislation camp. Stark believes the legislation will ensure that the "the kids, the amateurs and sociopaths" are "weeded out" of the superhero business. He believes that for the greater good it's imperative that super powered beings "be better-trained and publicly accountable" (Millar).

He is ideologically opposed by Captain America who sees the SHRA as an unconstitutional infringement by the government on the civil liberties of America's citizens; rights that are guaranteed by the Bill of Rights. He correctly fears that the law will split the superhero community "down the middle" and force them go to "war with one another." Cap believes that "super heroes need to stay above politics," lest they risk becoming partisan or unprincipled mouthpieces for the government (Millar).

In the *Civil War* spin-off, "The War at Home #6" (*Amazing Spider-Man* #537, Feb. 2007), which is written by J. Michael Straczynski, Captain America elucidates his reasoning by quoting from Mark Twain's *Letters from the Earth* (1909): "Each must for himself alone decide what is right and what is wrong, and which course is patriotic and which isn't. You cannot shirk this and be a man. To decide it against your convictions is to be an unqualified and inexcusable traitor, both to yourself and to your country. Let men label you as they may." In the same conversation, Captain America says:

> Doesn't matter if the whole country decides that something wrong is something right. This nation was founded on one principle above all else: the requirement that we stand up for what we believe, no matter the odds or the consequences. When the mob and the press and the whole world tell you to move, your job is to plant yourself like a tree beside the river of truth, and tell the whole world—"No, you move" [Straczynski].

Wasp echoes her colleague's concern, but with a different rationale, when she frets, "Pension plans and annual vacation time? It's ridiculous. What are they trying to do? Turn us into civil servants?" (Millar). In the Marvel Universe, being a "civil servant" is akin to working for the DMV, and that's just a step above being a supervillain. In essence, Wasp's complaint comes not from ethical reasons, but annoyance at the looming bureaucracy she will encounter.

While Iron Man and Captain America are steadfast in their beliefs, not all the heroes are entrenched in their views; some rethink their attitudes towards the SHRA. Spider-Man, for instance, initially has conflicting feelings concerning the legislation, but with cajoling from Tony Stark he changes his mind and participates in a press conference to demonstrate his support for it. During the press event, Parker, who in his own comic book titles has steadfastly protected his identity to shield his Aunt May and wife, Mary Jane, from harm, now proudly declares, "My name is Peter Parker and I've been Spider-Man since I was fifteen years old" (Millar). And just like that, Peter Parker comes out of the superhero closet.

However, after making such a bold show of support for the SHRA, he again reconsiders his position. He flip-flops once more and quits the Avengers after Goliath, a superhero who opposes the legislation, is killed by an out of control clone of Thor. In "The War at Home #4" (*Amazing Spider-Man* #535, Nov. 2006), Parker confronts Stark about imprisoning superheroes without due process and in "The War at Home #5" (*Amazing Spider-Man* #536, Dec. 2006), he says that the price of supporting the SHRA is "the cost of silence is the soul of the country ... if the cost of tacit support is that we lose the very things that make this nation the greatest in human history—then the price is too high" (Straczynski).

Some Avengers refuse to take sides. Doctor Strange, for example, doesn't endorse either faction. Instead, he protests the situation by fasting—a nonviolent method human rights leader Mahatma Gandhi employed to protest England's rule of India. From Strange's point of view, "there is no right or wrong in this debate. It is simply a matter of perspective..." (Millar).

Civil War generated a number of spin-off and tie-in series, including the aforementioned "War at Home," where other writers were given an opportunity to further explore the themes that were introduced in *Civil War* and played out in scores of other comics, among them *The Amazing Spider-Man, Iron Man, The New Avengers,* and *Wolverine*—usually with subtitles that further reinforce the "war" theme, including *Front Line, Battle Damage Report, War Crimes,* and *Casualties of War.* In these stories, writers weren't bound to align themselves with Millar's main book, which took a pro-legislation stance.

One interesting dissenting view was explored in *The New Avengers* #22 (Sept. 2006), in which Iron Man tries to convince Luke Cage, an African American superhero, to support the SHRA. However, Cage argues that the SHRA is an unjust law that should be disobeyed until it is repealed. He reminds Iron Man that "slavery used to be a law" too. Cage likens the initiative to other systemic abuses of power when he says, "Is it Mississippi in the 1950s now?"—clearly referring to the Jim Crow segregation laws that lasted from 1876 to 1965 and took its name from a song and dance act in which a white performer in black face pejoratively caricatured African Americans (Bendis).

It's not totally surprising that billionaire industrialist Tony Stark is a little too trusting in his government. As a rich, white man his interests are sometimes served and protected by siding with the government. But other heroes, like Luke Cage and Falcon, are sensitive to the ways that racism, prejudice, and legal and financial inequality can be reinforced and eventually institutionalized by bad legislation.

The anti-registration theme adopted by other writers surprised Millar: "A lot of the tie-ins were interesting because the other writers chose to go *against* registration, but I don't believe for a second people would feel that way in the real world" ("Mark..."). Millar is right that in the "real world" most people would object to masked vigilantes. But real world ideology and the heightened reality of comics cannot always amicably, or dramatically, co-exist. In the comic book world, the Avengers are necessary because the government cannot sufficiently protect its citizens from these oversized threats. The Avengers represent a national fantasy that was shattered in 2001: the belief that the citizens of the United States could be shielded from external harm.

In comics the Avengers are positioned as the moral center of their universe, and as a result readers empathize with them. So it's profoundly disconcerting when superheroes like Captain America are depicted as the bad guys. Millar has to work harder to sell that premise, which helps to explain why he made Nitro's victims young school children. He bet that readers would be so outraged at the loss of so many innocent lives that they too would *want* superhero accountability. In fact, Millar and the editors at Marvel upped the violence that begins the series in order to ensure that readers would understand the need for the SHRA. In early drafts, the story began with the death of just one person (at different stages Tony Stark's friend Happy Hogan and a "little kid" were suggested as sacrificial lambs) but as the scope of the series increased it was decided that a more dramatic inciting incident was needed ("Civil War Room" and "Civil War Sketch Book").

Millar elicits further comparison to 9/11 when in the wake of the fictional tragedy of the destruction of the school the Avengers descend on ground zero of that destruction. Iron Man, Captain America and other superheroes join rescue workers as they search for survivors. The scene deliberately evokes images of the devastation and recovery efforts at the World Trade Center.

The entire series is filled with thinly veiled references to post–9/11 America. Stark tells Peter Parker, "We live in a time when everyone has to make sacrifices of their privacy. Wiretaps. Increased surveillance. Random searches at airports. Do you really think we would be immune to [sacrifices of our personal freedoms] for long? After what happened in Stamford?" (Straczynski).

In an effort to give a voice to the victims of the tragedy, Millar invents Miriam Sharpe, whose child was killed in the explosion. Sharpe believes that superheroes are teaching impressionable youth that they can "live outside the law as long as they're wearing tights." At her son's funeral she tells Stark that the "blood of my little Damien is on your hands." She accuses him of misguiding America's children by teaching the dangerous lesson that "all you need are some powers and a badass attitude, and you can have a place in [Stark's] private super-gang" (Millar).

Super-gang is an interesting choice of words. "Gang" connotes a group of unsavory characters who make their own rules and act outside the law, often by means of brute-force and intimidation. Gangs are often linked by ethnicity—the Latin Kings, the Jews of Murder Incorporated, the Italian and Irish Mafias, to name a few. In the case of the Avengers, the "gang" is linked not by ethnicity (although many members are white males) but by superpowers.

Despite the reoccurring presence of Miriam Sharpe, the debate about the SHRA becomes steadily less concerned with the victims of the school tragedy and more concerned with the political repercussions of the legislation. Before he becomes a fatality in the civil war Goliath warns Ms. Marvel, a pro-legislation hero, that one probable consequence of the tragedy will be a series of "witch hunts" (Millar). Goliath is referring to Senator Joseph McCarthy's House Un-American Activities Committee, which was established in 1938, but gained great notoriety in the early 1950s, when Senator McCarthy conducted a series of hearings intended to expose the internal threat to America posed by communists and communist sympathizers and to root out American citizens suspected of communist ties. Under the guise of keeping America safe, the reckless McCarthy injured or destroyed many innocent lives and stoked the flames of fear that made many Americans suspicious of one another.

In "The War at Home #4," Reed Richards, a pro-legislation superhero, talks about his Uncle Ted, who was called before McCarthy's HUAC committee, and refused to "name names" and as a result was blacklisted, "lost his life savings, his home, and in the end … it killed him" (Straczynski). But despite knowing the personal costs to its long-term well-being as a democratic society when the government abuses its power, Reed still believes it's necessary to follow the law, irrespective of whether it's just or not.

Civil War is, in many ways, a referendum on George W. Bush and the American government's response to 9/11. The story mirrors how the administration of President George W. Bush sought to justify the suspension of many civil rights as a means of finding, capturing, and killing terrorists. President Bush also signed into law the Patriot Act, a piece of legislation that extended the government's powers that was drafted and voted upon by the overwhelming majority of members of both parties in the aftermath of 9/11. The Patriot Act empowered the government to perform warrantless wiretaps, suspend due process, and to engage in other previously unconstitutional forms of surveillance and law enforcement, even condoning torture.

The Patriot Act became widely criticized for abridging the rights of Americans and trampling on the U.S. Constitution. The American Civil Liberties Union, the civil rights watchdog group, maintains that since the inception of the Patriot Act the U.S. has become a "surveillance society," that "the government has asserted sweeping power to conduct dragnet collection and analysis of any American's telephone calls and e-mails, web browsing records, financial records, credit reports and library records. The government has also asserted expansive authority to monitor American's peaceful political and religious activities" ("America's...").

The erosion of civil liberties is further dramatized when Tony Stark and his operatives lock up superheroes who oppose the SHRA in "Number Forty-Two," a detention center in the Negative Zone, a dimension chiefly absent of life. "Number Forty-Two" is Marvel's Guantanamo Bay detention camp, the controversial military prison whose prisoners can be held indefinitely and without legal rights.

There are numerous other allusions to politics and war thrown into this superhero stew. Anti-registration supporters are referred to as "rebels" who have joined the "resistance." While Captain America remains imprisoned, a "small band of Cap's followers remain radicalized in the Underground Movement" (Millar). They are offered "amnesty" if they turn themselves in. Superheroes are referred to as "weapons of mass destruction" and reporters are "embedded" in their ranks.

In the final battle, Hercules, the Greco-Roman hero, fights a clone of Thor, the Norse god of War. During the melee, Hercules wields Thor's hammer and crashes it down on the cloned Thor's head while shouting, "I knew Thor ... Thor was a friend mine ... And you know something imposter? Thou art no Thor!" (Millar). The line is an allusion to the 1988 Vice Presidential debate, when Senator Lloyd Bentsen turned to the inexperienced and callow Dan Quayle, who was comparing himself to John F. Kennedy, and said, "I served with Jack Kennedy. I knew Jack Kennedy. Jack Kennedy was a friend of mine. Senator, you're no Jack Kennedy" (Holley). Quayle never recovered from Bentsen's smack down, and neither does the Thor clone.

Deconstructing Superheroes

Although *Civil War* is primarily a meditation on how abused government powers can curtail civil liberties it is also an examination of the superhero genre. In the seventh issue, Captain America calls on the anti-legislation superheroes to fight against Iron Man's army with the familiar battle cry, "Avengers Assemble!" However, his call to action catches some pro-legislation heroes off-guard including Bishop, a former member of the X-Men, who wonders, "What's he talking about? I thought our side was the Avengers" (Millar). Bishop's confusion raises the crucial question of the essential nature of the Avengers.

The Avengers, a rotating roster of superheroes, is not a fixed group; it is a team that is in constant flux. In the first issue of *The Avengers* published in 1963, the founding members are Iron Man, Thor, Hulk, Henry Pym and The Wasp. But over the years the group's ranks swelled to a massive number of characters who have obtained Avengers membership.

Who were the true Avengers during *Civil War*? Was it Iron Man and his supporters or Captain America and his allies, who sometimes call themselves the Secret Avengers? The idea that different constituent members reshape the whole but, somewhat paradoxically, that individual members cannot easily be separated from the whole is addressed in a passage from Corinthians. "For the body does not consist of one member but of many. If the foot should say, 'Because I am not a hand, I do not belong to the body,' that would not make it any less a part of the body. And if the ear should say, 'Because I am not an eye, I do not belong to the body,' that would not make it any less a part of the body.'

Millar's *Civil War* is bursting with ideas and story threads that can't be properly explored in just seven issues. Tantalizing ideas, questions and provocations are dropped—waiting for other writers to pick them up and run with them. One small example concerns heroes with multiple identities: when the anti-legislation heroes go underground they are forced to assume new secret identities because their old ones have been compromised. Millar introduces the idea of a *triple* identity. Captain America ceases to be Steve Rogers and becomes Brett Hendrick a "security supervisor at a shopping mall in Queens" (Millar). Though it seems degrading for Captain America to become a rent-a-cop, even in the guise of this new persona, he's serving the community. But what happens if a hero has to sustain a new fraudulent identity over a long period of time? Might it gradually chip away at his original identity and begin to transform him? Might it eventually alter his nature, his values and his behavior? In his novel *Mother Night* (1961), Kurt Vonnegut writes, "We are who we pretend to be, so we must be careful about who it is we pretend to be" (qtd. in Fingeroth).

By the story's end, the government learns the secret identities of many of the heroes in the Marvel Universe. But in an era where websites like Julian Assange's WikiLeaks are devoted to publishing classified intelligence, it's just a matter of time before the wrong people get their hands on the information. How would the superhero genre change if secret identities didn't exist? Would that enrich storytelling possibilities or limit them?

Other ideas that were introduced include an ominous-sounding initiative, which calls for "at least one super-team in every U.S. State." The goal is "decentralizing this [superhero] community from a single coast and building a super-power for the twenty-first century" (Millar). This initiative is intended to mirror the design of Congress, which was created to spread both the power and the responsibilities of the government and ensure that the particular needs of every state are addressed. But isn't the idea of a superhero group in every state an instance of overreach? Might multiple teams lead to turf wars and confirm Miriam Sharpe's belief that superheroes are nothing more than gangs?

Who Won?

Because *Civil War* is not the *Face the Nation*, a forum for political discussion, the story ends not with measured and well-reasoned closing arguments, but with a slugfest. In the final grudge match, Captain America gets the better of Iron Man and bashes him repeatedly with his shield. Iron Man's armor splits open and just as Captain America is ready to deliver a punishing blow to his old friend he is stopped by a group of outraged EMTs and paramedics who try to restrain the star-spangled hero. Rather than risk harming these civilians, Captain America surrenders. In the end, Captain America is sent to prison, Tony Stark is named director of S.H.I.E.L.D. and the SHRA remains the law of the land.

So, who won? According to Millar, "Cap's fans will be happy because he won the fight and Tony's fans were happy because Tony won the argument" (Mark..."). Millar is only half right in his assessment. Readers, I believe, are not left with the feeling that both Captain America and Iron Man have won, but rather that both of them, and the country, have lost—Captain America has been arrested, Tony Stark has lost the moral battle, and both have been diminished by the experience.

At a story conference regarding the finale of *Civil War*, comic book writer and eventual writer and director of the big screen blockbuster *The Avengers* Joss Whedon advocated giving the story a decisive winner ("Mark..."). For practical reasons Tony's side had to "win" and the Super Hero Registration Act had to be passed. With it in place, Marvel set up potential conflicts and storylines that would be played out in many different titles for years to come.

For instance, the revelation of Spider-Man's secret identity led to *One More*

Day (2007), in which after Aunt May is killed, Parker makes a deal with a demon to bring his beloved aunt back to life; but the cost of doing so is that his marriage to Mary Jane is erased from time. Another equally seismic shift plays out in *The Death of Captain America* (2007), in which the titular hero is shot and (seemingly) killed. It would take a little over two years before Steve Rogers returned as Captain America.

In the story's coda, Stark meets with Miriam Sharpe, whose child's death brought about the SHRA. Stark tells her that they named the Guantanamo Bay–esque detention center "Number Forty-Two" because it was one of 100 ideas that he and his colleagues cooked up to build a "safer world." If one of the ideas was the highly controversial prison, will the other 99 ideas also curtail people's civil rights and diminish their dignity or will they lead to beneficial reforms that preserve civil rights while also protecting the country? Benjamin Franklin warned that, "Those who would give up essential liberty to purchase a little temporary safety deserve neither liberty nor safety" (Isaacson).

In the final panel Tony Stark and Mrs. Sharpe stand on the observation deck of an aircraft, and they are bathed in the orange rays of the sun. The image evokes Benjamin Franklin's observation about George Washington's chair, which had a sun painted on it. As the Constitution of the United States was being written and bitterly debated, Franklin saw the sun as a metaphor for the bright prospects of the new country. Franklin said that he "often in the course of the Session, and the vicissitudes of my hopes and fears as to its issue, looked at [the sun] behind the President without being able to tell whether it was rising or setting: But now at length I have the happiness to know that it is a rising and not a setting sun" (Isaacson).

The scene between Stark and Sharpe is clearly meant to end the story on a hopeful note and restore the reader's faith in the moral and ethical judgment of Avengers. However, due to the troubling implications represented by the passage of the SHRA, it is necessary to consider that unlike the painting on George Washington's chair, the sun in the Marvel Universe is a setting and not a rising sun.

Let's return, one last time, to the question at the heart of *Civil War*: Are there times when national security trumps civil liberties? In the Marvel Universe, the troubling answer is yes. To reshape a political axiom: "As the Avengers go, so goes the Nation."

Works Cited

"America's Surveillance Society." ACLU.org. Accessed March 2014.

Bendis, Brian Michael (w), and Leini Yu (a). *The New Avengers*, #22, September 2006, Marvel Comics.

Brubaker, Ed (w), and Steve Epting (a). *Captain America* #25, April 2007, in *The Death of Captain America*, 2007, Marvel Comics.

Brubaker, Ed (w), Bryan Hitch (a), and Butch Guice (a). *Captain America: Reborn* #1–6, 2009–2010, in *Captain America: Reborn*, October 2010, Marvel Comics.

"Civil War Room #1. Tom Brevoort Debriefs Civil War #1." Newsarama.com. 25 May 2006. http://www.newsarama.com/marvelnew/CivilWar/WarRoom/01/WarRoom01.html. Accessed 9 May 2014.

Fingeroth, Danny. *Superman on the Couch: What Superheroes Really Tell About Ourselves and Our Society*. New York: Continuum, 2004.

Holley, Joe. "Lloyd Bentsen; Texas Senator, Vice Presidential Candidate." *The Washington Post*, May 24, 2006. Accessed April 2014.

Isaacson, Walter. *Benjamin Franklin: An American Life*. New York: Simon & Schuster, 2003.

Lee, Stan (w), and Jack Kirby (a). *Fantastic Four* #34. January 1965, Marvel Comics.

"Mark Millar's Civil War Post-Game Show." *Newsarama*, February 26, 2007. http://archive.today/jyd5a. Accessed March 2014.

Millar, Mark. *Civil War Script Book*. Appendix. Marvel Comics, 2007.

Millar, Mark (w), and Steve McNiven (a). *Civil War* #1–7, 2006–2007, in *Civil War*, 2007, Marvel Comics.

Shakespeare, William. *Romeo and Juliet,* Act 1, Prologue. Waxkeep Publishing, 2013.

Straczynski, J. Michael (w), and Ron Garney (a), *The War at Home* #1–7, *Amazing Spider-Man* #532–538, 2006–2007, in *Civil War: Amazing Spider-Man*, 2007, Marvel Comics.

Straczynski, J. Michael (w), Joe Quesada (w, a), and Danny Miki (a). *Amazing Spider-Man* #544, *Amazing Spider-Man* #545, *Sensational Spider-Man* #41, *Friendly Neighborhood Spider-Man* #24, 2007, in *Spider-Man: One More Day*, 2008, Marvel Comics.

Twain, Mark. *Letters from the Earth*. 1909. New York: HarperCollins, 2004.

Vonnegut, Kurt. *Mother Night*. Introduction. New York: Fawcett, 1961.

Islamic Invaders

Secret Invasion *and the* Post–9/11 World of Marvel

DYFRIG JONES

This essay will examine the way in which the consensus-liberal approach to American politics that has dominated for much of Marvel's history (see Costello) comes under challenge following the terrorist attacks of September 11, 2001. While the argument here exists in the context of a narrative arc that begins in 2006 with *Civil War* and continues until the end of *Siege* in 2010, the focus is on a single cross-over event, *Secret Invasion*. This storyline, which was published in 2008, will be analyzed in the context both of the Avengers' own history, and broader changes that occur in American popular culture during the same time period.

Secret Invasion **and the Post–9/11 Alien Invasion Narrative**

The premise of *Secret Invasion* is that a race of shape-shifting aliens, the Skrulls, have managed to disguise themselves as both humans and superhumans, and are plotting an invasion of earth. They have taken advantage of the divisions and mistrust which has resulted from the civil war between superheroes, and the splitting of the Avengers into two factions. Both factions within the superhuman community have become aware of the Skrulls' disguised presence on earth, but do not know the extent of the infiltration. The Secret Invasion storyline involves the Skrulls' open assault upon earth, and the superhumans' attempts to defend their home planet.

Generically, *Secret Invasion* can arguably be located within a specific subgenre of science fiction narratives who's history can be traced back to the late 19th century, the invasion narrative. Growing out of what Matin has described as "English literature of espionage and invasion"—a counter-factual literary genre that imagined Britain under assault from its Geo-political rivals—the invasion narrative was given an extra-terrestrial twist by H.G. Wells' *The War of the Worlds*. Alien invasion narratives are a mainstay of pulp science-fiction publications between the two World Wars, before transferring to the cinema in the post-war era. Murphy, in an influential early essay on the subject, argued that 1950s invasion narratives were "more characteristic of the Fifties than any other kind of film is characteristic of its time" (31), stemming from a fear of immediate destruction which came in the wake of the development of the Atom Bomb, and the increasing influence of technology upon the daily lives of ordinary people. In the same issue of *Popular Film*, Gregory argues that *Invasion of the Body Snatchers* is a "cry of frustrated warning against the conformity and uniformity of a society that was living in the best of all possible worlds" (4). Others have suggested that these films go beyond exploring the fear of technology and communist infiltration, with scholars such as Mann arguing that a fear of immigration play as central a role as the fear of communism.

The aftermath of 9/11 sees a reinvention of the genre, both on film and television. Many of the post–9/11 alien invasion narratives were direct adaptations of previous texts—Spielberg's *The War of the Worlds, The Day the Earth Stood Still* (Derrickson), *Battlestar Galactica* (Moore), *V* (Peters)—while others contained less direct, but nonetheless influential, references to previous works (for instance, JJ Abrams' *Cloverfield* and *Super 8* are both clearly indebted to the Godzilla movies and Spielberg's alien invasion films of the late 1970s and early 1980s respectively). Where the science fiction and monster movies of the 1950s drew upon specific fears about political and social changes that occurred in the immediate post-war era, the alien invasion narratives that emerge in the first decade of the 21st century reflect upon the social and political response to the terrorist attacks of 9/11; *Battlestar Galactica* has been described as "the best show on American television to deal with the complex realities of life post–9/11" (Hussain 57).

As the remainder of this essay will argue, *Secret Invasion* is a typical example of the post–9/11 alien invasion narrative. Like many of the post-war alien invasion films, it is primarily concerned with the fear of an ill-defined other that is conspiring against the USA, and a paranoia that this other is being assisted by co-conspirators within America itself. Where some of this paranoia is vague and generalized, the argument of this essay is that the post–9/11 paranoia that is on display in *Secret Invasion* is specific and pointed. An emphasis on religiosity as a threatening factor—particularly a religiosity that is coded as being separate from Western religion—is combined with a visual aesthetic that is distinctly post–9/11 to strongly suggest to the reader that the threat facing the Avengers should be understood as a specifically Muslim one.

The Politics of the Marvel Universe

While differing political pressure groups may have sought to recruit Captain America and his fellow heroes to their respective causes (see Phillips), the question of how comic narratives betray ideological positions is one that has long formed part of the scholarly discussion of the medium. Mondello, in his 1976 analysis of Spider-Man, argues that the character's attitude towards issues such as the Vietnam War, racial bigotry, drugs, organized crime and pollution indicates a hero that was a "resolute defender of traditional American liberalism, especially the liberalism fashioned by Franklin D. Roosevelt and other New Dealers" (236). Writing in the same year MacDonald argues that Captain America occupies a similar position on the political spectrum, having undergone a metamorphosis during the 1960s and 1970s that saw his attitude shift from the jingoism of a previous era to a more nuanced questioning of American domestic affairs. Both characters' embrace of liberalism (or New Deal liberalism, to be more specific) needs to be understood in its historical context, however. The rise of the New Left and its rejection of New Deal liberalism in favor of an ill-defined radicalism (Matusow 310) created a flank to the left of Lyndon B. Johnson's Democratic Party. And liberals within the Democratic Party itself, briefly united in their efforts to push through Johnson's civil rights and Great Society legislation had split by the end of the 1960s, chiefly over the Vietnam War. Mondello's decision to describe Spider-Man as a New Dealer is particularly apt; Johnson himself had been the head of the Texas National Youth Administration, was close to Roosevelt during his time in the House of Representatives, and saw the Great Society as the continuation of the New Deal.

While the Marvel Universe contains a diverse range of characters, making it possible to find exceptions to the rule, there was a trend during the 1960s and 70s for the Marvel superhero to occupy an ideological position that was broadly on the center-left, aligning themselves with the mainstream of the Democratic Party of the time, but more fundamentally with a broader world-view that can be typified as consensus-liberal. This is an argument that has been made at length by Costello, and Dittmer has also drawn attention to the limits of Marvel's liberalism during this period, and the way in which characters such as Captain America often worked to contain radicalism.

During the early–1980s, however, the center-ground of American politics began to shift to the right, and the New Deal liberalism that informed much of Marvel's writing during the 1960s and 70s was marginalized by the rise of Reganism. Costello has argued that the early 1980s saw Marvel superheroes partially retreat from discussing the public and political issues that had driven the books of the previous two decades, concentrating instead on their private lives. The rise of Reaganism did not result in a de-politicized Marvel Universe, however. As DuBose has noted, the mid–1980s saw Captain America facing up to two key antagonists, Flag-Smasher—an anti-nationalistic anarchist—and Super Patriot, both the creations of Mark Gruenwald, whose decade writing Captain America stories would be typified by overtly political story-lines Indeed, it is Captain America who—in his refusal to swear allegiance to the government, and his battles with villains on the extreme left and the extreme right—is the keeper of the "liberal tradition" of superheroism (Mondello) during the 1980s.

The mid–1990s, when the shadow of corporate and commercial ruin was cast over Marvel Comics, saw the company's creative arm wrestle with the twin issues of declining sales and a ballooning narrative universe. It would take the events of September 11, 2001, to draw Marvel Comics back into a sustained discussion of American politics, and while the early 2000s would arguably prove to be the most commercially successful period in Marvel's history—largely due to its expansion into film-production and acquisition by Disney—there are questions as to the extent to which the consensual politics of the previous era would survive into the new century.

Superheroes After 9/11

The initial reaction of the comics industry to the events of 9/11 is one of shock. Jenkins has argued that in the immediate aftermath of the attacks, "comic book artists rejected fisticuffs and vigilante justice in favor of depicting the superheroes as nurturers and healers" (79). This new emphasis on non-violence is short-lived, however, and superhero narratives soon return to familiar themes. Yet while the reader is soon plunged back into "fisticuffs and vigilante justice," within the Marvel Universe there is a distinct shift in attitude. The (relatively) apolitical 1990s give way to a post–9/11 narrative universe that is sustained by a number of significant story-lines that are primarily concerned with examining both America's place in the world, and American domestic responses to conflict and terror. This attempt to politicize the Avengers takes center-stage with the launch of the *Civil War* cross-over event of 2006–2007. The main storyline of Civil War follows an inciting incident in which a battle between superheroes and supervillains results in the deaths of over 600 civilians. Following this incident, the government passes a Superhero Registration Act, which forces each superhero to reveal his or her secret identity to the government, and to register as an employee of the state. This causes a split within the Avengers, with Captain America choosing to oppose the Act, while Iron Man gives it his full support. This leads to the creation of two rival teams of Avengers that become the focus of the Marvel Universe over the next four years. During *Civil War* the two most significant other teams of heroes are marginalized, with the Fantastic Four splitting themselves between the pro- and anti-camps, and the X-men formally declaring their neutrality. The conflict between the two sides is framed in terms of civil liberties, and the series deals in part with the erosion of civil liberties in post–9/11 America.

In many ways, the conclusion to *Civil War* is typical of Marvel's consensus-liberal approach to American politics. The anti-registration Avengers ultimately succeed in pushing the pro-registration faction to the point of defeat, but the ordinary citizens of New York—where the battle is located—draw Captain America's attention to the fact that the conflict between the two factions is damaging the very people that the heroes purport to protect. Captain America orders his followers to stand down, and surrenders himself to arrest. Ultimately, the clash of values is abandoned in favor of pursuing an attempt at ideological compromise. As Costello points out (238–241) this attempt at consensus building is short-lived, however. The original Captain America, Steve Rogers, is soon assassinated; the war between the factions continues, and Rogers' shield is soon accompanied by a gun, wielded by his successor—the newly resurrected Bucky Barnes, who eschews consensualism in favor of division and revenge. In the period between the end of *Civil War* and the beginning of *Secret Invasion* the Avengers—and consequently the rest of the Marvel Universe—remain at war with each other.

The 9/11 Aesthetic

The argument that *Secret Invasion* should be read as a comment upon a specifically post–9/11 America can be made in reference to the visual aesthetic adopted by the writer and artists. While it is a story about an invasion of earth, and while key chapters in the story take place in non–American settings, the focus of the narrative is on the Skrull attack on New York. This is, in one sense, entirely in keeping with the Marvel Method (see Costello 11), yet the perspective on New York which is presented in *Secret Invasion* is a distinctly post–9/11. Scenes of destruction are often presented as seen from a civilian viewpoint, rather than from the elevated position of the superhero. Melnick talks of a "snapshot culture" (64) which rose in the aftermath of 9/11; the prevalence of amateur footage—both video and photographic—help to construct a public perception of the attacks as witnessed by the ordinary citizens of New York, and this street-level perspective is found throughout *Secret Invasion*. The Skrulls initially attack New York by destroying the top floor of the Baxter Building, a Manhattan sky-scraper which is home to the Fantastic Four. In *Secret Invasion* #2 (July, 2008) we see the aftermath of the attack from the perspective of ordinary New Yorkers: they are looking up at the skyscraper that is missing a top section, and one of them holds up a mobile phone to photograph the action. This street level per-spective of the battles in New York occurs time and again throughout the nar-rative. *Secret Invasion: Frontline* (Oct. 2008) follows Ben Urich, a journalist working with an alternative newspaper in the city, during the attacks. The nar-rative contained in *Frontline* follows his attempt to assist his fellow New Yorkers, while recording the events as journalistic record. We follow Urich and his fellow civilians to a besieged hospital, which is attacked by a Skrull suicide bomber. This is accompanied by a storyline in which civilian visitors to Stark Tower— a skyscraper that is home to the Avengers—are trapped inside the building that subsequently comes under attack (20). Much of this narrative takes place within the building's stairwells, and follows the civilians' attempt to escape from disaster. The final issue of *Frontline* sees Urich unable to write about the events, due to the trauma that he has suffered. However, while reflecting upon this trauma, he makes a direct connection between the events of *Secret Invasion*, previous fic-tionalized assaults on New York, and real-world terrorist attacks.

Paranoia and Conspiracy

Within *Secret Invasion*, both the humans and the Skrulls are involved with conspiratorial secret societies. During the lead-in to the Secret Invasion story-lines, writer Brian Michael Bendis revealed the existence of the Illuminati, a secretive committee of superhumans who gathered to decide the fate of humanity (*The New Avengers: Illuminati*. May 2006). This story functioned as a retroac-tive change to continuity, or retcon (see Wolk 69), which described how the Illuminati had played an instrumental part in key events in the history of the Marvel Universe—including the Skrull-Kree war of 1971–72. The choice of name is significant; conspiratorial secret societies called The Illuminati are a recurrent presence within the paranoid style, stretching from the anti–Masonic conspiracies of the 1820s (see Hofstadter) to the present day.

The actions of the Illuminati are supplemented by a wider human conspir-acy, in which the super-heroic community, in collusion with various government agencies, have been responsible for secretly changing the course of history. In *Mighty Avengers* #15 (Aug. 2008) we witness a conversation between the Avenger Hank Pym, and a British college student that he is dating. The student talks of her interest in conspiracy theory, and links real world conspiracy theories—the deaths of John F. Kennedy and Marilyn Monroe—to events in Marvel's narrative history including the first Skrulls attack on earth (in *Fantastic Four* #2, Jan. 1962), the *Secret Wars* storyline (Shooter and Zeck). Pym responds to her questions by saying "In my experience, most conspiracy theories are true." By grouping together fictional and "real world" conspiracy theories, Bendis places the events of Secret Invasion within a wider paranoid style. Human conspiracy is supplemented in the narrative by the conspiracy of the Skrulls. During the events of Secret Invasion, as well as the comics which precede the crossover event, the reader is privy to numerous scenes where the Skrulls gather together to plot the downfall of humanity.

Proponents of the consensus view of American politics, most notably Richard Hofstadter, have argued that conspiracies play a central role in creating the political narratives of marginal, extreme groups. Hofstadter's famous 1964 essay, *The Paranoid Style in American Politics*, argues that the demonization of ethnic, cultural and religious sub-cultures is a hallmark of the kind of coarse populism that was alien to the stabilizing American consensus. Hofstadter drew particular attention to the anti-communism of figures such as Senator Joseph McCarthy, but argued that this tradition of paranoia reached back to the earliest days of the republic. The prominence given to paranoia and conspiracy within *Secret Invasion* can be found in any number of other film and television texts post–9/11, and point towards a worrying resurgence in the paranoid style within American popular culture. In the context of the Avengers, however, it is additionally troubling, as it suggests a deviation from the consensus-liberal perspective that has formed such a key part of the characters' history.

Islam and Islamism

Where *Secret Invasion* is most explicitly post–9/11 is in its discussion of religion and religiosity; in its tendency to emphasize the role played by religious fundamentalism in motivating the external threat to America; and most importantly in the pointed way in which the narrative directs the reader to understand this threat not as generally religious but specifically Islamic.

From the outset of *Secret Invasion* there is little doubt that the Skrulls of 2008 are a distinctly pious breed of aliens. Their scientific research is undertaken by "Priests of the Science" (*The New Avengers* #44, Oct. 2008), and their soldiers are accompanied by military chaplains, who bless the attack on earth (*Secret Invasion: X-Men* #1, Oct. 2008), declaring that they are embarked on a "Holy War" (22), a designation which is echoed by the superhero-god Hercules, who declares that "for these aliens, this is a religious war" (Pak and Van Lente, 2008: p. 6). During the first issue of the series a number of Skrulls who have assumed the identities of key superheroes and their allies trigger acts of violence or sabotage, each of which is instrumental to the Skrulls' coordinated invasion of Earth. Each character utters the line "He loves you" before triggering the attack, and—to avoid any misunderstanding on the part of the reader—the "He" is clearly identified as "God" in the sixth issue of the series (Nov. 2008).

Painting the Skrulls as religious, or even as religious fundamentalists, does not necessarily mean that they should be read as Muslims. In the context of post–9/11 America, a critique of political religiosity could easily be read as a response to the evangelical "moral framing" (Spielvogel 549) of the War on Terror and a critique of the Bush Administration's War on Terror. Taken as a whole, the Avengers narrative arc that begins with *Civil War* in 2006 and concludes in May 2010 with the end of the *Siege* storyline contains pointed criticisms of Bush's presidency. Equilibrium returns to the Avengers only following the election of Barack Obama as President, whose pardoning of Steve Rogers (who surrendered his Captain America identity following his apparent death and subsequent resurrection). Yet while the story of division and reconciliation that typifies the Avengers books between 2006 and 2010 is one that broadly fits the consensus-liberal pattern of previous decades, *Secret Invasion* stands out as the chapter that sits uneasily both within its specific narrative arc, and the broader history of the characters and their universe. This is largely due to the fact that while the religiosity of the Skrull invaders might have been used to address the failings of politicized religion in general, it is an opportunity that Marvel passed over in *Secret Invasion*.

Where Marvel Comics has sought to criticize Christian Fundamentalism in the past, it has done so using recognizably American figures—such as the Reverend William Stryker, an anti–Mutant zealot who is openly identified as being a Christian minister, and who eventually leads a paramilitary force known as the Purifiers. Story-lines featuring Stryker and his purifiers often serve as discussions of morality and religious fundamentalism (see Claremont and Anderson; Brubaker et al), yet this discussion is always conducted within a domestic American context, using openly Christian figures. Secret Invasion is distinct in that it seeks to place a similar discussion within the context of an inter-species war. What we witness is not a fight between two factions within the same religion or culture, but rather the invasion of the (American) Earth by religious fundamentalists that belong to a different civilization.

This invasion is resisted by a range of Marvel characters that represent a range of non–Muslim religions. While the Norse god / superhero Thor plays a relatively marginal role within *Secret Invasion*, his fellow Avenger—and Greek god—Hercules is tasked with bringing together a team of divine superheroes in order to battle the Skrull gods. Hercules' team, The God Squad, is made up of characters who stand in for Inuit, Japanese and Egyptian deities; a team that is geographically, racially and culturally diverse enough to stand in for the entire globe, but which remains firmly allied to an American world-view. As this union of per–Christian deities take on the Skrull gods in their divine realm, the Skrulls are presented as being explicitly anti–Christian. Nightcrawler, a long-standing and prominent member of the X-Men, is one of the few explicitly religious superheroes, having trained as a Catholic priest. During the events of *Secret Invasion*, Nightcrawler discovers a Skrull artifact which communicates with him telepathically (*Secret Invasion: X-Men* #3. Dec. 2008). This artifact attempts to convert Nightcrawler to the Skrull Religion, and Nightcrawler resists by quoting the Lord's Prayer.

On the one hand, therefore, *Secret Invasion* deliberately excludes certain Western religious and pre-religious creeds from its criticism of religious violence. If this were not enough by itself, there is an equally deliberate attempt to point the reader towards the one religion that is not excluded from criticism. Perhaps the clearest indicator that we are to equate the Skrulls with Muslims is the use of the specifically Muslim term *Jihad* which occurs three times within the series. In *Nova* #16 (Oct. 2008) a Skrull defector named Kl'rt describes the invasion as being driven by a "jihadist fervour" (24). This use of the term Jihad is repeated in *Guardians of the Galaxy* #6 (Dec. 2006), where the Guardians encounter a group of pacifist Skrulls who are opposed to the invasion. Again, they make reference to "the Jihadist regime" (15) and explain that they are in hiding, since they are being hunted by a "Jihadist Hardcore" (14). The use of Jihad has the immediate and unambiguous effect of linking the Skrull Invasion to Islamic terrorism, due to the fact that it remains one of the few Islamic terms which is familiar to (although often misunderstood by) a general audience, and which would be associated with the actions of Islamist terrorists (Ruthven 116).

Jihad is a rare example of an aspect of Islam which has found common currency within Western culture. There are references to other, less familiar, aspects of Islam which are also to be found within Secret Invasion. When the Skrull army reveal themselves to the people of earth in *Secret Invasion* #6 (Nov. 2008), they seek their acquiescence in the invasion, explaining that their invasion need not be taken as a threat. "Do not fight against yourselves" is the message to humanity, explaining that the Skrulls intend to abolish all modern nation states, and that they are battling for the common good of mankind. This emphasis on a global community could be read as making reference to the Muslim concept of Umma—or rather as a reference to the use which Islamists, most notably Osama Bin Laden, have made of the concept of Umma. The Umma literally refers to the community of believers which makes up Islam, and has no connection to terrorism. However, Bin Laden's public rhetoric has placed great emphasis upon this concept, often appealing directly to the Umma for their loyalty, and relating his grievances against the West to transgressions against the Umma (Milton-Edwards 204). In addition, Bin Laden has outlined the duty of the Umma to establish "an Islamic state, that abides by God's law, and raises the banner of His unity" (98). For Bin Laden, therefore, the outcome of the war against America and its allies is the establishment of a global Islamic state to supersede all current nation states. The Skrulls' direct appeal to the people of earth to help establish a global state is clearly a reference to Bin Laden. The sinister implication of this reading is underlined by the images which accompany the Skrulls' call. As the Skrulls appeal to the humans to abandon their resistance, and to accept the global state which they intend to establish, we see panel which is marked "Israel" showing the Israeli superhero Sabra being killed by a Skrull. The abolition of all nation states is therefore tied directly to the abolition of a single nation state, an outcome which Bin Laden has described as "the most important ... of our issues" (198).

It is important to underline the fact that the "Islam" which is presented within Secret Invasion is an American construct which bears little relationship with the Muslim religion. Edward Said described the misuse of the label "Islam" as "unacceptable generalization of the most irresponsible sort" (xvi), arguing that the tendency to reduce Islam to a "monolithic, enraged, threatening and conspiratorially spreading" (xxviii) entity is the reason why Americans fundamentally misunderstand Islam. Said argues that the Orientalist Western perspective on Islam is rooted in the late 18th century, and stems from a fear that this particular Eastern "Other" represented a religious, cultural and political threat to the dominance of the European Christian Empires (4). Within a contemporary American context this Orientalist discourse has involved the creation of a single, and vastly reductionist, understanding of what is meant by "Muslim" and "Islam." For Said, this has involved the predominance of a "caricature" of Islam, which by the mid–1990s was of Muslims as "oil-suppliers, as terrorists ... as blood-thirsty mobs" (6) with "Religious intensity of a particularly violent kind [being] ascribed solely to Islam" (33). It is this mis-representation of Islam which features prominently in Secret Invasion, in the form of the Skrull religion.

Fictional depictions of Muslims in Hollywood film has been extensively cataloged by Jack G. Shaheen, who has examined over 900 films which feature Arab characters. Like Said, Shaheen finds a number of stereotypical renderings of Muslim characters, which coalesce around a number of themes. Positive depictions of Arabs are few and far between, and Arabs are predominantly included in Hollywood films as villains or buffoons. Islam is linked to "male supremacy, holy war and acts of terror, depicting Arab Muslims as hostile alien intruders" (Shaheen "Reel Bad Arabs" 9). Shaheen's subsequent analysis of post–9/11 Hollywood films found that although the number of positive portrayals of Arabs on screen had increased, the negative stereotypes continued to dominate. Post–9/11, greater emphasis was placed on the Arab villain as a terrorist, with no the majority of films making no attempt to present Muslim characters which condemned or challenged terrorism ("Guilty" 26). Again, Shaheen found that the vast majority of Hollywood films strongly identified Muslim characters with terrorism, religious fundamentalism, and holy war. The fictional Muslim who appears in Hollywood films, as identified by Shaheen, can also be found on the smaller screens which are found in many American homes. News discourse following 9/11 served to reinforce many of the stereotypes perpetuated by Hollywood. As Karim argued, "[news] interviewers sought confirmation for their perceptions about an endemically violent Islam" (105). The views of non-violent (and even irreligious) Muslims were obscured, with the news media giving undue prominence to Islamic fundamentalism within "the Bush administration's polarized narrative frame of good versus evil" (106).

While, as Said argues, the tendency to caricature Muslims as violent religious fundamentalists existed long before 2001, the effect of 9/11 is to strengthen the association in the American public's mind. While the stereotypes identified by Shaheen could easily be associated with other religions, post–9/11 any discussion of violent religious fanaticism is almost automatically linked with the specter of Islam in the American public's mind. Reading Secret Invasion, it is clear that the threat presented by murderous religious fanatics is the single dominant theme of the narrative. The themes identified by Shaheen and Said dominate the way in which the Skrulls are portrayed within Secret Invasion. They are typified by their fanaticism, their fundamentalist religious zeal, and their disregard for innocent life. Moreover, they are depicted as a single, monolithic culture. While they have the ability to assume the shape—and the superpowers—of earth's inhabitants, their native appearance is uniform. One Skrull is almost indistinguishable from another, and major characters are only identifiable within the narrative because they retain their "human" disguise.

Conclusion

Since the 1960s, the Avengers have functioned as "superheroes in the liberal tradition" (Mondello). They have been staunch defenders of the consensus-liberal position; tolerant, open to new ideas, concerned with questions of social justice, yet resistant to radical challenges to the status quo of the center-left. During the Bush Era, the overarching theme of their narrative has been an examination of how these ideas face challenge as the United States comes under direct attack. Taken as a whole—a story that begins with *Civil War* in 2006 and concludes with the end of *Siege* in 2010—we see the Avengers re-affirm the values that have informed the majority of their existence Yet in the middle of this narrative arc, *Secret Invasion* stands out as a departure from the consensual norm. In this particular storyline, the writers of the Avengers have retreated into a xenophobia and paranoia that is more in keeping with the jingoism of the late Golden Age of comics, when Captain America would briefly become the "Commie Smasher." Fear of a racial other is made explicit, trustworthy American heroes are shown to be complicit in conspiring against their own people, and the entire package is wrapped up in the imagery of 9/11. As interesting as it may seem from a scholarly viewpoint, the tone and theme of *Secret Invasion*, and the contribution that it makes to popular American discourse surrounding Islam and Islamism marks it out as one of the less edifying chapters in Marvel's recent history.

Works Cited

Abnett, D. (w), A. Lanning (w), and Paul Pelletier (a). *Guardians of the Galaxy* #6 (Dec. 2008). New York: Marvel Comics.

Abnett, D. (w), A. Lanning (w), Alves Wellington (a) and Geraldo Burges (a). *Nova* #16 (Oct. 2008). New York: Marvel Comics.

Bendis, B. M. (w), and J. Cheung (a). *The New Avengers* #42 (Aug. 2008). New York: Marvel Comics.

Bendis, B. M. (w), and A. Maleev (a). *The New Avengers: Illuminati* (May 2006). New York: Marvel Comics.

Bendis, B. M. (w), and J. Romita, Jr. (a). *Mighty Avengers* #15 (Aug. 2008). New York: Marvel Comics.

Bendis, B.M. (w), and B. Tan (a). *The New Avengers* #44 (Oct. 2008). New York: Marvel Comics.

Bendis, B. M. (w), and L. Yu (a). *Secret Invasion* #1 (June 2008). New York: Marvel Comics.

Bendis, B. M. (w), and L. Yu (a). *Secret Invasion* #2 (July 2008). New York: Marvel Comics.

Bendis, B. M. (w), and L. Yu (a). *Secret Invasion* #6 (Nov. 2008). New York: Marvel Comics.

Bin Laden, O. *Messages to the World*. London: Verso, 2005. Print.

Brubaker, Ed (w), et al. *X-Men: Messiah Compex (Trade Paperback)* New York: Marvel Comics, 2008.

Carey, M. (w), and C. Nord (a). *Secret Invasion: X-Men* #1 (Oct. 2008). New York: Marvel Comics.

Carey, M. (w), and M. Sepulueda (a) *Secret Invasion: X-Men* #3 (Dec. 2008). New York: Marvel Comics.

Claremont, C. (w), and B. Anderson (a). *X-Men: God Loves, Man Kills (Trade Paperback)*. New York: Marvel Comics, 1982.

Coogan, P. *Superhero: The Secret Origin of a Genre*. Austin: Monkeybrain Books, 2006. Print.

Costello, M. J. *Secret Identity Crisis: Comic Books and the Unmasking of Cold War America*. London: Continuum, 2009. Print.

Dittmer, J. *Captain America and the Nationalist Superhero*. Philadelphia: Temple University Press, 2013. Print.

Dubose, M. S. "Holding Out for a Hero: Reaganism, Comic Book Vigilantes, and Captain America." *The Journal of Popular Culture* 40.6 (2007): 915–935. Print.

Gregory, C. T. "The Pod Society Versus the Rugged Individualists." *Journal of Popular Film* 1.1 (1972): 3. Print.

Hofstadter, R. *The Paranoid Style in American Politics*. New York: Harpers Magazine, 1964. Online.

Hussain, A. "(Re)presenting: Muslims on North American Television." *Contemporary Islam* 4.1 (2010): 55–75. Print.

Jenkins, H. "Captain America Sheds His Mighty Tears: Comics and September 11." *Terror, Culture, Politics: Rethinking 9.11* (2006): 69–102. Print.

Karim, Karim H. "Making Sense of the 'Islamic Peril': Journalism as Cultural Practice." *Journalism After September 11* (2002): 101–116. Print.

Lee, S. (w), and J. Kirby (a). *Fantastic Four* #2 (Jan. 1962). New York: Marvel Comics.

Lee, S. (w), and S. Ditko (a). *Amazing Spider-Man* #1 (Mar. 1963). New York: Marvel Comics.

Macdonald, V. "Sold American: The Metamorphosis of Captain America." *The Journal of Popular Culture* 10.1 (1976): 249–258. Print.

Mann, K. "'You're Next!'": Postwar Hegemony Besieged in *Invasion of the Body Snatchers* (1956)." *Cinema Journal* 44.1 (2004): 49–68. Print.

Matin, A. M. "'We Aren't German Slaves Here, Thank God': Conrad's Transposed Nationalism and British Literature of Espionage and Invasion." *Journal of Modern Literature* 21.2 (1997): 251–280. Print.

Matusow, A. J. *The Unraveling of America: A History of Liberalism in the 1960s*. Athens: University of Georgia Press, 2009. Print.

Melnick, J. *9/11 Culture*. Chichester, West Sussex: Blackwell Wiley, 2009. Print. Milton-Edwards, B. *Islam and Politics in the Contemporary World*. Cambridge: Polity Press, 2004. Print.

Mondello, S. "Spider-Man: Superhero in the Liberal Tradition." *The Journal of Popular Culture*. 10.1 (1976): 232–238. Print.

Murphy, B. "Monster Movies: They Came from Beneath the Fifties." *Journal of Popular Film* 1.1 (1972). Print.

Pak, G. (w), and F. Van Lente (a). *Hercules* #117 (July 2008). New York: Marvel Comics.

Phillips, F. "Captain America and Fandom's Political Activity." *Transformative Works and Cultures* 13 (2013). Online.

Reed, B. (w), and M. Castiello (w). *Secret Invasion: Frontline* #1 (Sept. 2008) New York: Marvel Comics.

Reed, B. (w), and M. Castiello (a). *Secret Invasion: Frontline* (Oct. 2008). New York: Marvel Comics.

Said, E. W. *Covering Islam: How the Media and the Experts Determine How We See the Rest of the World*, 2d ed. London: Vintage, 1997. Print.

Shaheen, J.G. *Guilty: Hollywood's Verdict on Arabs After 9/11*. Northampton, MA: Olive Branch Press, 2008. Print.

_____. *Reel Bad Arabs: How Hollywood Vilifies a People*. Moreton-in-Marsh: Arris Books, 2003. Print.

Shooter, J. (w), and M. Zeck (a). *Secret Wars* (trade paperback). New York: Marvel Entertainment, 2005.

Spielvogel, C. "'You Know Where I Stand': Moral Framing of the War on Terrorism and the Iraq War in the 2004 Presidential Campaign." *Rhetoric & Public Affairs* 8.4 (2005): 549–569.

Wolk, D. *Reading Comics: How Graphic Novels Work and What They Mean*. Philadelphia: Da Capo, 2007. Print.

"The one with the kids
on the island"
Avengers Arena *and*
Teenage Dystopian Fiction

Joseph J. Darowski

Hunger Games with Superheroes

"Yes, this comic's concept of a teenage death match is derivative of The Hunger Games, which is derivative of Battle Royale, etc." (Yehl). "If this sounds a little bit like "The Hunger Games" (or going further back, "Battle Royale" or even "The Long Walk"), you aren't alone in that assessment" (McElhatton). "It seemed as if Marvel was just capitalizing on the trend set forth by *The Hunger Games*" (Richards).

As the above reviewers, and many, many other readers of *Avengers Arena* have noted, on the surface *Avengers Arena* feels though someone pitched, "What if the Hunger Games were crossed over with superheroes?" While there is undeniable accuracy in that description (in the first issue the villain of the piece announces that he got the idea for his scheme "from a couple kids' books I read"), there are elements to the series that elevate it beyond that simple conceit (Hopeless, "Worse Things"). *Avengers Arena* brings into sharp focus concerns about virtual identity and the negative impacts of technology while still embracing the expected tropes of superhero comic books. Virtual identities can project a false façade, and cyberbullying can be an act of supervillainy in the Marvel Universe.

However, a brief summary of the series makes it clear why the connection was one that so many instantly reached when hearing about the premise or after reading the first issue of the series. The supervillain called Arcade kidnaps sixteen young heroes and traps them in his secret base called Murder World. The heroes are told that this is a kill-or-be-killed situation, the last one left alive after 30 days will be allowed to leave. Then they are left alone to try and survive, with continual manipulations from Arcade to ensure they fight and murder one another. Arcade is not only the villain that instigates the situation, he also takes on the role of director in a control room where he films the proceedings.

The sixteen heroes are a mix of established members of superhero teams such as the Runaways (Nico Minoru and Chase Stein), the Avengers Academy (Hazmat, Mettle, Reptil, Juston Seyfert and his Sentinel), preestablished Marvel characters (X-23, Cammi, Darkhawk, and Red Raven), and brand new creations (Anachronism, Apex, Cullen Bloodstone, Death Locket, Kid Briton, and Nara). Through an 18 issue run alliances are formed, betrayals enacted, and a body count rises.

With that premise, it is easy to identify close ties to *The Hunger Games*. Teenagers are put in a contained environment with the express purpose of killing one another. The events are filmed in both instances, though in the case of *Avengers Arena* they are not sent out live. The teenagers are a mix of bloodthirsty individuals out to kill anyone and those who wish to be anywhere else. Romance blooms in the unlikely setting. Uneasy and temporary alliances are made with the understanding that they must inevitably be broken. There is a larger external threat that the participants are aware of (the government/Arcade), but they must focus on surviving before they can even begin to address that issue.

It seems as though the combination of a presently popular premise with the young superheroes would be a natural pitch to Marvel. In truth, though, we know that Dennis Hopeless, the author of most of the 18-issue run of *Avengers Arena*, did not have any intent to write a tale of teenagers in mortal combat. As Hopeless explains in a letter to readers that is found in the final issue of the series, "Full disclosure, AVENGERS ARENA isn't the book I wanted to write. Not at all" (Hopeless, "Untitled"). He goes on to explain that his initial pitch to Marvel Comics was purely teen drama in the vein of *Veronica Mars*, *Friday Night Lights*, and the Marvel Comic book series *Runaways*.[1] Axel Alonso and Tom Brevoort, Marvel's editor-in-chief and executive editor/senior vice president of publishing, reviewed Hopeless's pitch and zeroed in on a brief reference to what Hopeless considered to be a potential third story arc of his series. Because this was proposed to be a storyline more than a year after the series had launched, it only had a vague description of "our kids competing in a tournament with other Marvel Universe schools that turns into a death match when a supervillain takes control. The Triwizard tournament meets *The Hunger Games*" (Hopeless, "Untitled"). But that is the part of the pitch that stood out to Alonso and Brevoort, and so that is what they requested Hopeless focus on for his new series.

Hopeless defended the premise of the series, while acknowledging that the success of *The Hunger Games* was a factor, explaining:

> Some of our harshest critics have thrown around the words "cash grab" and "rip off" to describe the series. In reality, these sorts of decision are far simpler and less nefarious than all that. Marvel editors help us develop plots with an eye to marketability. They're always searching for strong story hooks that can be used to sell the idea of the books to readers. Battle Royale in the Marvel Universe or Teenage Super Hero Hunger Games are ideas readers can quickly understand. Marvel leaned into those comparisons with the marketing. That's their job. As creators, it was our job to deliver a unique and compelling story that went beyond simple homage [Hopeless, "RE: Academic]."

Throughout the series, and in his letter to fans, Hopeless does not disguise the types of stories which his series makes homage. Hopeless name drops Harry Potter, *The Hunger Games,* and *Battle Royale,* while also alluding to *Lord of the Flies.* Hopeless also adds that television series like *Survivor* and *Lost* and films like *The Running Man* and *Mad Max: Beyond the Thunderdome* were influences, admitting that he had "been a fan of life or death competition and survival stories for as long as [he] can remember" (Hopeless, email). In the character interactions and quieter moments readers can also see the influence of teenage dramas on his writing. Hopeless also identifies the British television series *Skins* as an important influence, particularly in that series' "rotating POV structure and character-driven perspective shifts" which helped to shape *Avengers Arena*'s structure and also in helping to give the "British characters believable voices (Hopeless, "RE: Academic").

All stories have elements of other creative works, that's nature of storytelling. There are myriad other narratives that mine similar territory to what is seen in *The Hunger Games,* from the classic short story *The Most Dangerous Game* to previous Marvel mini-series such as *Secret War* or *Contest of Champions.* But there are several unique aspects of *Avengers Arena* that situate it with contemporary issues, with the hopes and fears of modern society. These nuances help to turn the series into something more than an homage or rip-off.

Virtual Identity

Comic books are not created in a vacuum. It has already been established that the success of *The Hunger Games* and similar stories was a factor in Marvel editorial guiding Hopeless into telling this particular tale. But there are many contemporary issues that are reflected in the series besides the popularity of other book and film series. The concerns that are layered into the narrative are demonstrative of modern society and, particularly, the pervasiveness of our online culture. Issues such as virtual identity, interpersonal communication, and even cyberbullying are important themes within this series.

Because the captives in Arcade's Murder World are kidnapped teenagers the story requires some explanation as to why their absence is not noted. Particularly when many of the teenagers are under the care and supervision of superheroes who would no doubt pursue their charges if they suspected they were captives of an insane supervillain. At first there is little explanation for why there is not a massive ongoing search from heroes outside of Murder World for these characters. Some readers felt that, for the first twelve issues, this was an omission that was hurting their ability to suspend disbelief and immerse themselves in the story. *Avengers Arena* #13 (Oct. 2013), the issue that finally explains how their absences have not caused a worldwide manhunt by the superhero community, featured a break from the regular creative team. Christos Gage was the writer and Karl Moline the penciler for "The Devil's Greatest Trick," which explains how, exactly, a supervillain like Arcade could kidnap more than a dozen superheroes, most of who belonged to teams or training schools, without anyone coming to rescue them. While fill-in issues are often lamented for a disruptive tone that distracts from the larger story the regular creative team is telling, this issue "is a rare instance of a fill-in issue which doesn't just contribute to the series, but feels essential" (Hunt).

Avengers Arena #13 (Oct. 2013) reveals that Arcade manipulates the online profiles and social media of his captives to make it appear that they've all chosen to depart from their respective teams and schools for various reasons. This is done so well that adults don't question their absence. The lack of personal interaction or personal connection that is so frequently lamented as a result of our contemporary culture is what allows Arcade to carry out his plan. Arcade sets up a computer to use "the contestants' body scans. Voice prints. A.I. software that reconstructs their personalities—such as they are—-flawlessly. Plus access to every password, pixel, and pin" in order to maintain online profiles of the kidnapped teenagers (Gage).

A Google trends analysis reveals that the search term "social media" has seen a consistent rise in interest, from a low ranking of 3 or 4 in 2007 to a high ranking of 99 in 2014. Social media has become much more pervasive in our culture, becoming a primary means of communication for many and also a source of identity formation.

Simultaneous with the rise of social media a concern has developed about how it changes those who use it in any form, from early Myspace accounts to recent Tumblrs, from text messages to Twitter. These fears can be seen in news articles like "Texting, Tweeting and Social Networking are to Behind 'Rough Behavior' of Teens, says Pratchett" from 2012. The fantasy writer Terry Pratchett laments the degrading communication and interpersonal skills of teenagers, arguing that "social networking sites such as Facebook and Twitter lead to children being unable to communicate properly, meaning they express themselves through bad or violent behaviour" (Titcomb). In the same article, educational psychologist Dr. Kairen Kullen warns that Pratchett is "making some big claims" about the effects of social media, but acknowledges "that social media and texting can damage children's ability to relate to each other" (Titcomb).

Also in 2012, *Forbes* published an article by Susan Tardanico titled "Is Social Media Sabotaging Real Communication?" (Tardanico). The article title implicitly concludes that social media is somehow artificial communication and certainly inferior to personal communication. The content of the article explicitly states this. "Awash in technology, anyone can hide behind the text, the e-mail, the Facebook post or the tweet, projecting any image they want and creating an illusion of their choosing. They can be whoever they want to be. And without the ability to receive nonverbal cues, their audiences are none the wiser" (Tardanico). This is the precise problem that Arcade exploits to cover his actions in *Avengers Arena*. Tardanico laments that "we are more connected—and potentially more *disconnected*—than ever before." Is a virtual connection a real connection? A computer can project the reality that Kid Briton is off playing hooky from the Braddock Academy and nobody can tell.

Avengers Arena #13 (Oct. 2013) clearly demonstrates the way social media can be used for inauthentic communication. Arcade delivers lies through the sixteen superheroes's online accounts that are convincing enough that few question why they haven't seen them in person for some time. Hopeless notes that "Modern teenagers have lived with reality television and social media their whole lives. [...] They all have websites and instagram and tumblr on which they project some version of themselves out over the Internet" (Hopeless, "RE: Academic"). These false, virtual versions of themselves deflect concern from their real selves, who are currently dealing with the heightened threats of the superhero genre. Interestingly, the virtual identities of the Marvel superheroes are using several of the decidedly less superheroic concerns that plague contemporary teenagers to explain why they have run away from their caretakers. Issues such as overbearing parents, young love, and feelings of abandonment are addressed by their digital selves as explanations for why they are avoiding personal interactions with their friends and mentors.

The only person who suspects something is amiss is the youngest member of the Runaways, Molly Quinn. She insists that "Bad guys stole my friends" (Gage), but her concerns are dismissed by most others because her friends, Nico and Chase, "left a note. Said they were going away for a bit" to figure things out. Molly's concerns do inspire Hank Pym to look a little more closely at things, and he does become suspicious because so many teenaged heroes disappeared at about the same time from various training facilities (Gage). Tigra concludes that Hazmat and Mettle left together because her "parents were going to pull her out of school because they didn't want her dating Mettle. I can't really blame them for running off together" (Gage). Arcade makes it appear that Reptil texted his friends to let them know he "had a line on finding his parents. Something to do with other dimensions ... magic" (Gage). Wolverine is unconcerned that his adopted daughter, X-23 (a cloned version of himself) has disappeared, explaining that "Laura went on walkabout. Sleep rough a while, get some peace. I used to do it myself before I opened this damn school" (Gage). X-23 texts Jubilee when she has cell phone reception, so there's nothing to worry about. Captain Britain is relatively unconcerned about the students who disappeared from his school because "It's not as if they've cut off communication." thanks to Arcade's updates Captain Britain believes his students "Delight in updating Fritter and Wastebook with their latest adventures. Always after they've moved on, of course. By the time I arrive there's just a dreadful mess I have to pay for" (Gage). Arcade goes to greater measures to explain Juston's disappearance, sending a mechanical Life Model Decoy to his home to convince his parents that Juston has come home.

Hank Pym is still bothered by the number of students who have disappeared from various locations and continues to look into the matter until Arcade plays his "trump card" (Gage). Arcade covers a robot with Mettle's remains[2] (Mettle was the first victim of Murder World) and sends the robot to talk directly with Hank Pym. Pym scans the robot, but concludes its DNA and retina are a match for Mettle, while Mettle insists he and Hazmat are fine and are simply spending some time alone. It is this personal contact that finally puts Pym's mind at ease (mostly), demonstrating the primacy of one-on-one communication versus virtual communication through the internet or cellular technology. However, this is troubled by the fact that this personal communication is as false as the virtual communication that misled so many others. Both Juston's Life Model Decoy and the robot wearing Mettle's skin are lies that dissuade others from probing into the truth. Deception is not the sole domain of online communication.

The Cyberbully as Supervillain

Arcade's final act of supervillainy is also predicated on our modern concerns regarding the internet and its influence. While many of his captives do die in Murder World (Apex, Juston Seyfert, Kid Briton, Mettle, Nara, Dania, and perhaps Reptil[3]) in the end his plan to end with only one survivor is thwarted. When some of the heroes enter Arcade's control room he teleports away before they can exact any revenge on him. Eight of the heroes leave Murder World under their own power. In *Avengers Arena* #18 (Jan. 2014), as the surviving heroes prepare for SHIELD and superheroes to come and provide transport out of Murder World, Cammi says "We need to get out story straight. Decide what we want to tell, what we don't" (Hopeless, "Boss"). Hazmat insists, "We don't say a word. We make a pact. [...] A pact that we won't talk about this hellhole or anything that happened here. Ever" (Hopeless, "Boss"). Knowing that their actions in Murder World, even in self-defense, would horrify the world, they pledge to never tell what they did to each other and to the others who died.

In the final two pages of the series we see a newscaster reporting about "Sixteen teenage super heroes kidnapped and held captive for thirty days. Nearly half of them dead and the wounded so traumatized they remain unwilling to talk about what transpired" (Hopeless, "Boss"). Then it cuts scene cuts to Arcade watching the news in a white bathrobe and popping champagne. In front of him is a laptop where he is uploading a video with the title "What Really Happened in Murder World? 1/30." The final two panels show the view count rising from 8 views to 16 views, leaving the reading with the ominous knowledge that the videos he took in Murder World are about to go viral (Hopeless, "Boss").

As evil as the kidnapping of adolescents was, as vile as forcing them to kill each other was, it is publishing the videos online that is Arcade's final triumph over the heroes. The survivors had planned to avoid as much of the negative fallout from the events of Murder World as possible by not speaking of them. Believing themselves to be the possessors of the truth, if it wasn't shared, nobody would know. "Audiovisual media presents an unquestionable truth, even after an editing process, while anything that does not take place on the screen, ironically becomes virtual due to the absence of images. That which is not by images in the media ceases to be real, it becomes a non-event" (Pagnoni). Arcade victimizes the heroes one final time by releasing to the world the "real" events. Of course, we don't know just how real the video that Arcade releases is, as he was acting as the director and editor from his control room. In *Avengers Arena* #17 (Jan. 2014), Arcade even acknowledges that he can manipulate the footage he has in any way. After Apex, who has been the most vicious in killing others and betraying friends, breaks into his control room and attempts to hack into his system, Arcade offers her a positive edit.

> **Arcade:** A storyteller needs to know his ending before he can tell a tale. I haven't released any video. Not yet. Hear me out. The way I see it, there are two possible endings. Ending number one: Keep doing what you're doing there. Shut it all down and maybe save a couple lives. I'll be forced to release the tape as is. Not a win for me, but close enough. But you ... you'll walk out of here a pariah. A natural born killer. The real villain of Murder World. Then there's ending number two in which I give you complete con-

trol of the system right now. We let this thing play out naturally. Tie up the loose ends. I get my win. [...] After a little creative editing, you become Murder World's charismatic lead. Tragic. Beloved. The sole survivor of this horrific ordeal [Hopeless, "Boss Level Part 4"].

If Arcade was prepared to manipulate his footage to make the most villainous of the heroes look good, what could he have done to the footage of the eight survivors? Will he release the footage unedited and let their actions still be condemned? Will they be made to look the most monstrous?

Hopeless acknowledges that this is a different world because of the internet and social media, and the conclusion to *Avengers Arena* reflects our contemporary world.

As for why teenage death match stories resonate right now, I think it's because effective satire reflects our society. Modern teenagers have lived [... in a world] in which bullying doesn't just follow you home, it lives on your cell phone. [...] they get to weather the unfiltered judgment that bounces from the Internet. Add to that a 24-hour "celebrity" news cycle that turns teen idols into social pariahs. Throw in an economy that requires a college education without guaranteeing employment once you have one. Teenage life isn't a literal death match but its definitely dog eat dog [Hopeless, "RE: Academic"].

The situation the heroes find themselves struggling through in *Avengers Arena* is a vastly exaggerated and hyperbolic representation of what many modern teenagers experience in modern society.

Cyberbullying represents the dark, uncontrolled side of the internet. As Laura Hudson puts it, "The behavior is so prevalent that it's seen as an inextricable part of online culture," to the point that many just ignore the negativity because there seems to be little that can be done about it. But that attitude pretends that there are few negative side-effects from cyber bullying. Hudson condemns this approach:

But the Internet is now where we socialize, where we work. It's where we meet our spouses, where we build our reputations. Online harassment isn't just inconvenient, nor is it something we can walk away from with ease. It's abhorrent behavior that has real social, professional, and economic costs. And the big social networks where most Americans spend time online—Facebook, YouTube, Twitter, and the rest—aren't doing nearly enough to address the problem.

The phrase "cyberbullying" has a similar upwards movement on a Google trend search to that of social media. It had a low ranking 3 or 4 in 2005 but rises to a high of 100 in 2013, though dipping back down to 86 in 2014. The real-world effects of virtual negativity is something that is increasingly being scrutinized, particularly when it comes to social media and children and adolescents. In its most tragic cases, as seen in several news cases around the world, cyberbullying is a contributing factor in a victim's suicide.

In considering why the upload of the Murder World videos to the internet is such a villainous act, Hopeless explained:

> Put something on the Internet and it's there forever. Arcade didn't just break these kids down and turn them into killers, he shared their descent with the whole world. He made them famous for the worst 30 days of their lives. Some of them may have survived Murder World but now they'll never escape it [Hopeless, "RE: Academic"].

Lawsuits abound in contemporary society regard material that is placed online that damages a person's reputation. But, with the internet, even when the information is removed from one location, it may be impossible to permanently delete it.

Rip Off?

Every narrative shares elements with other narratives. Joseph Campbell famously identified repeated tropes in myths from around the world. Christopher Booker argued that there are seven basic plots that are recycled and remixed, but remain the same at their core. When a story is told well and features interesting themes, complex characterizations, and a quality narrative it can be embraced even when similarities can be easily identified. When it has no depth, shallow characters, and is poorly told it is dismissed as a rip-off. Very well received works can have obvious narrative antecedents, such as *Harry Potter* and Arthurian legend or *Watchmen* and an episode of *The Outer Limits*. But they are forgiven if they are well-told and they have something to say. I believe *Avengers Arena* says something interesting about contemporary culture, adolescent identity formation, and the role of the internet in our lives. This elevates the series above the accusation of mere "Rip off" of *The Hunger Games* ... or *Battle Royale* ... or *The Lord of the Flies* ... etc.

Notes

1. Several members of the cast of Runaways are featured in *Avengers Arena*, so in a way Hopeless was able to continue the tradition of his "all time favorite Marvel comic" (Hopeless, "Open Letter").

2. The splash page in which Mettle dies in the first issue is meant to be shocking and shows his entire body being ripped apart and basically disintegrated. It is unlikely there was enough material left to cover a robot as is shown in this issue, but suspension of disbelief is a primary requirement of reading superhero narratives.

3. Reptil's body is fished out of the water after SHIELD Agents enter Murder World and it is never confirmed if the character is alive or dead. Of course, with the on-again, off-again relationship superheroes have with death, it is possible any of these dead characters may be retconned back to life or resurrected in some manner at a future date.

Works Cited

Gage, Cristos (w), Kev Walker (a) and Karl Moline (a). "The Devil's Greatest Trick." *Avengers Arena* #13 (Oct. 2013). New York: Marvel Comics, 2013.

Hopeless, Dennis. "RE: Academic Inquiry Regarding *Avengers Arena*." Message to Joseph Darowski. 6 May 2014. Email.

_____. "Untitled Letter to Fans." *Avengers Arena* #18 (Jan. 2014). New York: Marvel Comics, 2014.

Hopeless, Dennis (w), and Kev Walker (a). "Boss Level, Part 4 of 5." *Avengers Arena* #17 (Jan. 2014). New York: Marvel Comics, 2014.

_____, and _____. "Worse Things." *Avengers Arena* #1 (Feb. 2013). New York: Marvel Comics, 2013.

Hudson, Laura. "Curbing Online Isn't Impossible. Here's Where We Start." Wired.com. 15 May 2014. http://www.wired.com/2014/05/fighting-online-harassment/. Accessed 15 May 2014.

Hunt, James. "*Avengers Arena* #13." Comicbookresources.com. 19 August 2013. http://www.comicbookresources.com/?page=user_review&id=6347. Accessed 28 April 2014.

McElhatton, Greg. "*Avengers Arena* #1." Comicbookresources.com. 12 December 2012. http://www.comicbookresources.com/?page=user_review&id=5475. Accessed 28 April 2014

Pagnoni Berns, Fernando Gabriel. "War, Foreign Policy and the Media: The Rucka Years." Ed. Joseph J. Darowski, *The Ages of Wonder Woman: Essays on the Amazon Princess in Changing Times*. Jefferson, NC: McFarland, 2014.

Richards, Ron. "Advanced Review: *Avengers Arena* #1 (Spoiler Free)." 26 November 2012. http://ifanboy.com/articles/advanced-review-avengers-arena-1-spoiler-free/. Accessed 28 April 2014.

Tardanico, Susan. "Is Social Media Sabotaging Real Communication?" Forbes.com. 30 April 2012. http://www.forbes.com/sites/susantardanico/2012/04/30/is-social-media-sabotaging-real-communication/. Accessed 28 April 2014.

Yehl, Joshua. "The Hungry Avengers Royale Begins." IGN.com. 11 December 2012. http://www.ign.com/articles/2012/12/11/avengers-arena-1-review. Accessed 28 April 2014.

About the Contributors

José **Alaniz** is an associate professor of language and literature at the University of Washington–Seattle. He is the author of *Komiks: Comic Art in Russia* and *Death, Disability and the Superhero: The Silver Age and Beyond* (both University Press of Mississippi, 2010 and 2014, respectively). He also chairs the Executive Committee of the International Comic Arts Forum. His research interests include disability in Euro-American graphic narrative and the history of Czech comics.

Todd Steven **Burroughs** is the co-editor, with Jared Ball, of *A Lie of Reinvention: Correcting Manning Marable's Malcolm X* (Black Classic Press, 2012) and the co-author, with Herb Boyd, of *Civil Rights: Yesterday and Today* (Legacy, 2010). He is working on a monograph of Gil Noble and WABC-TV's "Like It Is" and a journalistic biography of imprisoned journalist Mumia Abu-Jamal.

John **Darowski** is a Ph.D. student at the University of Louisville, where he continues a lifelong love of comic books by researching their role in society. Other areas of interest include anime and manga, popular culture and the Gothic. He has previously been published in *The Ages of Superman*, *The Ages of Wonder Woman*, and *The Ages of the X-Men* (all from McFarland, 2012, 2014, 2014, respectively).

Joseph J. **Darowski** is a member of the English Department at Brigham Young University. He is on the Editorial Review Board of *The Journal of Popular Culture*. He has previously edited *The Ages of Superman*, *The Ages of Wonder Woman*, and *The Ages of the X-Men* (all from McFarland, 2012, 2014, 2014, respectively) and is the author of *X-Men and the Mutant Metaphor: Race and Gender in the Comic Books* (Rowman & Littlefield, 2014).

Mark **Edlitz** has written about superheroes and popular culture for numerous publications, including *The Huffington Post*, *Los Angeles Times Hero Complex*, *Moviefone*, Sirius/XM's *Slice of SciFi* and *Empire* magazine online. He has worked as a writer-producer for the National Geographic Channel and for ABC News. He wrote and directed the award-winning independent film *The Eden Myth* and produced and directed *Jedi Junkies*, a film about extreme Star Wars fans.

Nathan **Gibbard** is a Ph.D. candidate in the Religious Studies Faculty at McGill University. He studies religion and media, with a special interest in how religious images, objects, and ideas are used in creating cultural symbolic shorthand for media consumption and use.

Dyfrig **Jones** is a lecturer in media at Bangor University, Wales. He was appointed to this position following many years as a media practitioner, working as a factual television producer and director. He is pursuing a Ph.D. in media policy with a focus on public broadcasting in the United Kingdom and the United States.

Paul R. **Kohl** is a professor of media studies at Loras College in Dubuque, Iowa, where he teaches courses in film, television, and popular music. He published "The Struggle Within: Superman's Difficult Transition to the Age of Relevance" in *The Ages of Superman* and "Wonder Woman's Lib: Feminism and the 'New' Amazing Amazon" in *The Ages of Wonder Woman*.

Jason **LaTouche** is an associate professor of sociology at Tarleton State University. His work on superhero comic books has appeared in *The Ages of Superman*, *The Ages of Wonder Woman*, and the *Critical Survey of Graphic Novels*. He has presented papers on superhero comics at the Popular Culture Association conference and created and taught a course entitled "The Sociology of Superheroes."

Peter W. **Lee** is a Ph.D. candidate at Drew University, where he focuses on American cultural history and youth history. He has contributed to numerous publications, including *The Ages of Superman*, and his work has also appeared in *Thymos: The Journal of Boyhood Studies*, *The Bright Lights Film Journal*, and *Studies in Medievalism*. His research interests include cultural expressions of children's media during the early Cold War.

Lori **Maguire** is a professor of British and American studies at the University of Paris 8 (Vincennes–St. Denis). She has published many articles and books on the political history and foreign policy of Great Britain and the United States and the presentation of the Cold War in popular culture.

Giacomo Matteo **Miniussi** graduated from the University of Pisa with a degree in philosophy; his thesis was on philosophical hermeneutics. He continued his studies in theology at the Albert Ludwig University in Freiburg (Germany); his dissertation was on the thinking of T.W. Adorno and E. Levinas in relationship to European nihilism. He collaborates with Gallery Mario Mazzoli, a gallery of sound art and film, editing critical texts on works of art.

Morgan B. **O'Rourke** is an independent scholar who has co-written a book on the history of the Wooster High School Speech and Debate team, *A Good Town Speaking Well*, with Dan O'Rourke. In the area of comic books he has authored "Redefining Superman in the Age of Reagan," "The Death of Captain America," and "John Byrne's Re-Imaging of Superman," all with Dan O'Rourke.

Jason **Sacks** is a co-writer and co-editor of *The American Comic Book Chronicles: The 1970s* (TwoMorrows Press, 2014). He is also a contributing writer to *The American Comic Book Chronicles: The 1980s* (TwoMorrows Press, 2013) and *The*

Flash Companion (TwoMorrows Press, 2008), and he is a former editor for *Amazing Heroes* magazine, among other books and magazines.

Laurie **Schwartz** is a composer and independent radio producer based in Europe. Her music has been released by Esopus, Academy, Edition Zeitklang, Cantate-Musicaphon, and Zeitkratzer. Her translation work includes the books *Music of the Arabs* (Touma) and *Skizo-Mails* (Berardi).

Liam **Webb** is a freelance writer and editor of online content, film scripts, news articles, blogs, comic books and short story books. He interned at Marvel Comics and for the past two years has been building his own publishing company, Red Branch Publications, focusing on comics, children's books and short stories.

Index